Over My Shoulder
2

Over My Shoulder 2

A Collection of
"Over My Shoulder" and "Passed Times" Columns
published in *The Post-Star* from 1994-2003
Volume 2: 1998-2000

by

Joseph Cutshall-King

matchless books

OTHER WORKS BY CUTSHALL-KING

FICTION
2011: *The Burning of The Piping Rock*; a historical mystery novel; (Matchless Books).

HISTORIES
2019: *Over My Shoulder 2; A Collection of "Over My Shoulder" and "Passed Times" Columns published in The Post-Star from 1994-2003; Volume 2: 1998-2000*. Matchless Books®, publisher.
2018: *Over My Shoulder; A Collection of "Over My Shoulder" and "Passed Times" Columns published in The Post-Star from 1994-2003; Volume 1: 1994-1997*. Matchless Books®, publisher.
2017: *WATER & LIGHT: S. R. Stoddard's Lake George*. Chapman Historical Museum, Glens Falls, NY, publisher.
2008: *Cornerstone of the Future*; history of First Presbyterian Church of Glens Falls, NY. First Presbyterian Church of Glens Falls, NY, publisher.
2001: *Con Amore – The Italian History of Fort Edward*; with Italian Heritage Committee of Fort Edward Historical Association, Inc., publisher.
1987: *Hospital by the Falls*; History of the Glens Falls Hospital, publisher.

NEWSPAPER COLUMNS
1994-2003: *"Over My Shoulder"* – Weekly column of history and commentary in *The Post-Star*, Glens Falls, NY.
1994-1995: *"Passed Times"* – Seasonal column of history and commentary in "The Time of Our Lives" tabloid of *The Post-Star*, Glens Falls, NY.
1975-1985: *"Chapman Museum"* – Weekly column of history and commentary in *The Post-Star*, Glens Falls, NY.

AS CONTRIBUTING AUTHOR
2005: Section on "Washington County, NY" in *The Encyclopedia of New York State*, 1st ed. Syracuse, NY: Syracuse University Press.

AS CO-EDITOR
1996 - *Sherlock Holmes: Victorian Sleuth to Modern Hero*. Scarecrow Press/University Press. Co-editor with Charles R. Putney and Sally Sugarman; collation of presentations from conference "Sherlock Holmes: Victorian Sleuth to Modern Hero."

RADIO
1978-1988: Author/producer of *LEGACY*, weekly program of history and commentary broadcast on WWSC AM/WCKM FM, Glens Falls, NY.

Table of Contents

Foreword 1
Introduction: Welcome and welcome back! 2
SECTION 1: Glens Falls History 3
    One site's sad history 3
    Reality falls short of a dream 4
    History of Union Square 6
    Women's group put focus on intellect 7
    Council promotes education for women 9
    Local man's early calls to impeach president 10
    A "pure heart" drove politician 12
    Recalling area's 1st Congressional Medal of Honor recipient 13
    Arthur deserves a marker 14
    A lover of education and parks 16
    One good effort leads to another 17
    A family's twisting history 18
    A name comes full circle 20
    Scandalous general spent youth in Glens Falls 21
    Civil War officer noted for gaff at Gettysburg 23
    Joseph's may have closed, but the memories linger 24
    A virtual historical tour of downtown Glens Falls 25
    Web tour of city updated with latest information 27
    Newspaper celebrates 90 years as The Post-Star 28
    Glens Falls once had its own version of Saratoga 29
    Going back in time to find The Post-Star's origins 31
    Continuing the journey through Post-Star history 32
    Writer recalls pride in being first with the day's news 34
    Chamber of Commerce began by buying cotton bale 35
    Today offers second chance to honor fallen heroes 37
    Empire Theatre started 20th century in grand style 38
    South Street still the lovable bad boy of Glens Falls 40
    South Street hustled and bustles with little attention 41
    Gangland murder, Prohibition tarnish South Street 43
    New Millennium brings hope for Street of Dreams 45
    Adirondack Pipes and Drums celebrates 50 years 46
    Bridging the gap, more than once, over the falls 48
    Hudson River's bridge experienced identity crisis 49
    Crossings began to define Glens Falls to the world 51
    Iron bridge undone by progress and pachyderms 52

Column, historian's office mark anniversaries 54
Start of county's historic tourism aided by Sue Wade 55
Sue Wade set standard for future county historians 57
Gompers brought eloquence to Washington County 58
City's first Labor Day celebration was huge affair 60
Municipal water system boon to firefighters 62
Celebrating paintings' homecoming 63
Empty spaces hold much history 65

SECTION 2: Area History 67

Putting the focus on temperance 67
The early days of an IP mill 68
Putnam's roots stretch to Scotland 70
Tale of Prince Taylor 71
Important date for Fort Ann 72
A girl, a boy and a dunking 74
Tales from the tannery 75
Mystery of a silent film star 76
The early abolition movement in Greenwich 78
Douglass' powerful presence 79
Baroness' mystery of the Red House 80
The Red House mystery solved 82
Friends, feathers in Easton 83
Quakers' impact on our region 84
A legal case for the books 86
The war against the flu 87
Giving Culver his due 89
"Ordinary hero" is honored in Whitehall 90
100 years for DAR chapter 91
Tracing the roots of Ticonderoga's first high school 93
Old-time obituaries raise intriguing questions 94
Born as property, slave emerged as free person 96
Pigs nowhere to be found on modern Bolton streets 97
Bolton offers summer cottages, museums, arts 98
Chester's bicentennial chance to reflect on history 100
Pember museum, library honor 90 years of history 101
History washes up on shores of Lake Champlain 104
Researchers gain knowledge of early occupants 105
Village of Fort Edward celebrates long, historic past 106
Railroad key to creation of Fort Edward village 108
Crown Point Bridge, first one for cars, turns 70 109
Residents recall dedication of Crown Point Bridge 111

Simultaneous parades complete bridge's dedication 112
Washington County to mark namesake's death 114
Recalling coincidental childhood memories with pal 115
Recollections of growing up, working in the pharmacy 116
Changes came slowly during the "good old days" 118
Reese, Rebel flag boosters have skewed view of history 120
Honoring a radical endorsed by Civil war history 121
Appreciate monuments for the stories they hold 123
Martha Barnes showed what country is all about 124
Call Mel: Battle of Saratoga would make a great movie 126
Local battle would make great climax for movie 128
County Historical Society has rich 60-year history 130
Club celebrates 100 years of leisurely pursuits 132
Historical association celebrates long history 135
Revisiting Henry Knox's 1775 trek 137
Knox trek highlights region's role in history 138

SECTION 3: Personal and Family Memories 140
Sweet sales pitch of George A. 140
A baby and a circus 141
Memories of Bobby Kennedy 142
Cruising your way through summer 144
A cool dude's guide to cruising 145
All the marbles 146
Leopard Girl finally sees the candy light 147
Sounds served as bookends for 1938 149
Strike up the band for a lesson in tolerance 150
A very special Santa 151
New Year's Eve dance will spin on forever 153
The gradual transformation from a child to an adult 154
Old Saratoga racing brochure a family heirloom 156
Preparing for atomic bomb hard lesson to forget 158
Memories of holidays gone by, via the back porch 159
Laundry and life lessons from the Christmas Cat 160
Days of enlightenment: Sampling the taste of paste 164
Way to grandma's heart - through your stomach 165
Historical events create an eruption of memories 167
Unexpected package conjures up Father's Day memories 168
Warm and wild flashbacks to Summer in Saratoga 170
Fall brings bright colors and warm memories 171
Unforeseen results of picking the wrong president 175
Christmas, Sinatra, a store's end 176

Friend wrote annual poem for 'New Yorker' 178
Afterward 180
Index 182
Endnotes 198

Foreword

The gift of a good storyteller is to take you outside of yourself and then subtly draw you back again, unfolding bits of the tale that remind you of yourself, and make the characters in the story relatable—no matter how long ago, nor fantastical the tale may seem.

I grew up having my father read to me at night. The Grimm Brothers and Mother Goose come to mind, but so do the tales he created from his memory and imagination. Once, out of desperation, he read to me from the biography of Elizabeth I; hundreds of pages long, it was dull reading bound to lull a child to sleep. I was hooked; I wanted to know what she did next, and why—as my father (I imagine) equally hoped to know the same about my sleep patterns, and when they would kick in.

That is the gift (and in that case, curse) of the true storyteller in action; I was in a time and place I'd never be able to conceive of, but I felt that I could. A story connects us, no matter who we are or what we've experienced. We understand because we're reminded that we are human, and that time and space separate little when it comes down to it.

My father's columns—whether you're familiar with them or not—foster that connection. I'm honored to have been able to edit them and know that you, dear reader, will enjoy them as much as I have.

Julia C. Cutshall-King, Editor

Introduction: Welcome and Welcome Back!

When City Editor Bob Condon first discussed my returning to write for *The Post-Star* in 1994, perhaps he was a little trepidatious. I certainly was! It had been nine years since my last column, written while I was Director of the Chapman Historical Museum. However, Bob said Managing Editor Ken Tingley had approved my starting out with a column called "Passed Times" in a quarterly tabloid section, "The Time of Our Lives."

That tabloid was discontinued in 1995. However, the column had garnered enough interest from past and new readers by then for *The Post-Star* to offer me a bi-weekly column, "Over My Shoulder," combining local history and commentary. In 1996 it went weekly and stayed as such until March 2003. I ended it when I took a job out of the region.

In all, I wrote more than 400 columns, all but eight were "Over My Shoulder." This book is a selection from all columns from January 1998 to December 2000. As *The Post-Star* covers Warren, Washington, and Saratoga Counties, I wrote columns covering from Ticonderoga (Essex County) in the north to Saratoga in the south, east into Vermont and west into the Adirondacks. I wrote local history as well as commentary on events of day. Most of the latter were rants and, thanks to the editorial work of Julia C. Cutshall-King, you have been spared columns too dated, too topical, or just too dull. Spelling and punctuation have been corrected when necessary. An occasional endnote was added for clarity or to update information.

Speaking of editors, Bob Condon was not my only one. Others included Will Doolittle, Dave Blow, Fred Daley, and Mike Mender, to name a few. Bob comes to mind most often, as he was also my editor when I was a correspondent from 1995 to 1997, reporting on news of towns and villages in southern Washington County and eastern Saratoga County. I learned from all my editors and am grateful to them.

This is not a scholarly book. I have always written knowing history can be deadly but hoping I could make it enjoyable enough for all to read. However, I always used primary and secondary sources. Primary included newspapers, public records, booklets, pamphlets diaries, journals, correspondence, audio and video recordings, many of them mine. Secondary included every published history I could buy or borrow. Some have been cited; others not. Our house groans under the weight of paper collected. I wrote these before the internet had become the trove it is today. Since then, to my wife Sara's distress, I have added more paper to my own library, not to mention hundreds upon hundreds of gigabytes of scanned and downloaded documents, maps, photographs and the like. My mania.

So, I thank you for reading these columns. I really hope you will enjoy them!

Joseph Cutshall-King

SECTION 1: GLENS FALLS HISTORY

NOTE: These first two columns provide a history of the Glens Falls Civic Center and, more broadly, of the Glens Falls Urban Renewal site bounded by Warren Street, Glen Street, Oakland Avenue, and Church Street. I was going to omit these columns but decided to keep them for two reasons. First, my compilation of the businesses, the buildings, and the one whole street lost to Urban Renewal in 1968-1970 is not duplicated elsewhere. Second, and sadly, what I had listed as having been built on that site as of 1998 has not changed in twenty-one years. However, and happily, the one major difference since the column's first publication rests in the optimistic prospects for the future of the Civic Center, thanks to work of The Adirondack Civic Center Coalition.

"OVER MY SHOULDER" COLUMN FOR JANUARY 18, 1998
One site's sad history

Yesterday marked the 18th anniversary of the Glens Falls Civic Center's Heritage Hall of Fame.

In the January 19, 1980 edition of *The Post-Star*, then "Women's Editor" Hermine Sherman[i] wrote enthusiastically: "Heritage Hall was launched Thursday night in an atmosphere of conviviality. Wall to wall people gathered... Many hope it is the beginning for a new era of prosperity for the city..."

Accompanying photographs showed the Civic Center's earliest proponents, such as banker Hubert Brown, attorney Francis W. McGinley and the honored guest of the evening, Oliver Laaskso. The presence of Assembly woman Joan Hague and Queensbury Supervisor Frances Walters[ii] underscored the regional support for the new Civic Center, and the Heritage Hall of Fame.

The January 17th event was hosted by the Adirondack Regional Chambers of Commerce. As Ms. Sherman wrote: "It was a happy crowd – one that was eager to hear what had transpired and what the future might bring."

The future is here and what constitutes "Heritage Hall"[iii] is being moved out into the hallway, where the folding chairs are stacked, and the whole Civic Center is being viewed as a loss. What happened to the dream of 1980? Were three "miracle revivals" on the same site simply too much?

Let's look at the site's history. Between 1966 and 1969, the Urban Renewal Agency took all of the land bordered by Warren Street, Glen Street, Church Street, and Oakland Avenue. Between 1969 and 1970, it demolished every building and obliterated all of Berry Street, which had run between Church and Glen Streets since 1835.

The plan was to renew Glens Falls. Instead, the parcel sat empty. Now, disaster had occurred twice before on all, or much of, the same site: once during the fire of 1864, which consumed almost every building on that later Urban

Renewal location; and in the fire of 1884, which destroyed the buildings on Warren Street and part of Glen. In both cases, all the burned out buildings were replaced within a few years.

That didn't happen in 1970 and the site sat vacant for nine years until the Civic Center was created. Using the 1961 edition of Manning's city directory, I've compiled a listing of the site's businesses. While a few may have moved or have gone out of business before Urban Renewal, the list still gives a fair, if heartbreaking, epitaph of the vitality Urban Renewal eradicated. On Glen, from Oakland to Warren: The Old Irish Inn and Annex; S&W Furniture; Glens Falls Commercial Sales; The Outlet; Northway Floors; Glen Pastry Shop; Hertz Jewelers; Silverman Clothing; Economy Dry Goods (later the Joy Store); Stein Clothes; Wedgeway Barber Shop; Glens Beauty Shop; Louis Fisher, Tailor; The Palace Lunch; The Sugar Bowl; Collins Newsroom; Boxers Drugstore.

Warren, from Glen to Church: Boxers (same store); Cervera Studio; Patten, Dentist; Stylair Beauty Shop; Palace Lunch System; Red Cross Shoe; Park Studio; Bartlett & Diers, Att.; Spiegel's Men's Shop; Stern's; John Wiley Shoe; Walk Over Boot Shop; Winch Signs; Western Union; Shine Realty; Micks, Osteopath; Rialto Theatre and Hotel; Colburn, Osteopath; Albert, Hairdresser; Steiner's Wallpaper; Clement's Delivery; Royal Typewriter; Kansas Restaurant; The Canteen; Alverson, Optometrist; Hart's Aluminum Prod.; Nat Stores; Goodson's Dress; Warren Co. Democratic Headquarters; Glidden Paint; Electrolux; Smart Set.

From both sides of Berry Street: Adirondack Credit Service; Medical Arts Dental; Rothbards; Robert Rhinelander, Architect.

Over 50 businesses, plus numerous private residences, located there in 1961 were gone by 1969. Dozens of buildings flattened. With them went a community unto itself and one of "valves" of the heart of downtown Glens Falls.

Now, twenty-nine years later, only two businesses occupy that site: Burger King and the Civic Center – and now people talk of the possible demise of the Civic Center.

Next week: some instructive history of the Urban Renewal site and the Civic Center from 1978 to 1998.

"OVER MY SHOULDER" COLUMN FOR JANUARY 25, 1998
Reality falls short of a dream

This week we trace the history of, and past dreams for, the Glens Falls Urban Renewal site and Civic Center from 1978 to 1998.

Actually, we'll start from Feb. 24, 1977, when Mayor Robert J. Cronin first presented the idea of the Civic Center in *The Post-Star*. He defended the idea, saying it had come from Oliver Laakso, who was president of Kamyr, one of the city's largest tax-paying corporations, and certainly experienced in business.

Laakso was supported by the region's top business leaders, who held a mutual hope for downtown's renewal. Not everyone embraced the Civic Center dream, leading First National Bank of Glens Falls President William Clark to criticize publicly the negativity of its critics.

But most of us shared *Post-Star* Editor Don Metivier's vision for Glens Falls' rebirth, as stated in his article, "An Optimistic Look at Glens Falls," inspired by the Center's opening in May 1979.[iv]

But there was substantial difference between Mayor Cronin's $6 million proposal and the $7 million reality.

The 1977 architectural rendering showed two stories of subsurface parking. The article stated that the 4,000-seat center would feature an ice rink, a movable stage, a boxing and wrestling ring, and a basketball hard court. The area arts community's desires were solicited, too, and it was understood the Center would be the new home of the Glens Falls Opera Festival,[v] then seeking its own facility.

By 1978, seating had been increased, but subsurface parking had been eliminated and the arts' involvement, particularly the Opera Festival's, had not taken place.

Those last two "omissions" proved to be very weakening factors.

Nonetheless, in 1978 Ned Harkness was hired as the first director. The Red Wings franchise was secured that year, with Bill Purcell as coach. Performances by Ringling Brothers Circus were booked. Edward Bartholomew succeeded Mayor Cronin in the fall of '78.

On May 18, 1979, both mayors officiated at the opening of the Glens Falls Civic Center. Two days later, the Center's opening act was the Beach Boys, introduced by Mayor Bartholomew, who asked the audience, "Are you ready to rock 'n' roll?"

We all were, and, over time, acts like the Grateful Dead and Aerosmith came to help.

The Heritage Hall of Fame opened in January 1980. When the 1980 Winter Olympics' torch paused at the Urban Renewal site, it seemed like "the time" to develop the rest of it.

Mayor Bartholomew proposed an ambitious design. Essentially like a mini-mall, it included a huge theater, a movie house, retail shops, subsurface parking and a combined museum to house the Chapman Historical Museum and The Hyde Collection.

The idea, the last integrated plan for the whole Urban Renewal site, never materialized. In October 1984 the present Burger King opened on the corner of Warren and Glen Streets.

The outcry was unreal: only one business where many used to be?! In 1985, two office buildings were erected on Warren Street adjacent to Burger King.

More outcry. Last fall, the two empty office buildings were up for sale. There has been no outcry.

And the Civic Center?

It still lives, but the circus and the Beach Boys no longer appear there, thanks to Albany's Pepsi (formerly Knickerbocker) Arena, and there is the ever-growing question of whether the Wings can afford to stay.

The team is still here because of - among others - their fans and the Center's four directors: Ned Harkness, 1978-1982; Jack Kelly, 1982-1993; Alan Vella, 1993-1994; and now, Donald Ostrom. Somehow, those directors have kept the Center going despite such disadvantages as poor parking, the Pepsi Arena, the Northeast recession and a city without a plan.

However, for the Urban Renewal Site as a whole, this thumbnail history shows that the sad reality of 1998 certainly does not match the hopeful dream of 1977.

"OVER MY SHOULDER" COLUMN FOR APRIL 5, 1998
History of Union Square

David Blow's March 26 *Post-Star* article "Entrepreneur reveals plan to transform center of city," raised the question about the origin of the name "Union Square."

Dave reported on Richard R. Emerson's plans for redeveloping a commercial block at the corner of Broad and Pine Streets in the City of Glens Falls. This was originally the York Shirt factory. He wrote, "By the end of the summer, the corner of Broad and South Streets will be known as Union Square."

Technically, it has been known as "Union Square" since 1891, although in recent times the name's use has faded a bit. "Union Square" was derived from "Union School No. 2," the 12-room, brick school building erected at Broad and South Streets in the Village of Glens Falls in 1891. The new school was built by the Union Free School District No. 1 of the Town of Queensbury and replaced an 1864 2-room school.

On page 200 of the book *Bridging the Years*,[vi] there is a photograph of Union School No. 2 in all its glory. It was a school until 1931, when the Broad Street School replaced it. Although the school moved, the name for the intersection stuck. The building was later used for county offices, then razed. On the site today is a Rite-Aid Pharmacy.[vii]

While Mr. Emerson may use the phrase "Union Square" in his new address, the possessor of the address "One Union Square" is Frank Colotti, owner of the building at 1 Broad Street, where he operates Colotti's Shoes Sales and Service. Frank said that when Michael Dolan, Jr., built on 1 Broad Street in 1904, he petitioned Glens Falls to allow the building to be officially listed as both "1 Broad Street" and "One Union Square."

Frank maintains both addresses for the building, which he purchased in 1975.

"Niagara Mohawk bills me under the address of One Union Square," while others use the 1 Broad Street address, Frank told me last Monday.

Shortly after Frank moved in, he commissioned artist Max Tupper to create the sign "One Union Square," which now hangs on the front of the building.

Richard Emerson's plans focus on several buildings on Broad Street, down to the corner of Pine Street. The brick structures on the plot will remain, while the wood frame structure to the right of the brick ones will be razed. Mr. Emerson is searching for any information on the site and, with that in mind, I spoke with architect Robert Joy last Tuesday. Bob had been involved in two recent attempts to redevelop the same property, once for medical offices and another time for a hotel. I'd mentioned that I was sad to see the one building having to be razed, but as Bob pointed out, the building is a wooden "balloon frame" and unlike buildings with "heavy timber frames," does not meet city building codes.

Ralph Shapiro of Glens Falls told me that, until third grade, he went to "the South Street School," as the Union School No. 2 was called. He recalls stopping by the old York Shirt factory to watch the workers make their own boxes in the cellar. After World War II, it was owned by the Patrick family and briefly used for shoe or slipper manufacture. It was then rented to a Granville clothing firm. Neither lasted long. Dennison's had a lingerie factory on the top floor. On the second floor, there was a wholesale candy and toy dealer.

I know the Chapman Historical Museum has some great panoramic shots of Union Square. Perhaps you have some history of that site? Please contact me care of *The Post-Star* and I'll include it in an upcoming "part two" of the Union Square story. Thanks![viii]

"OVER MY SHOULDER" COLUMN FOR MAY 3, 1998
Women's group put focus on intellect

As promised, some history on the origins of the organization "Friends in Council," one of the oldest continuously running study clubs for women in New York State. My thanks to Friends members, Helen Cackener and Harriet Cederstrom, for sending me the history of the organization, written in 1974 by Kathryn O'Brien.[ix]

Friends in Council began in Glens Falls in 1884. To put the organization's beginning in perspective, let's look at the what had been happening in the region.

In the days after the Civil War, women began to find greater opportunities for self-expression outside of the home. In only a few generations, the descendants of the women who had lived in the frontier region of eastern New York and western New England of the 1760s had become housebound. Although the frontier women had never had the same rights as men, they enjoyed a shoulder-to-shoulder equality of frontier work. During the

Revolution, women and men shared equally the misery of invading soldiers, being driven off their lands, being kidnapped, or having their homes burnt out from underneath them.

By the early 1800s, women lost much of what they had gained and their "expected place" in the "model Victorian world" was in the home raising children, especially women living in villages and cities. Fewer women went to school than men. By the Civil War, it was usually only religious organizations that afforded women the chance to get out of the house, although in this region the activism of Quakers and Methodists in social causes of education, abolition, suffrage and temperance brought area women into the mainstream.

The Civil War itself spawned women's organizations to help the war effort. In the post-war decades women's organizations such as the W.C.T.U. thrived. In the 1870s laws were being enacted to allow women to divorce, to own property and have other rights. The suffrage movement had gained power. The powerful Chautauqua movement with its emphasis on home study started in 1874. State laws were enforcing more schooling for girls and boys. And perhaps most significantly in the 1870s and 1880s, jobs began to open up for women in textile mills and other factories, and in shops and offices.

Still, there was a need to be met, a need for intellectual fulfillment. In 1884 Glens Falls, while more and more females were going to public school, unlike their male counterparts, few were going to college. And by extension, few were using and expanding their intellectual gifts.

In 1884, two women from the west side of Glens Falls decided it was time to remedy that. "Miss Anna Murray...and a friend, Mrs. James H. Bain met with a definite purpose: to read and study; to broaden their horizons; and to go more deeply into the subjects studied." Anna Murray would serve as "principal of 3rd and 4th grades in the Union St. School" on Broad Street. As Kathryn O'Brien noted, both women were knowledgeable about the Chautauqua method of home study and they hoped to "achieve even greater success on a local level."

The two organizers invited eight women to join them. Eventually the number would increase and stay steady at between 17 and 18, perhaps due the fact that the Friends have always met in their homes.

The Quaker beginnings of Glens Falls show up in the name "Friends in Council," a term used in the 1860s by Quakers for "prayer and thought." No religion was involved here, however, and proof of this was in the group's first choice for study: Darwin's "Origin of the Species." A lava-hot topic even in 1884, the choice inspired one member to resign due to her religious differences with Mr. Darwin's theories!

Next week, we'll finish our history of the Friends in Council.

"OVER MY SHOULDER" COLUMN FOR MAY 10, 1998
Council promotes education for women

We are looking at the early years of the women's study club "Friends in Council." It was mentioned in last week's column how the Friends' first study issue, Charles Darwin's "Origin of the Species," had caused one of the groups' initial members to drop out due to religious differences.

That, however, was an exception to the rule for Friends in Council, begun in Glens Falls in 1884. As the name suggests, these women were friends and strove to stay as such. Though social in organization – the group has always met in each other's homes – "improvement of the mind was the main objective," member Kathryn E. O'Brien wrote in her 1974 history.

Ms. O'Brien also wrote that unwritten rules gradually emerged. Everyone had to approve a new member, although memberships could be passed down from mother to daughter. "Only serious students were accepted into membership" and "gossip and trivialities were taboo."

Some of the informality left in 1904 with the creation of officers, printed programs and minutes. In 1906 the Friends became "federated," that is registering with other study clubs in the state, which like the Friends in Council were flourishing at this point. A statewide convention in Saratoga Springs was held in 1906, with the main consideration being "illiteracy in New York State," still a problem 92 years later.

Federating did not yield much, and the Friends concentrated upon their own program. From the early 1900s, courses were being outlined as in a college syllabus. One subject per year was studied, such as French History or German History, although the Reformation took two years.

Each week one woman presented a paper, and everyone had homework. Even after 1910, when meetings dropped to once every two weeks, this was certainly a serious commitment to scholarship.

I'm impressed by all who were members and select one as an example of the kind of women who were in Friends in Council in those early decades, in this case during the first decades of the 20th century. She was Eva Judkins, listed in the history as "Mrs. Charles O. Judkins," who joined the Friends in 1904. She was a perfect example of the "new woman" of that time.

Among her accomplishments, she was an early member of the Women's Civic Club, helped found the local Red Cross Chapter in 1916, was deeply involved in the suffrage movement and was not only the first woman to serve on the board of Education of the Glens Falls City School System, but the first to serve as its president.

O'Brien's history notes that the state Commissioner of Education from 1913 to 1921, John H. Finley, had told a member that the "Friends in Council as a study club ranks second to none in the state." The courses of study that were followed were rigorous and everyone participated – and persevered. Neither World War I, Prohibition, flappers, the Great Depression, nor World War II caused them to stop meeting.

However, by the late 1940s, Kathryn O'Brien wrote, there was "a gradual lessening of intensity" in the study materials. It's speculation, but perhaps it was due to several things. During the war, many women had worked or served in the military. More women were going to college, more to work. Some of the members had grown older, while some incoming members filling newly vacated seats were also busy creating "the baby boom."

Now in 1998, in spite of the frantic changes of the last fifty years, the 114 year-old Friends in Council remains a resilient organization for intellectual discussion among women, some of whom are "baby boomers." Congratulations to Friends in Council, a contributor to the progress of women's education over the last century.

"OVER MY SHOULDER" COLUMN FOR MAY 17, 1998
Local man's early calls to impeach president

NOTE: There is no little irony in the fact that the first sentence of this column can be stated again today, twenty-one years later, with equal validity.

Impeachment is being whispered, almost to a shout, around Washington these days, the second time in twenty-five years.

The first attempt at presidential impeachment was against President Andrew Johnson in 1868. Among his antagonists was an assemblyman from the Town of Queensbury – Orange Ferris.

Before we look at Ferris' role, we need background on the case against Johnson.

The attempt to impeach Johnson is often seen solely as a straightforward attack on the powers of the presidency, which under Lincoln had grown beyond what the Constitution allowed. Yet, Lincoln was in a war and had reluctantly assumed powers of the Supreme Commander. With Lincoln's death, Radical Republicans buried him and his plans for a Reconstruction based on clemency and forgiveness, pushing instead to punish the South, leaving it embittered and unrepentant, essentially losing the gains of war. This loss eventually included the rights given to ex-slaves by the Radicals' own 14th and 15th Amendments, later negated by the South's "Jim Crow" laws. How fast would civil rights have advanced had Lincoln lived?

But in addition to punishing the old Confederacy, the Radicals sought to reorganize our government in a way to make Congress the supreme authority of the land, like a parliament, with the 1789 Constitution's checks and balances of both the president and Supreme Court effectively gone.

Congress created two laws. (Both were eventually overturned.) One, the

"Command of the Army" Act, ended the president's Constitutional role as the civilian head of the military by forcing all military orders to be issued through a "General of the Army" who could only be removed by Congress. Second was the "Tenure of Office" Act, denying the president the right to remove any appointees, even cabinet members, from office without Senatorial approval. Johnson fired Secretary of War Stanton and Congress had its excuse to start his impeachment.

Johnson's personality and its effect upon partisan politics clouds the "straightforward" interpretation. He was elected vice president in 1864 as a "War Democrat" – from Tennessee but opposed to secession. After the assassination, Democrat President Johnson tried to follow Republican President Lincoln's principles, but lacked Lincoln's political ability or power of speech.

Johnson's pugnacity, biting tongue, and lapses in judgment figured largely in the 1866 congressional elections that saw Queensbury Republican Orange Ferris elected Representative to the 40th Congress. Johnson stumped for his party, forgetting forgiveness, making foolishly vindictive statements, and ironically, considering the war just fought, raising the issue of "states' rights."

Many fellow Democrats, as well as Republicans, opposed Johnson personally without necessarily supporting Republican Radicals. More importantly, he lost support of the Northern press, pulpit, and people. As early as 1866, impeachment was being proposed.

Ferris, a Republican, was ardently pro-impeachment. Born in the Village of Glens Falls in 1814, Ferris was educated at the Glens Falls Academy and the University of Vermont. He studied law under Judge William Hay and first dipped his feet in political waters in 1839 as a "Whig," when he became Justice of the Peace. In 1840, Gov. William Seward appointed him as Inspector of Common Schools. He served as Surrogate Judge from 1840-45, County Judge from 1851-63, and US Representative from 1867-69 and 1869-71.

What pushed Ferris toward impeachment is difficult to tell outright, as most of my facts on Ferris come from Dr. A. W. Holden's 1874 *History of Queensbury* and his contribution to the 1886 *History of Warren County*. And Holden was hardly impartial about Ferris. He wrote in 1874 that Ferris was "Like Caesar's wife...above suspicion," and "in a corrupt age, surrounded by demoralizing partisan influences, he has escaped...political contamination with clean hands and a pure heart."

Next week, I'll attempt to "read between the political lines" to examine the pure of heart.

"OVER MY SHOULDER" COLUMN FOR MAY 24, 1998
A "pure heart" drove politician

We are reading between "the political lines" in an attempt to examine the motivations of Representative Orange Ferris of Queensbury, a Republican who came to Congress in 1867 and joined the chorus for the impeachment of President Andrew Johnson, a Democrat.

I said that most of my information on Ferris came from historian Dr. A.W. Holden, who wrote in 1886 that Ferris "commanded universal respect." I also looked through the Crandall Library's newspaper microfilms at issues of "The Republican," ironically, the local Democratic paper. (There are no Glens Falls pro-Republican papers of the era surviving.) Interestingly, while *The Republican* blasted Congress' call for Johnson's impeachment, it did not attack Ferris.

Also interesting is that Holden wrote for *The Republican*. Certainly, Ferris' views had to conflict in some ways with Holden's, which I assume would have followed his newspaper's party line to a certain degree. Like Republicans, the Democrats had been pro-Union, but unlike Republicans, more appeasing to the South. The Democrats split over secession, with some like Andrew Johnson favoring war and becoming "War Democrats." (Holden himself was the first to open a recruiting office in Glens Falls in answer to Lincoln's call for troops in April of 1861.)

Unlike fellow Democrat Johnson, "The Republican" was virulently against Lincoln, Emancipation (the paper was a racist rag), and his compassionate Reconstruction policy. Democrats supported what I would call a "forgive and forget" Reconstruction policy, the opposite of the Radical Republicans' desire to punish and remember.

Ferris called for impeachment, but I think his motivations were above those of the Radicals. Ferris seemed to be no slave to party line when in 1867, he attacked fellow Republican Secretary William Seward's proposal to purchase Alaska. (Seward had given Ferris his first political appointment.) According to Judge John Austin, Ferris has ended up in "The 41 Worst Predictions of All Time" for saying that possession of Alaska "will always be a source of weakness and expense, without any adequate return."

On March 2, 1868, Ferris addressed Congress in support of impeachment. He said that the Civil War had been "a contest...between republican ideas...and aristocracy, the pilgrims and the cavaliers. Jamestown typifies the one...Plymouth Rock the other. Weeds and thistles" had overgrown Jamestown, "but Plymouth Rock remains." Long after that rock disappeared, "the free civilization and social ideas of New England will be doing their work..." (Holden, the Democrat, quoted the entire last paragraph of Ferris' impeachment speech in his 1874 town history.)

On March 3, "The Republican" newspaper again came out against impeachment, calling the Radicals "Destructionists," ironically including

President Johnson in that group. In a blast against the Radicals' promoting racial equality, the paper said that Radical Senator Ben Wade (who would become president once Johnson was ousted) had already picked his cabinet members, including "the negro, Fred. Douglass...The end is approaching!"

But nothing was written at any time in the paper against Ferris for his support of African American rights. There Ferris had already taken his stand in that March 2nd speech to Congress. Here's the rest of the previous quote: "the free civilization and social ideas of New England will be doing their work...inculcating a love for liberty which is as broad in its philanthropy as the universe, and knows no distinction of race or color."

Impeachment failed by a vote. But shortly thereafter Ferris' color-blind philosophy became law in the 15th Amendment, which states "the right...to vote shall not be denied...on account of race, color or previous condition of servitude."

I have come to believe that while Ferris may have been misguided in the case of Johnson's impeachment, he shared none of the Radicals' ulterior motivations for power, but truly operated from what Dr. A. W. Holden called a "pure heart."

"OVER MY SHOULDER" COLUMN FOR MAY 31, 1998
Recalling area's 1st Congressional Medal of Honor recipient

In honor of Memorial Day, originally started as "Decoration Day" on May 30, 1868, here is a timely story about the first person from Glens Falls and Queensbury to be awarded the Congressional Medal of Honor. I thank Nancy Barrett of South Bay for her research.

A "Congressional Medal of Honor" was created in 1861 for the U. S. Navy and in 1862 for the U. S. Army "for conspicuous gallantry and intrepidity at the risk of life, above and beyond the call of duty." The first honoree from Glens Falls and Queensbury was Franklin Johndro – ironically born in Highgate Springs, Vermont. Somewhere in the late 1850s, he married Emeline Philo, of Philo Street – right next to the Bay Street Cemetery – in the Village of Glens Falls. Frank, as he was called, moved to the village.

On August 8, 1862, he enlisted in Company A of the 118th Regiment of the New York Infantry. That regiment's story was beautifully recounted in *Three Years with the Adirondack Regiment*, the memoirs of Colonel John Cunningham, whose book, as we'll see, presents an interesting "twist" concerning Johndro's citation.

Johndro was nearly four years in the army, not being "mustered out" until June 20, 1865. It was almost miracle that he lived to perform the heroism that won him the Medal of Honor, and definitely a miracle that he ever lived to receive it.

The highest and lowest points in Johndro's military career occurred within five months in 1864 in Virginia. His 1888 pension application tells a horrific tale. In June of 1864 at Yorktown, he contracted rheumatism, then suffered sunstroke. Then in July at Petersburg the breech pin blew out of his rifle, severely wounding his left eye. He fought on through a horrendous summer.

Then, glory came to Johndro on September 30, 1864 at Chapin's Farm. Cunningham's diary entry tells it in the typical understatement of a war-seasoned soldier: "After the third assault, in the lull following, we sent out a few sharpshooters as a picket of observation. Franklin Johndro, Company A of our regiment, was in this detail and found some twenty-five of the enemy hiding in the bushes not daring to reveal themselves so near the fort, waiting for darkness to retire or...probably to surrender... Anyhow Johndro with his seven-shooter...persuaded them to `come in' with him." (Some documents put it at 50 soldiers captured, but even 25 is phenomenal.)

Johndro was in triumph. One month later he was a Confederate prisoner, captured at "Second Fair Oakes" and held until March, 1865, at Salisbury, North Carolina, under wretched conditions that left him permanently deaf in his left ear.

After his release, he was placed in a hospital in Hampton, Virginia. On April 6, 1865, he was awarded the Congressional Medal of Honor by Sec. of War Stanton, according to government records. But Cunningham, whom I believe was a truthful writer, stated that "Johndro received an honor medal from President Lincoln," as opposed to Stanton. My belief in that is buttressed by Nancy Barrett's having found that Lincoln was at City Point that very day, only two miles from Johndro. What a mystery.

After the war, Frank and Emeline moved to Bay City, Michigan. There they lived until their deaths (hers in 1898, his in 1901), when they were returned to Glens Falls. On April 8, 1901, four veterans, three of whom had served with Johndro, accompanied him on his last march, this time to the Bay Street Cemetery to join Emeline and to become the first Congressional Medal of Honor winner buried in Glens Falls and Queensbury.

"OVER MY SHOULDER" COLUMN FOR JUNE 21, 1998
Arthur deserves a marker

Greenwich town historian Cathy Sharp[xi] has "a good problem."
The "good" is that the boyhood home of President Chester A. Arthur is located in the Village of Greenwich. The "problem" is that she can't find sufficient funding to have a New York State historic marker placed in front of it.

There is a REPLICA of the Fairfield, Vermont, house Arthur was born in. Also, there is a New York State historic marker in the Town of Hoosick in Rensselaer County, because he lived there. But the ACTUAL HOUSE in which he lived is no longer there.

So, logically, Cathy would like to place a marker in front of the ONLY existing boyhood home of President Arthur, on Woodlawn Avenue in the Village of Greenwich.

Why is it worth it? I have put together some information Cathy sent me, along with some additional research, in order to tell you.

Chester Alan Arthur was born in Fairfield, Vt., on Oct. 5, 1830. His father, a poor Baptist minister, relocated with his family to Greenwich in 1839 to preach at the Greenwich Baptist Church on the corner of Woodlawn and Church Streets. However, the church then was a wooden structure.

Nearby was the parsonage where the Arthurs lived until 1844. I'll come back to that shortly. Chester A. Arthur spent 9 formative years in Greenwich, before moving to Schenectady. There, at age 15, he entered Union College and graduated in 1848 at age 18! Ironically, Arthur was there at the same time as James A. Garfield, whose assassination in 1881 vaulted Arthur into the presidency.

After graduation, Arthur taught school in North Pownal, Vermont, where Garfield also taught after graduation. In 1852, Arthur moved to New York City to practice law. Sadly, he became part of the corrupt "New York machine" run by Roscoe Conkling.

Conkling ruled New York State's Republican party as a tyrant, doling out political patronage jobs to 7,000 people, including Arthur, for whom he secured a job in the New York Customs House, where Arthur got into corruption up to his neck. Conkling "owned" him.

Conkling then got Arthur the vice-presidency under James A. Garfield. We would have totally forgotten Arthur had it not been for a mentally unhinged office-seeker, Charles J. Guiteau, who shot Garfield. Garfield died September 19, 1881 and Chester A. Arthur was sworn in as President.

Handsome, a widower with three children, Arthur brought elegance and fun to the White House. It could have stopped there. Instead, this "bought" attorney regained his moral bearings. He went against the "New York machine" and after corruption, canceling a wasteful bill to benefit New York City and routing out post office fraud. Most dramatically, he championed the Pendleton Civil Service Reform bill that would strike at the heart of the very political patronage system that had put him in office! Congress passed the Pendleton bill in 1882.

The Republicans dumped him, choosing someone else to run for President for 1884. Arthur had sacrificed his political career. Imagine that. He had placed the good of the people above political gain. He died in Albany in 1886.

Meanwhile, in 1880, Arthur's Greenwich home had been moved to Gray Avenue. Later, it was moved again, this time to Woodlawn Avenue, where it stands today.

What an honor it is for this whole region to have the boyhood home of President Chester A. Arthur, the President who regained his honor. However, the cost of creating and installing a historic marker is around $1,000, far beyond the meager budget of a town historian.

It would be sad not to commemorate the boyhood home of Arthur, all for the lack of $1,000.

Or, looking at it another way, all for the price of 5 pairs of name-brand sneakers.

"OVER MY SHOULDER" COLUMN FOR JUNE 28, 1998
A lover of education and parks

When I tell you the story of Henry Crandall, I tell you of a person born with three strikes against him, who went on not just to make a fortune in the Horatio Alger mode, but to use it to enrich this region. Henry was born in 1821 in Harrisena, Town of Queensbury. His first strike was to be born out of wedlock, then hypocritically regarded as rare, and subject to censure. Second, his mother was NOT wealthy. Third, he received scant education, coming away with minimal reading abilities but an incredible head for business. His spirit overcame those adversities, but today I feel that spirit is misunderstood.

In 1839, at 18, Henry literally walked to North Creek, became involved in lumbering and by 1849, (1) had saved $1,000, a LOT of money then, and (2) was listed among the major names of lumber in the region – Finch, Morgan, Wing, and Van Dusen, significantly all from the booming Village of Glens Falls.

Crandall took his $1,000 and went to Glens Falls, where, in addition to the lumber industry, he emerged as a business partner in every enterprise that smelled of money, including being a co-founder of today's Evergreen Bank[xii] and a board member of today's Glens Falls National Bank and Trust Company. In the post-Civil War era, his fortune expanded, unimpeded by subsequent recessions.

He married, and he and Betsy built a beautiful home near where Crandall Library is today. He became involved with other than business. He was a village trustee, a major supporter of the Presbyterian church, and a vestryman for the Harrisena Church.

Significantly, in 1881, the boy with little formal education became a proponent of it as he joined the original board of education of today's Glens Falls City School System. Then he created a boys club that changed the lives of many boys whose beginnings were like Henry's, perhaps motivated by the fact that he and Betsy had no children.

Most significantly, in 1893 Crandall, definitely not a reader, approached Superintendent of Schools, Dr. Sherman Williams[xiii], with a proposal to create the Crandall Free Library – "free," as Henry would have no charging for books. It was established in a business block adjacent to their home.

Henry then created Crandall Park in 1898, a magnificent gift that pleased his adopted village. He tended it like a private garden and he and Betsy were later buried there, in the monument bearing his log mark[xiv], a huge star.

Not everything he did pleased others, such as fighting the village water system in the 1870s. (He lost.) Or putting an unwanted fence around the Civil War Monument. The night after he died, Feb. 19, 1913, city crews removed it. Powerful people can be powerfully disliked.

In death, he caused problems. His will's many codicils included ones to endow his Crandall Park, and to buy what little land around his house he didn't own, build a library building and use the rest for a park. Trouble arose as the will was contested, especially by those claiming Henry as their father.

About thirteen years later the will was settled and Henry Crandall's last project was begun. Completed in 1931 very near the site of his home, Crandall Library was the pinnacle of his philanthropy, for it spoke to what he had lacked, but had wanted for others.

My interpretation is that Henry provided what we call today "City Park" as a place for the library to be built and to expand outward, as it has once already. I believe if he could speak today, the man who was not a reader, but who loved equally education and parks, would say, "Save some of City Park, but above all, let Crandall Library grow."

"OVER MY SHOULDER" COLUMN FOR JULY 26, 1998
One good effort leads to another

The Tri-County United Way celebrated its 75th anniversary on May 31st this year.

But did it actually begin earlier?

"Monopoly" players are familiar with "Community Chest" and today's Tri-County United Way began in 1923 as the "Glens Falls Community Chest" at a public meeting held in the offices of the Glens Falls Insurance Company, then located on the northwest corner of Glen and Bay Streets in Glens Falls. Seventy-five people attended.

That the Community Chest's founding meeting was in the insurance company's offices is not surprising, for it was there that the Glens Falls Hospital's founding meeting occurred in 1897 and there the Adirondack Chapter of the American Red Cross had its first offices from 1917 to 1919.

Of the 75 people attending, sixteen served on the first board of the Community Chest: George F. Bayle, Sr.,[xv] board president; John Bazinet[xvi]; Louis M. Brown[xvii]; Robert G. Clark; Daniel H. Cowles; Louis F. Hyde[xviii]; Byron Lapham[xix]; John R. Loomis; B. F. McCreery; T. J. McGillicuddy; James McPhillips; James E. Singleton; Frank M. Smalley[xx]; George Tait[xxi]; E. West[xxii]; and C. M. Wilmarth[xxiii].

Each was a powerful and able person. Board president George F. Bayle was an excellent example of them all. Bayle had moved to Glens Falls from

Washington County and started as a clerk in a dry goods store, eventually establishing his own highly successful "Boston Store" before becoming head of the Glens Falls Portland Cement Company. He helped lead the drive to create the City of Glens Falls and served on its first common council. His intelligence and initiative were perfect for the Community Chest.

In 1923, when the average annual salary was about $1,800, the board set a fund raising goal of $65,525 for these original "member agencies": the Glens Falls (now Adirondack) Chapter of the American Red Cross, the Salvation Army, the Tri-County Association for the Blind, the Boy Scouts, and the Girl Scouts.

I'd mentioned that possibly our United Way could claim an earlier starting date than 1923. Follow along with me. The concept of a Community Chest – where area charities would unite in a common fund raising effort – had begun in Denver in 1887. However, the Community Chest concept got a huge boost throughout the United States and Canada in 1918, during World War I, when each of many thousands of communities established what was called a "War Chest."

Glens Falls had. Considering that the city's drives for money and *materiels* for the war effort often exceeded those of larger communities, it was sensible to create a common funding mechanism for agencies such as the Red Cross, which were helping the war effort, as well as those civic organizations vital to the health of the community, such as the Glens Falls Hospital.

In fact, in May of 1918, the hospital was deeply in debt as its traditional community support had been diverted to the war effort. The hospital board turned to the War Chest and asked for $5000.

The War Chest's president sent its board members to investigate, resulting in the War Chest approving triple that request, $15,000, to help the hospital clear all its debt, an action that spurred the community to rally behind the hospital. The three investigators were George Tait, B.F. McCreery and J. E. Singleton. Sound familiar? They were among the 1923 Community Chest founding board. And the War Chest's president? George F. Bayle.

With war's end, the War Chest also ended. But did it? Obviously, the spirit lived on, for only four years later Bayle and, as far as my research shows, the original members of the War Chest founded the Glens Falls Community Chest.

So, in my wishing the Tri-County United Way a happy 75th anniversary, I'll wish it a happy 80th, too!

"OVER MY SHOULDER" COLUMN FOR NOVEMBER 1, 1998
A family's twisting history

What follows is a story breathtaking in its complexity.

Often American descendants of Canadian French immigrants can only trace their family to Canada. Sometimes, fortunately, the family even knows the family's place of origin in France, but like so many of us, are left wondering why their ancestor emigrated to the New World.

Here is a true story of one such ancestor, Jean Bail and how several of his descendants, including Robert Bayle of Queensbury, New York, answered that question.

Bob Bayle was fortunate in starting his search, as his father, Francis, had written down what he remembered of the family history. In a past column, I mentioned Bob's grandfather, George F. Bayle[xxiv], who had been born at Bald Mountain in the Town of Greenwich in 1860. He later moved to Glens Falls, where he began in the dry goods business. Possessing incredible drive and ability, George excelled in the dry goods business, working in New York and New England and eventually establishing his own store in Glens Falls, The Boston Store. His business abilities led him, among his many accomplishments, to become president of the Glens Falls Portland Cement Company.

That wasn't totally unusual considering that the Bayle family had become involved in a related business, lime making at Bald Mountain, after emigrating to Washington County from Quebec.

In his history, Francis wrote that George knew that the Bayles had come from Metz. (Presumably this was from oral tradition, though Francis Bayle did not indicate as such.) On a buying trip in France in the 1880s, George looked up his family. He discovered that they spelled their name as "Baille" and that they had been wealthy but had lost their fortune in the Franco-Prussian war of 1870-71.

So, much was known of the Bayle family history, including that a Bayle ancestor had emigrated from Metz to Chambly, Province Quebec, Canada, and from there to Greenwich. Overall, a pretty straightforward line of march, typical of many French Canadians who would settle here in the 1800s. But had it been that way?

The story took on a fascinating twist, when one of Bob's cousins began to look more deeply. Essentially, he had that itch to know "why" the Bayles came to Canada. Researching in Quebec, he had found more information had helped but it was primarily of the Bayle's and their descendants in Canada.

It was a 1984 monograph by a researcher named Virginia DeMarce that put a whole new angle on the Bayles. It was entitled, "Settlement of the Former German Auxiliary Troops in Canada after the American Revolution."[xxv] In it, they learned of the Hesse Hanau Regiment, also called the Grenadier Regiment Erbprinz, or Grenadier Regiment Crown Prince, for the Crown Prince of Hesse-Kassel.

Among the recruits serving in the Crown Prince's Infantry was a Jean Bail, also called Jean-Baptiste Bail, born in Metz, on the Moselle River in France, only about 40 miles from Germany. It would be an easy thing for a man from Metz to join the Hesse Hanau Regiment, which was assigned to fight under the Baron von Riedesel, a German noble acting as a mercenary under the orders of

Frederick II, who supplied his troops to King George of England.

Have you guessed it? These were the very "Hessian" troops sent to fight against the rebellious colonists in the American Revolution. Jean Bail was one of them. He served five years, mustering out in 1783 in Quebec, where he remained. For in 1782, he had married Margaurite Monsciau dite Deslormeau and some of their descendants would move to Washington County and call themselves "Bayle."

Had Jean Bail served in this area, possibly even fighting against the very colonists whose descendants would be the neighbors of his descendants? Certainly, the Baron von Riedesel was here, and though he was captured at Saratoga in October of 1777, not all those under his command were there. Further research will tell.

"OVER MY SHOULDER" COLUMN FOR NOVEMBER 8, 1998
A name comes full circle

Colonel John Glenn, now Senator Glenn, has once again returned to earth from a mission in space.

In a recent article in *The Post-Star*, David Blow reported on the day in February of 1962 when the City of Glens Falls was officially renamed "Glenn's Orbit" to commemorate Glenn's first trip around the earth.

The irony was that, in the renaming, the city was more historically accurate than it knew.

Let me explain by telling you a bit about the person for whom the City of Glens Falls is named.

According to Holden's 1874 history of Queensbury, John Glen was born in Albany in 1735. His actual name was Joahannes Glen, showing his Dutch ancestry. His great-great grandfather, Sander Leendertse Glen, had come to the Albany area from Holland in 1633.

When our John Glen stopped calling himself Joahannes is not known, but if not before, it could have been during the French and Indian War. Being a British subject and serving with British soldiers, he may have sought to minimize his "Dutch-ness." The Revolutionary War General Philip Schuyler had done something similar in 1761, anglicizing the spelling and pronunciation of his name.

Glen had been commissioned as an officer and thereafter would be referred to by his rank, more about which below. In 1772, he became a partner in the crown grant of land, "the Kayaderosseras Patent," in northern Saratoga County. While I will say that part of the land was especially allotted to Glen, it's up to you to understand the whole patent. Should you ever feel the need for self-punishment, wade through descriptions of the colonial land grants. It's the next best thing to hell.

In 1775, just at the onset of the Revolutionary War, Glen bought a parcel of land from the Parke family who lived in what is now the Town of Moreau. He created a summer home in today's South Glens Falls on the site of the Encore Paper Mill. He would come there from his main house in Schenectady.

Glen assembled a massive amount land locally, but apparently wanted more. After the Revolution, he rebuilt the South Glens Falls mills that had been destroyed. From his adjacent summer home, he would have looked down into the huge, deep chasm through which the Hudson plunged, over the falls and around the island in the center. Later, quarries on both sides would greatly diminish the incredible gorge.

Glen would also have been able to see Abraham Wing's sawmill across the river in Wing's Falls in the Town of Queensbury, where Finch Pruyn & Co. stands today. In between, the thundering Hudson would have been powering Wing's mill on the one side and Glen's on the other.

For reasons never stated but easy to guess, Glen wanted to own those falls. In 1788, so one of two stories go, Glen contacted Wing and proposed to pay for a wine supper for mutual friends in exchange for Wing's title to the falls. Wing agreed and within only days Glen had handbills posted from the falls to Albany proclaiming their name change to "Glen's Falls." In time, the village came to have that name as well.

I have held back two facts about John Glen until now, both of which make the city's name change in 1962 so ironic. First, during the French and Indian War, Glen had become a Colonel, a title he always used. Second, his last name was just as often spelled with a double "n" at the end.

In other words, the name of the person from whom Glens Falls derives its name is "Colonel John Glenn."

The very same name as America's first earth-orbiting astronaut.

"OVER MY SHOULDER" COLUMN FOR FEBRUARY 20, 1999
Scandalous general spent youth in Glens Falls

You may never have heard of Daniel Sickles, but any student of the Civil War will immediately recognize him as being either the war's greatest hero or greatest fool.

This region gave many of its finest men to the war, and it proudly claimed Sickles as its own. Actually, Sickles only lived for a brief time during his childhood in Glens Falls. That time was one the few in his life that was not scandalous.

However, most of his most whole life was. According to Holden's history of Queensbury, Sickles was the son of a George Sickles, who "carried on a mercantile business in the stone store under the hill," that is, at the foot of Glen Street near the river. At this point his son, Daniel, born in 1819 in Manhattan, was of school age and had been enrolled in the Glens Falls Academy. As Holden delicately puts it, young Dan was remembered as "bright, active, and somewhat unruly lad, who dominated over his playmates."

The Sickles family moved back to Manhattan and young Dan finished school, became a lawyer and subsequently a political boss in the Democratic machine at Tammany Hall. He served in the state Assembly in 1847 and Senate in 1856-7. He moved to national office in 1857, serving four years in Congress. During that period Dan Sickles made legal history, though not through his own legal prowess.

A recent article by Gary Rice, "Devil Dan Sickles Deadly Salients" (in the November 1998 issue of "America's Civil War")[xxvi] repeats the common knowledge that Dan gambled and drank too much, "defied authority," and was a "womanizer." On that last point, and very ironically, Sickles' own wife Teresa turned the tables on him and that was why Dan made legal history.

In 1859, in the middle of Sickles' Congressional service, Teresa had an affair with Philip Barton Key, a member of Washington society and son of national anthem composer, Francis Scott Key. Sickles, not at all troubled by his own philandering, flew into a jealous rage. He confronted Key on a pedestrian-filled public sidewalk in downtown Washington D.C., very near to the executive mansion, and shot Key to death.

Edwin Stanton, who would soon be Secretary of War under Lincoln, was Sickles' defense attorney. For the first time in American jurisprudence, the defense claimed "temporary insanity for the client, citing his marriage having been violated by Key. The jury acquitted Sickles after 22 days. In typically Victorian style he had made legal history – and had gotten away with murder.

From there our hero served out the remainder of his term. In his last year, 1861, war erupted in April after the fall of Fort Sumpter. Sickles got the governor of New York to authorize his raising an entire brigade of 5 regiments of volunteers. Sickles did it by May and Lincoln nominated him to be a brigadier general of this new "Excelsior Brigade." Lincoln may have been grateful, but the Senate, which had to confirm the nomination, looked at Dan in a more objective manner. Still, they conceded, and Dan got his commission.

A book loaned to me by Nancy Barrett, entitled *Reveille in Washington* by Margaret Leech,[xxvii] gives perspective to Sickles' generalship. While most of the generals in McClellan's new Union Army were West Point trained, Sickles was one of the few exceptions. None of the West Point regimen of military tactics and, especially, discipline was a part of Sickles' make up. He was hot headed, impulsive, and not prone to take orders.

As we will see next week, those aspects of his personality would prove disastrous for him...and more so for his Excelsior Brigade.

"OVER MY SHOULDER" COLUMN FOR FEBRUARY 27, 1999
Civil War officer noted for gaff at Gettysburg

By 1859, forty-year-old Dan Sickles was trying to get over a mid-life crisis of his own making.

He had gone to Congress via the stinkingly corrupt Tammany Hall machine. Mid-term he shot to death his wife's lover, son of the writer of the national anthem and darling of Washington society. He was acquitted by a sympathetic jury, who felt that Dan, a drunken gambler who cheated on his wife as a steady hobby, had cause to feel slighted by his wife's infidelity. He then took his wife back.

Now, in 1861, perhaps seeking to atone, Dan "convinced" New York's governor to allow him to raise the Excelsior Brigade of 5 regiments of volunteers. Lincoln nominated him for Brigadier General.[xxviii] Having charged nothing more than a bar tab, Dan Sickles was ready to lead the charge in the Civil War.

Civilian generals, common in the Revolutionary War, were now outnumbered by West Point officers, who led both the Union and Confederate Armies. Sickles' nomination appalled the professionals and it took the Senate months to confirm it. However, in 1862, Sickles fought well at Fair Oaks. Promoted to Major General, he took command of the Third Corps. But, as Leech notes in "Reveille in Washington," Sickles' Excelsior Brigade "was badly cut up" in the battles on the Peninsula that raged from March to July in 1862.

Considered hot headed and impulsive by some, he was daring and bold to others. To the dead of the Excelsior Brigade, it was a moot point.

Now in 1863, Sickles arrived at the Battle of Chancellorsville, Virginia, and subsequently the Battle of Gettysburg, Pennsylvania. At Chancellorsville, Sickles stretched his orders to hold his troops in reserve, according to author Gary Rice, in "Devil Dan Sickles Deadly Salients[xxix]." When he sent some troops on reconnaissance, the Confederates surrounded the Union soldiers, decimating thousands. Then Sickles was called reckless, but later, blamed outright.

His impulsiveness may have been forgotten, at least forgiven, if he had not absolutely disobeyed General Meade's orders at Gettysburg to occupy the area around Little Round Top. Sickles instead moved his troops where he thought best and the Confederates attacked through the gap left open by Sickles. They narrowly failed to win, no thanks to Sickles, himself hit in the leg by shrapnel during the Confederate charge. His leg was amputated and author Rice credits that amputation alone with saving Sickles from court martial.

Sickles, and his supporters, defended him to Sickles' dying day, although no one today can logically do the same. To the war's end Sickles served in other capacities and then from 1865-1867 as military governor of the Carolinas. Given a Medal of Honor for Gettysburg, he could have retired a hero.

But he thrived on controversy. In 1873, he was removed as ambassador to Spain, for meddling in Cuban affairs. Named the head of the New York State Monuments Commission in 1886, he was removed in 1912 for mismanagement of funds.

And yet, in spite of all that, our nation is in his debt. For it is commonly held that it was chiefly due to Sickles' political savvy that Gettysburg was saved as a national park. He attended its dedication in 1913. Shortly thereafter, he came to Glens Falls for the Warren County Centennial. Cheered in parades and at the soldiers' encampment on Miller Hill, Sickles called his return "one of the most pleasant...weeks of my life."

Earlier in boyhood and now to a 94 year old man, Glens Falls had given the controversial warrior what he seldom had throughout his turbulent life: unconditional acceptance. In a published letter Sickles wrote that the memory of the visit would "remain with me to the end of the journey."

That journey ended, without controversy, a year later.

"OVER MY SHOULDER" COLUMN FOR MARCH 13, 1999
Joseph's may have closed, but the memories linger

My wife, Sara, said it all: "It's the end of an era."

That was her reaction to the news that Joseph's Restaurant, on Warren Street in Glens Falls, had closed after sixty years.

Sara's comment comes from a very personal vantage point. Her family, the Cutshalls[xxx], long-time friends of the Josephs, had operated a dry cleaning business across the street from Joseph's for decades. The Cutshalls are no longer connected with that business.

What Father C. Michael Abraham had said was true: the restaurant's closing was "like a death in family." Father Michael, as we all know him, is a life-long friend of the Joseph family, and traces his roots to the Syrian community of the city's First Ward.

But Father Michael knows, just like all of us who have grown up in a family business know, that Bill and Jeff Joseph's decision to close the family restaurant is also very understandable – and very right. Running a small family business is so difficult. For all the good it gives – family togetherness, food, home, education – the downside includes long, grueling hours, working on days when everybody else isn't. It's seeing more of your family than sometimes you care to. Worse yet, sometimes it's fear, never knowing where the next dollar is coming from.

The end of a restaurant that spanned generations is undeniably sad, hard on us mortals, creatures of habit who resent change. We recall the good times we had there, the memories indelibly etched. I see my daughter there as a little girl. I will forever recall with pride that Joseph's catered my retirement party from the Chapman Historical Museum.

I won't be ashamed of the pangs in my heart when I drive down Warren Street and see the "closed" sign.

But I will also rejoice. For what we lose is actually the "theater" in which the Joseph family has performed since William and Elizabeth Deeb Joseph opened a fruit market there in 1939. The curtain may have come down, but the actors are very much alive and well, thank you. For Bill and Jeff Joseph are exercising the American dream. They are fulfilling their grandparents' and great-grandparents' fondest wish.

Their grandmother, Elizabeth Deeb Joseph, known as Boe, told me she and her husband were born in America to families who had come from Syria. They married in 1937. Chance brought them to Glens Falls, while visiting relatives in Whitehall. They liked it, stayed and opened their fruit market in 1939.

Boe said service was the core of their success. She recalled when "a rich woman pulled up in a chauffeured car. It was drizzling and I went to the car to take the order." It never occurred to her to do otherwise.

Respect for the customer was also at the core. Boe said, "When a person walked in your premises, they were known, and their name was said aloud." This was true when the Joseph's kids worked there, then when her son "Doc" and his wife Jean took over, and then when their kids, Bill and Jeff did.

Those who know the Josephs, know they care for family first. "That's why we succeeded," said Boe. So, while she was saddened by the boys' news about the closing, she knows they're doing the right thing.

Boe is right. They have succeeded. The whole family has – exercising the American dream. Look at Boe's son, Doc, now vice president of the Adirondack Regional Chambers of Commerce. Her daughter-in-law, Jean, going back into teaching.

And now their sons, Bill and Jeff. Closing with "only" success, with "only" the love and respect of family and friends, as their legacy for the future.

Follow my tears down my cheeks. You'll see they run over my huge smile.

"OVER MY SHOULDER" COLUMN FOR MAY 15, 1999
A virtual historical tour of downtown Glens Falls

Welcome to the Over-my-Shoulder website.

Our featured special today is a virtual bus tour of downtown Glens Falls, on an open-roofed, double-decker bus, with selected views of the upper areas of many buildings in downtown Glens Falls. Click on the Downtown Tour button to join our tour, already in progress. (Click the audio button to listen.)

At the moment, we're stopped in the middle of Glen Street hill, just south of where Glen Street intersects with Warren Street, Ridge Street and Hudson Avenue. We passed the headquarters of Finch Pruyn and Co., Inc., but those just joining us can click your zoom button to see the symbol in the weathervane atop the 1906 building. It's the British pound symbol, the logmark used by Finch to tell its logs from the tens of thousands floated down the Hudson every year until 1951.

Atop the huge stone wall right next to us is J. E. Sawyers. At the base of it on Glen Street zoom in on the 1837 Calvin Robbins Blacksmith Shop, said to be the oldest building in the city. It's now home to Edmond De Rocker Design. We're where Park Street intersects with Glen. The building at the southwest corner of Park and Glen is the old *Post-Star* building. Click on zoom to see the facade of the building next to it, the 1911 Park Street Theater, the region's oldest building, still standing, ever to have served as a movie house.

We were going to have you click on the Park Street website to look at the 1861 home of business pioneer Samuel Goodman, but that building was "deleted" only recently. If you still wish to visit that website, click on "Parking lots."

Now, back on the western side of Glen Street, click the zoom button on the top two floors of the third building north of Park Street. See how that is made of brownstone? Called the "Old Brownstone," it was the home of Glens Falls National Bank and Trust Company before 1950.

Next to it, the Dolan Building tells you it was built in 1879. Zoom in on the words "Braydon and Chapman" atop the building next to Dolan's (at the corner of Hudson Avenue and Glen St.). Braydon and Chapman's was the place to buy sheet music, music printed on paper, and "records," flat, grooved disks with that played music. Until 1915, this building was home to Evergreen Bank's predecessor, First National Bank of Glens Falls. This, the Old Brownstone and Merchants Bank (where Scoville's Jewelers is today) led the intersection to be called Bank Square.

Zoom in on the top of the Cowles Building on the corner of Warren and Ridge, site of Abe Wing's Tavern. This was the first building built after the Great Fire of 1864. Zoom in on the "drip moldings," the brick decorations on top, so- called because they look like huge drips frozen in place.

Zoom up Ridge Street to the top of Monahan-Chase Caterers' building. See the words "The Star Building 1892"? *The Star* was the newspaper that combined in 1909 with *The Morning Post* to create the sponsor of this website. A website on the history of *The Post-Star* is under construction.

Stay on Ridge and zoom to the top of city hall. See the "City Hall" sign? Hit the "erase" button and when the sign disappears, you'll see carved in stone "Village Hall," which it was when first built in 1900.

The virtual bus is back on Glen Street, but our server is shutting us down until next Saturday, when you can click on this website for the most recent update of the Virtual Bus Tour.

"OVER MY SHOULDER" COLUMN FOR MAY 22, 1999
Web tour of city updated with latest information

Welcome to the next update on the Over-my-Shoulder website's Virtual Bus Tour of downtown Glens Falls.

We're on board a "virtual" open-roofed, double-decker bus, zooming in selected views of upper areas of several buildings in downtown Glens Falls.

We're cruising north on Glen Street toward Monument Square, the intersection with Bay and South Streets. Thanks to Jack Wiberg for construction help on this website.

On the west side of Glen Street, we'll click the "zoom button" on the building with the words "B. B. Fowler." Fowler's was the pre-eminent dry goods store downtown from 1869 on. This Chicago style building was constructed in 1905 to replace one that burned in 1902. (Click the "Love This Building" button.)

Across the street click on the upper story of Godnick's Furniture, the old YMCA building called "Ordway Hall" (zoom in on the name etched in the arch). The right-hand outer corner of the top floor has the figure of a woman, much like the prow of a ship. Who or what it may represent is a mystery.

Look next door at the Evergreen Bank facade. Can you find the physician's symbol by the main entry?

Scan back across Glen to the Associates of Glens Falls building. Click on the upper left corner of the building. In tiny letters you'll see the architect's name.

We're at Monument Square, named for the Civil War monument we're next to. The 1868 Civil War monument (dedicated in 1872) is under restoration thanks to a public-spirited group. Click on Zoom through the construction materials to see the lists of the battles fought and of those of Queensbury and Glens Falls who gave their lives.

The recent restoration has been removing years of grime and has been restoring pride. The original eagle that was on the top (please click your Zoom button) has been recreated as the original was too heavily deteriorated to leave there.

Click on downtown's third square, its name reflecting the Civil War, Union Square at the intersection of South and Broad Streets. Originally that was Haymarket Square. The wood building that was Varney's a 19th century feed store still stands. Can you find it with its pointed gable in front?

South Street is called the Street of Dreams, why exactly we don't know, but a guess is that it may be connected to the former Empire Theatre on your immediate right. (Click on Zoom.) The 1899 theatre at one hosted Sarah Bernhardt and the Barrymore Family. A 1976 recommendation by the architect of Wolftrap to restore the old theatre was not heeded. But now a community theatre is planned for Glen Street. (Click on "The old Woolworth's Store" next to Godnick's.)

Now zoom in on the building beyond the Monument, the one with the words "The Library" over the main door. Henry Crandall (click on "Crandall Park") built the first library here and left money for the present building, constructed in 1931, and designed by the famed Charles A. Platt.

Crandall's also created the park you see around the library (click on "City Park") bequeathing money for removing neighboring buildings to create space for the library to be built. Recently the Library wanted to expand but thought it could not because the City owned the land. However, from information recently found in a search of the land's titles and deeds, it appears the Library actually owns part of the park.

Hmm. A search of titles and deeds? For further comments, click on the chatroom "History Has Some Uses, After All."

The Library's expansion still needs the voters' approval. Click on "Hoping for a Happy Ending!" [xxxi]

The server's shutting us down. Want more? Click on "Visit the Crandall Library and the Chapman Historical Museum."

And visit this site next Saturday. We'll just use words, no buttons, the next time.

"OVER MY SHOULDER" COLUMN FOR JUNE 26, 1999
Newspaper celebrates 90 years as The Post-Star

NOTE: I am delighted that *The Post-Star* is still publishing a daily issue, both print and online, as it is the central news source for its region.

It is the 90th anniversary of *The Post-Star*!

The Post-Star actually made its debut on June 14, 1909. It was a merger of two newspapers, *The Morning Star* and *The Morning Post*," both dailies.

The first daily here, *The Glens Falls Times*[xxxii], was started in 1879 by Addison B. Colvin. On April 2, 1883, a second daily, *The Morning Star* was launched by the Star Publishing Company. As Brown's history of Warren County notes, the company's founders were "Jeremiah C. Mahoney, Beecher W. Sprague and Frederick Lupien. Later A. L. McMullen joined the company."

The Morning Star was typical of most newspapers of the 19th century prior to the 1890s in that covered mostly state and national news, all of it in the first pages, with local news on the back page. This may come as heart-stopping news for diehard sports fans, but the "sports page" did not exist as such in those primitive times.

Jeremiah Mahoney, originally from Adirondack, was the editor from 1883 until his death in 1904. At first the paper did not have a direct telegraph link, and instead got its news by daily mail from Albany.

The paper expanded its content and must have prospered, for in 1892 the company built on Ridge Street, a building that still stands just south of City

Hall. Star Publishing, like other publishers, owned its own presses, and so did all kinds of print work, books, letterhead, etc., to make additional revenue.

The newspapers were fiercely partisan in those days, endorsing political candidates and verbally assassinating political rivals. This is my own opinion, but I think local news got more coverage to help attract more readers and keep them long enough to read the political message.

The Morning Post, the other half of *The Post-Star*, was created in 1904 for expressly that purpose, politics. The leaders the local Democratic Party, George R. Finch, Winfield A. Huppuch, John A. Dix (later Governor, 1910-12) and Isaac Blandy hired Allen Eddy to print a campaign sheet for the elections that year.

Coinciding with the death of "Star" editor Jeremiah Mahoney in 1904 was the death of "The Glens Falls Republican," ironically a Democratic newspaper, the only one in Warren County from 1843 on. I assume the Democratic Party leaders hired Eddy, who had been editor of "The Sandy Hill Daily News," to help fill the void. The Democrats took a dive that year, with Republican Teddy Roosevelt re-elected as President, and Glens Falls native Charles Evans Hughes becoming governor of New York.

However, Finch decided to continue *The Morning Post* with his own money. He formed The Post Company, which bought *The Sandy Hill Daily News* printing plant, from where the paper was printed until it bought the plant of *The Glens Falls Republican*. Outside of fighting "the Republican machine," as Eddy said, it advanced newspapers in Glens Falls by being the first to affiliate with the Associated Press, which brought night telegraph service to Glens Falls.

The Morning Post built a new home on the corner of Glen and Park Streets, which stands today. It came out for progressive issues of the day, such as putting electrical wiring underground and for Glens Falls' becoming a city, the latter of which occurred in 1908. A year after that The Post Company bought *The Morning Star* and merged both papers to create the newspaper you're holding today, *The Post-Star*.

I will be doing more columns on the history of *The Post-Star*, including the reminisces of Florence McIlvaine, who began work at *The Post-Star* in the 1930s and was there for several decades. Do you have any reminiscences you care to share?

Then, while you're humming happy birthday to *The Post-Star*, you can be writing me care of that same place.

"OVER MY SHOULDER" COLUMN FOR JULY 31, 1999
Glens Falls once had its own version of Saratoga

The ponies are back at Saratoga, stirring a mix of images from Diamond Jim Brady and Lillian Russell to Damon Runyon's world of touts and nags.

Horse fever is deep-rooted here. B.C. – Before Car – horses were transportation, but horse-breeding and racing were passions, fueled by interest, pride and money.

And those stirred the more basic passions.

Glens Falls had its own flat track starting in the 1890s, but before that, the more formally organized racing was principally harness racing. That you'd find at any fairgrounds. In Glens Falls it was centered at the old Warren County Fairgrounds, which had moved to the Village of Glens Falls in 1868.

If you look at Burleigh's 1884 birds-eye view map of Glens Falls, you can see the fairground and track. In terms of today, it took in the land running from the north side of Lincoln Avenue, up through Coolidge and Horicon Avenues to the bottom of Crandall Park. On the west it was bordered by Kensington Road. Lincoln Avenue and Kensington Road were originally part of Dixon Road.

When the fairgrounds moved again in 1892, the land was subdivided for luxury homes and Lincoln, Coolidge and Horicon Avenues, and Kensington Road were created.

In 1893 a flat track was built called the Mile Track, where the Broadacres section of Glens Falls and Queensbury is today.

There is this long-time notion that flat tracks breed something unwholesome, while harness racing is a thing of purity. A line in the song "We Got Trouble" from the musical "The Music Man" comes to mind, in which Professor Harold Hill decries children going to horse races: "Not a wholesome trotting race, no," he sings, "but a race where they set down right on the horse."

I don't think anyone truly believed that one hundred years ago. In fact, one of the more disreputable spots that popped up as a direct result of the presence of that fairgrounds was "The Club House," on nearby Sanford Street, where the Sanford Street School stands today.

Ostensibly the Club House was a hotel, built somewhere in the late 1870s or early 1880s. It definitely was there in 1884. From 1891 to 1895 it was operated by Marcus E. Granger and after him, its name was changed to the Glen Park Hotel.

That's the "standard history." Frankly, it was essentially a male-only watering hole. It had huge barns in the back where horses were quartered and in that hotel a man could indulge in most of the "acceptable vices" of the day. When I first came to Glens Falls in 1975, I recall older men speaking in hushed tones about men of their father's generation who frequented the Club House.

The Club House was so bad that a woman couldn't walk by without receiving rude comments, catcalls and obscene gestures. The place was generally by-passed. One man confided to me that the place was known for roaring drunkenness, tumultuous fights, extremely high-stake gambling and, he looked furtively around and then said, "girls."

Which was a code word, a polite word, for "prostitutes." But in 1975, I was given to understand that we never spoke of such things in terms of "old Glens Falls." So, for the record, the Club House featured prostitutes, which, for the other record, did not exist in Glens Falls at that time.

The Mile Track folded in 1903, partly due to competition in other places, especially Saratoga. The Club House, a.k.a. the Glen Park Hotel continued until 1913, when fire destroyed it.

Did the Club House's "activities" then cease? Or were they available elsewhere? Let's just say that even after the fire, the Music Man would have sung "Oh-ho, we got trouble! Trouble with a capital "T" and that rhymes with "P" and that stands for...

"OVER MY SHOULDER" COLUMN FOR SEPTEMBER 4, 1999
Going back in time to find The Post-Star's origins

As promised back in June, some history of *The Post-Star* by Florence McIlvaine, in celebration of our paper's 90th anniversary.
Or is it?

Linda Jones, *The Post-Star*'s Educational Services Director, reminded me that our paper's masthead declares it to be the 95th year. Managing Editor Ken Tingley says that's because it dates to the beginning of *The Morning Post* newspaper in 1904.

The Morning Post had bought out the Morning Star in 1909, officially combining the two to make *The Post-Star*. But *The Morning Post*'s starting date is correctly that of today's *Post-Star*.

Thanks, Linda. First time I've ever gained five years in history without gaining the same on my age.

Florence McIlvaine began work at *The Post-Star* in 1936 and worked there until the 1970s. She has written some great history, some of which I have already shared with you. As promised, here is more.

We'll start with her beginning. Everything in quotes is hers. "When I began work at *The Post-Star* in 1936, the editorial staff was made up of H. Ralph Knight, managing editor; Edward J. Sherman, city editor; Donald O. Cunnion, sports editor; Gregory E. Faherty, copy editor; Frank Briggs, who monitored Associated Press news coming over the teletype and wrote front page headlines for Mr. Knight's approval; Sherman Litchfield, City Hall and police; Fred Carota, general purpose "swing man;" Minna Feigenbaum, society editor; Leo Dunn, Washington County copy; James Dineen; assistant sports editor; and me."

She was Florence Webster at that time, a graduate of the Glens Falls Academy, who had spent a year at Wellesley. She said her job was "to answer the telephone, greet people at the counter. . .and secure items for the Away and at Home column," which was "of particular concern" to Arthur P. Irving, general manager.

It says something of *The Post-Star* that Ralph Knight later became associated editor of *The Saturday Evening Post*.

In 1936, *The Post-Star* occupied the whole building on 100 Glen Street, at the southwest corner of Glen and Park Streets. From top to bottom you had the press room in the basement, the business office on the first floor, the editorial and composing room on the second.

Also, on that floor were "old newspaper files and an office where the cashier counted out the cash for our Thursday night pay envelopes." There are fewer and fewer of us who can say we were paid our weekly wage in cash.

The editorial crew worked from midday into the evening, even night. Florence noted, it was "a noisy workplace subject to all kinds of interruptions that everyone took in stride." It was "something between command post and a public information bureau," with people banging on manual typewriters, and in one corner a clacking teletype machine. If you have not heard the sound of a press room of that per-computer period, rent the Rosiland Russell/Cary movie, "His Girl Friday," for a sample.

Everyone was in plain sight, crammed into tight quarters, working cheek to jowl. A tiny conference room offered some privacy for personal interviews, but the everyday public "came upstairs" to the second floor "to tell us about lodge meeting, give us a news tip or look something up in the back issues."

There were also the uniformed Western Union and Postal Telegraph messengers coming in and out, and the "nightly visits from the man who sold numbers, an illegal but ubiquitous lottery based upon the U. S. Treasury balance," reported each day in the newspaper.

Florence writes that *The Post-Star* was "next door to the Salvation Army Citadel and sometimes people thought we were it." Or sometimes they "came upstairs to complain, if they found" the door to the Salvation Army locked.

Oops. Out of space. But we'll continue Florence McIlvaine's memories next week.

"OVER MY SHOULDER" COLUMN FOR SEPTEMBER 11, 1999
Continuing the journey through Post-Star history

We continue our history of Florence McIlvaine's career at *The Post-Star*. Everything in quotes is from what she has written.

Florence started in 1936, an exciting year. President Roosevelt was running for re-election, Jesse Owens was running at the Nuremberg Olympic games, and water was running for the first time from the Glens Falls Halfway Brook Reservoir.

Things at the 1936 *Post-Star* were the same as, and very different from, today's newspaper.

In the "same" (or similar) department, Florence was hired to fulfill one function, but "in practice most of us weren't confined to a particular slot," and "helped edit copy and wrote heads (headlines) under the eye of Greg Faherty," copy editor. Today's staff often fill in for one another.

In the "different" department, the 1936 staff had to understand all printing fundamentals. Her copy, written on a manual typewriter, was reviewed by a "copy man," then city editor, then laid out by the composing room's makeup man, then retyped on a "hot lead" machine that produced the proportioned type on plates for printing. Writing headlines "was an art because they were balanced (lines of equal length and centered)." To achieve this, "one had to know the print count of various type styles and sizes to make them fit the spaces as well as the story below."

Composing is done on computer today. Still, as in 1936, today's staff must comply with space limitations, for editors can still be ruthless. Sic semper tyrannis.

Florence agreed with my assessment that the 1940 movie, "His Gal Friday" offered a good representation of the newsroom then. Here she captures the newspaper office atmosphere: "Our typewriters were old Marvel Woodstocks, Underwoods and Remingtons in various stages of decay." Most of the men typed two-fingered, "about as fast as a woman who had learned the touch system. The editors and some reporters wore the trademark green eye shades."

The "atmosphere" included a constant, cigarette smoke. "Men had ashtrays on their desks; women retired for their cigarette breaks to the ladies' room on the first floor."

Amidst the smoke, typewriter and teletype clatter, people talking and shouting, customers coming in and out, there were telephones wailing incessantly. Five lines fed *The Post-Star*. Every desk had a phone, but there were no extensions. The switchboard operators left at 5:30 p.m. Then everybody answered calls, be it for news, complaints about home delivery or classified ads. When a call came for someone else, one just "called across the room to the person wanted."

"One of the first skills a neophyte learned was how to listen with all the racket going on."

And salaries? "*The Post-Star* didn't pay large salaries, although it was generally believed that the city editor was getting an impressive $100 a week." Florence "started at $12 with a promise of two dollars more if I survived a six week trial." She worked six nights a week.

And survived 90+ degree temperatures in a composing room with only a window on a back alley, and one large fan that blew papers off the desk. Air-conditioning, a child of the 1920s, hadn't found its way into the office yet.

Many today don't know of *The Glens Falls Times*, sister paper to *The Post-Star*. Both were published by the same company but had independent editorial staffs and represented different political positions. "The competition between the…editorial staffs was strong. When we came into work, we scanned the Times." Had its staff "scooped us on a story we shouldn't have missed?"

She muses, "probably we took ourselves too seriously," but "we assumed that people read what we wrote." A good assumption, with staff the likes of William Kennedy, who later went on to win the Pulitzer prize[xxxiii].

And the likes of Florence Webster McIlvaine, whose story continues next week.

"OVER MY SHOULDER" COLUMN FOR SEPTEMBER 18, 1999
Writer recalls pride in being first with the day's news

We conclude our three-part series of Florence McIlvaine's memories of her career at *The Post-Star*, which began in 1936.

We've focused on her earlier years, just a sliver of her more than 35 year as reporter, editor, columnist. As before, everything in quotes was written by her.

In the 1930s, and until the mid-1960s, Glens Falls was the center of the tri-counties. Along with its sister paper, *The Glens Falls Times*, it was the information center, the first, and the final, source of news.

"It was taken for granted that every day's happenings would be recounted in *The Post-Star* next morning. The left-hand box on the top of the front page promised `the latest news first' and we meant it. Not only fire, accidents and murders, but weddings, concert and drama reviews, births and deaths, graduation exercises, service club and church group meetings, and pinochle winners of the weekly card parties of E.M. Wing Relief Corps 128, auxiliary to the GAR."

The paper covered "in person and in detail..." everything from town and village meetings, "board of education, courts and commissions" to the meetings of "the Knights of Columbus," and "the Women's Civic Club." The staff went "to the Hospital Guild Ball, Priscilla Lee Baker's dance recitals...and the monthly meeting of the Broad Street School PTA." If it happened, they were there.

They also covered community projects such as "Operetta Club productions, Hadassah's `Night of Stars,' Community Chest Red Cross dinners.

"During the summer," readers learned of Bolton Road society and the Saratoga racing scene. Sally Brownell was in residence at the Sagamore to report on doings there and at the Lake George Club...Helen Irene Carroll did likewise for Saratoga society."

There were four editions, "the first for northern New York, the second" for all "Washington County outlying villages, the third aimed at Saratoga, and at 3:00 a.m., the final for Glens Falls." Plus "an occasional extra if some event warranted."

"Salaried officers in Hudson Falls, Fort Edward, Saratoga Springs, and possibly South Glens Falls," sent their "newsletters...twice nightly by" local bus. "Late breaking stories were dictated by phone."

Correspondents from other communities were paid "by the inch" and the paper used "junior and senior high school correspondents."

"People depended on the paper for information in other ways." If "you heard a fire whistle" or "felt an earthquake," you called *The Post-Star*. Friday nights there were "non-stop requests for basketball scores. From around midnight on, we settled what we assumed were barroom arguments: When did the Halfway House burn? or the Rockwell, or Fitzgerald's Hotel. We kept a card file."

Many called to discover Glens Falls' altitude. (Do you know?)

At World Series times, a special board placed on the front of the Glens Street building "plotted" the "progress of every game. "Ed Sherman regularly" leaned out the second story window to call out "blow-by-blow accounts of championship heavyweight matches as they came over the teletype" to the "cheering crowds below, lined up the parapet on Glen Street Hill." What an image!

We end with a glimpse of Glens Falls life now gone. "Most of the staff left after the first edition came off the press around midnight," but the city provided for these night denizens. "Johnnie's on South Street was open 24 hours, and did Tony deJulia's Palace Lunch ever close?" Across the street, Fitzgerald's offered a "bountiful lunch of left-over dinner specials' for 25 cents.

On Bay Street, "Frank Scully's Wonder Bar in the Rogers Building was our after-work haven. With the doors locked and the lights out, we and some other privileged owls could have ten-cent glasses of draft beer without fear of being raided." Editor Ralph Knight "was never a party to such doings, but the city editor was. What better place to pick up news tips than a friendly bar?"

And what better way to learn of a paper's glorious past than from one of its finest writers? Thank you, Florence McIlvaine. Sorry I had to play editor to your wonderful history.

You know, Florence, you've got a book there.

"Over My Shoulder" column for September 25, 1999
Chamber of Commerce began by buying cotton bale

My thanks to Joan Carswell Clarke of the Adirondack Regional Chambers of Commerce (the ARCC) for sending me an article a while ago about the beginnings of the Chamber.

Actually, today's ARCC and today's Glens Falls Chamber of Commerce trace their existence to one organization, The Glens Falls Chamber of Commerce that began on September 26, 1914.

Let's look at that parent organization's beginning years. In 1914, the City of Glens Falls itself was only 6 years old and bursting with self-confidence. Cars were beginning to cause traffic problems downtown, an enduring legacy. Reflecting a national trend, suffrage and temperance parties were in full swing in the area.

What would evolve into the first "world war" had started. Local papers were buzzing with news, not to mention fear that the US would be dragged into the fray. Interestingly, that far-away war would prompt the first official act of the newly created Glens Falls Chamber of Commerce.

But let's discuss that beginning first. We'll look to the April 24, 1939 special edition of *The Glens Falls Times*, published to commemorate the centennial of Glens Falls' becoming a village. The paper reported that the Glens Falls Chamber of Commerce was started by an energetic group of people who had "espoused (and accomplished) many projects for civic improvement and business development."

It went on to report that the campaign to organize the chamber "was started by the American City Bureau, with Lucius E. Wilson in charge of preliminary work. By September 26, 1914, 203 members had joined" and Wilson turned the governance of the new organization over to a committee headed by Daniel L. Robertson, a renowned businessman, whose involvement in the civic improvement of the area was phenomenal. His committee included J. Edward Singleton (a later president of *The Post-Star*), W. A. Buttrick, John J. Coy, A.E. Mason and F.C. Viele.

They held a meeting October 5th and elected a board of directors. The first officers were: Egbert W. West, president; John S. Davis, vice president; and A.E. Mason. Hazlett N. Clark was the first secretary, followed in November of 1914 by Walter K. Sumner. The board included: M.L.C. Wilmarth, Elmer C. West, George Tait, C.V. Peters, Beecher Horton and B. F. McCreery.

It was a powerhouse group, best symbolized by President Egbert W. West. Born on West Mountain, West went to work at 11 years old cleaning offices in the Glens Falls Insurance Company and eventually rose to become that company's president and chairman of the board.

The Glens Falls Times reported that "the first official act of the newly created Glens Falls Chamber of Commerce was the purchase of a bale of cotton." How did this have anything to do with the war raging in Europe? Because of that war, 8 million bales of Southern cotton had gone unpurchased, threatening the south with economic ruin. Everyone in the US was getting in on the "buy a bale of cotton movement," the Times said.

When the 500 pound cotton arrived in Glens Falls it was placed in the Glens Street display window of B. B. Fowler's fashionable emporium.

The paper said the chamber had three divisions "civic betterment; commercial and industrial development; and rural cooperation." In the first category, it "advocated an ornamental lighting system for Glens Falls...preservation of the city's trees" and shades of 1999, "worked for the extension of Crandall Library."

It launched a "buy in Glens Falls" program and worked to get the farm bureau started. It also began a project to create a new hotel. It took twelve years, but the Queensbury Hotel was the wonderful result. Shortly after that, in

1928, the chamber helped create the first airfield, the first "Floyd Bennett Field," on Aviation Road.

Now, 85 years later, today's Adirondack Regional Chambers of Commerce and the new Glens Falls Chamber of Commerce, reborn in 1994, carry on the legacy of that first chamber.

"OVER MY SHOULDER" COLUMN FOR OCTOBER 2, 1999
Today offers second chance to honor fallen heroes

The Civil War Monument in Glens Falls will be rededicated today, the culmination of three and half years of hard work.

We owe a debt of thanks to Chris Heidorf, the Soldiers' Monument Restoration Committee, and everyone who made its restoration possible.

So much has been written about the monument that I feared to add another word.

But not to would be to miss the opportunity to explore its many meanings. For the monument is more than stone. It is a visible link of the indivisible history of Glens Falls and Queensbury, the two communities which, when they were one, sacrificed sons to our country's most ferocious war.

Interestingly, in all the monument's original wording, only one municipality is named, and in the following inscription: "Erected to Their Memory by the Town of Queensbury."

The monument is also Glens Falls' and Queensbury's link in the chain of other communities where Civil War monuments stand, whether Hudson Falls, Ticonderoga, Manhattan or Washington DC. Meant as reminders, these monuments are now all too often forgotten. By restoring this one, we restore the honor of the other monuments and those people whom they commemorate.

Historian A.W. Holden, who led major recruitment efforts at the outset of the Civil War, wrote that soldiers from the Town of Queensbury served in "half the regiments of the state and in every branch of the service." This was true for men from all over this region. Although there were regiments drawn specifically from each town, people often joined regiments wherever they wanted.

Regardless of where they joined, they fought side by side with soldiers from all over this region, indeed, the country. So, the monuments we see in every town and city are really to every soldier and sailor.

And to every family. For the unspoken dedication on the monument, indeed every monument, is the sacrifice of the family. Tallied in the human cost of war, that sacrifice could have been expressed in the absence of a loved one for the duration of the war. Or it could have been the wound received, then carried throughout the remainder of life as a disability, depriving both the veteran and the family of the whole person. Or it could have been through the soldier's death.

When dedicated in 1872, the Civil War monument specifically named 82 people whose deaths were directly related to the war. The newly restored monument will add 13 names previously not listed.

The names of the dead tell us that the war took its toll from among all volunteers. I am struck by the variety of surnames, such as the French "Surprenant," the English "Crannell" or the Irish "O'Leary." And I know that Black veterans of the famed 54th Regiment of Massachusetts, lie in soldiers' graves in Fort Edward. They served and died, "regardless of race, creed, color or religion."

They served and died regardless of social status. The monument includes Lieutenant Edgar M. Wing[xxxiv], a descendant of Abraham Wing, founder of Glens Falls and Queensbury. He died at age 23, a "prisoner of war at Richmond," having been, "mortally wounded at the battle of Drewry's Bluff" in 1864.

But what of George Brumagym and Henry Brumagym, obviously from a single family. What is known of them? Were they brothers or cousins? Who grieved for them? What family members lost a part of their own lives when George and Henry lost theirs?

We do know today that at least the memory of their sacrifice lives on, enhanced by a monument newly restored. Let us all pause for a moment while scurrying to the library or waiting at the stoplight at Bay and Glen Streets to look at this renewed monument and, in that moment, remember those whose names are ennobled by these words: "Our Heroic Dead."

"OVER MY SHOULDER" COLUMN FOR OCTOBER 16, 1999
Empire Theatre started 20th century in grand style

Two recent *Post-Star* articles reminded me: this October marks the 100th anniversary of one of my most cherished buildings, the Empire Theatre on South Street in Glens Falls.

The first was David Blow's article (Oct. 2) on 10 year-old Chloe Blakeney-Carlson's love of the Park Street Theater. I share your feelings, Chloe.

The second was Maury Thompson's (Oct. 5) on Jerry Aratare's ongoing passion for bringing movie theaters back to various downtowns. Keep up the good fight, Jerry.

The Empire Theatre is the "grande dame" of area theaters. Incidentally, throughout this column, I'll use "theatre" when referring to a theater designed for live performances (termed legitimate theatre) and "theater" for one designed for movies.

William Brown wrote in his 1963 history of Warren County[xxxv], that when the Empire Theatre opened Oct. 6, 1899, "everybody thought that Glens Falls had arrived."

The 1,200-seat theatre was then the queen of the grand "opera houses" of

Glens Falls, Hudson Falls and Fort Edward. Now on the National Register of Historic Places, it is the last.

In 1899, the Village of Glens Falls had come of age, was cocky in its desire to emulate far larger communities. A group of wealthy, civic-minded businesspeople decided to enter the new century by creating a legitimate theatre that would rival any in Manhattan.

The group included A. B. Colvin, publisher and banker; Charles W. Cool, first mayor of the City of Glens Falls in 1908; brick manufacturer and builder Daniel DeLong; banker and later state historian James Holden; and architect E. B. Potter.

The finished building featured such novelties as electric lighting throughout, including for the staging areas. Its interiors, designed by Frederick Kettler of Manhattan, resulted in a theatre that not only looked as if had been snatched from the Manhattan theatre district, but also sounded that way. Its acoustics were reputed to have been the finest of any off-Broadway theatre in the Northeast.[xxxvi]

That feature attracted big-name stars, such as George M. Cohan, Harry Lauder, John, Ethel and Lionel Barrymore, and the legendary Sarah Bernhardt.

The theatre had many other deluxe appointments, including a third floor, which Richard Youngken's 1980 National Register nomination form stated "was reputedly the grandest ballrooms in the Adirondack region."

The ballroom had a chaperone gallery to allow the elders to keep an eye on the youngbloods.

But the eye should have been on the older men who had access, via an underground tunnel, to the bar in the Hotel Ruliff next door.

The gentlemen would scoot next door during intermission for a cigar and a snootful and then dash back. Boys will be boys at any age.

Among its features were a larger than usual fly gallery, metal ventilation domes, decoratively painted ceilings and ornate plasterwork. It had a stage made of hickory, so tough that in a play about Hannibal, live elephants trounced across it. (And given modern controversies, I will not make any mention of the elephant dung generated during the show.)

Its run was short. In the 1930s, movies were added to the Empire's offerings, but it was not destined to last, and in 1950, it was gutted. However, certain decorative elements remain, as does the stage, covered now by the first floor.

But I think of the Empire Theatre as it must have been on that opening night, Oct. 6, 1899.

Carriages and fancy barouches dropped off ladies in long gowns and gentlemen in top hats. The important people of the region poured into their seats, as the Empire's creators presided from their box seats, acknowledging the ovations of those below, while all waited for the curtain to rise on the first play, *Way Down East*.

It was 1899 and the first night of the first play to be held in the new Empire

Theatre.

It was the eve of the 20th century.

"OVER MY SHOULDER" COLUMN FOR OCTOBER 16, 1999
South Street still the lovable bad boy of Glens Falls

The other night on South Street in Glens Falls I experienced "a homecoming" and it seemed only right to share it with you.

The homecoming was brought about when Tim Weidner, the Executive Director of the Chapman Historical Museum, invited me to be the featured speaker at the annual meeting of the Glens Falls-Queensbury Historical Assoc..

The association is the parent organization of the Chapman Historical Museum, of which I had been director for 10 years. Now I was coming back as guest speaker. Actually, that was part one of this homecoming.

The annual meeting was held at Melucci's Restaurant on South Street in Glens Falls and I was asked to talk about – what else? – South Street.

South Street was part two of the homecoming. No, I've never lived there, but I have a "thing" for South Street. Also, as a local historian I have come to prize South Street for a history that ranks it among what I call "the crucial travelways" of the north country, whether those travelways are streets, roads or even overgrown trails.

A perfect example of a crucial travelway is the military road Sir William Johnson built in 1755 from Fort Edward to Fort William Henry. Today, it embraces parts of Broadway in Fort Edward and Main Street in Hudson Falls, all of Warren and Glen Streets in Glens Falls and Queensbury, and Route 9 between Queensbury and Lake George Village.

So, it was easy to say "yes" to Tim's invitation to enjoy a delectable dinner, then speak about South Street. Over the next few columns, I'll share with you that talk plus some other history of South Street, and a few of my own memories.

I started my talk by saying that, in days of old in England an often heard story was of the family cursed with the prodigal son, a real rascal who drank, gambled, chased women, and squandered his inheritance. But he was so witty, so smart and, oh, so lovable. He was what is called today a "bad boy."

The end to that story was often that the bad boy went off to colonial America and by dint of his brains and charm made a fortune – and became one of our country's founding fathers.

Like families, towns and cities also have their "bad boys." Over time, South Street has come to be the "bad boy" of Glens Falls. On the one hand, South Street is known as "the Street of Dreams." On the other hand, it has a wicked reputation, built over many decades and not necessarily in keeping with the realities of today.

To paraphrase Winston Churchill, South Street is a promise wrapped in a problem wrapped in a dream. Those with time, money and love invested in South Street have dreamed of its becoming the city's next downtown. Some dream of a tree-lined boulevard thronged with shoppers, all waiting to see the most recent off-Broadway play at the restored Empire Theatre.

But wrapped in the dream, the "problem" comes from a wicked reputation born of a century and a half's worth of gambling, booze, drugs, prostitution, and murder. Oh, what a bad boy. But, oh, how lovable.

And that lovability leads to the promise. But before we get to it, we need to look at South Street's history to see what this bad boy has been up to.

South Street could be called The Street of Controversies. Its first, let me warn you, is one only historians get agitated about. I'll have other, juicier, things for you to mull over, but we'll take them one at a time.

Controversy number one: when did South Street begin? Unlike most, I believe the street goes back to the beginning of Glens Falls and Queensbury, when the former was just a hamlet in the latter and both were a part of Albany County.

Abraham Wing and his Quaker group founded Queensbury In 1762. To the west in today's Luzerne was the settlement of the Jessup Brothers. My theory is South Street began as the road to the Jessups. It started at Glen, hooked right onto today's Broad Street and headed west.

Am I alone in this thought? Next week we'll see how history both supports and denies it. And over the next two columns, we'll explore the world of firehouses, families, theater and murder that make up the history of South Street, the Street of Dreams.

"OVER MY SHOULDER" COLUMN FOR OCTOBER 30, 1999
South Street hustled and bustles with little attention

We continue our history of South Street, "The Street of Dreams," an unusual nickname.

Something else unusual about South Street, which is 1.6 miles long, is that when people refer to it, they are generally thinking of its first two blocks, between Glen and Broad streets.

Also unusual is that historians can't even agree when South Street began. Some say the late 1700s, others the early 1800s. I say the first two blocks of South Street were the beginning of the colonial trail leading to the Jessup brothers' settlement in Luzerne.

This trail intersected with the 1755 military road in place when Abraham Wing and his fellow Quakers came to live in Queensbury in 1763.

Histories by A. W. Holden and Louis F. Hyde[xxxvii] both suggest South Street was part of the colonial period intersection called the "Four Corners," but you can't tell from either of them whether the Four Corners was at today's

Monument Square or Bank Square.

So, what's the big deal if South Street were the beginning of the colonial trail to the Jessups?

It would make it an original colonial street of Queensbury and Glens Falls, giving it the "pedigree" of Glen and Warren streets. God knows it deserves it after the shabby treatment it received before the 1890s.

We can cite occupancy on South Street as early as 1795, when John Eddy built a house on South Street (near Broad) that would stand until 1934. Yet, from the 1790s to the 1890s, South Street appears to have been the "service sector for Glen Street," and was ignored because of it.

As Glen was the main commercial route to Lake George, hotels popped up on Glen, such as the American House on the northwest corner of South and Glen. Built in 1835, it served the carriages that came from Saratoga and Washington counties.

Its stables were – where else? – on South Street. Significantly, the American House, which burned in 1879, never had a main entry opening onto South Street, only onto Glen.

Speaking of service, in 1823, South Street blossomed with the creation of the Feeder Canal. South Street became known as the "Road to the Feeder Dam." But, remember, traffic from the Hudson River came into Glens Falls via South Street. When the Feeder was widened for boat traffic in 1832, that traffic increased.

People doing river business – lumberjacks, teamsters, etc. – came to town. "Gin mills," gambling spots and houses of prostitution grew along Canal Street, lower Glen Street and South Street.

However, all was not unsavory on South Street. Other businesses grew, as did homes, with children.

In 1823, Queensbury created a school at the corner of South and Broad (then West) streets. The original 1823 school was later replaced in 1863, which in turn was replaced in 1890 by a brick structure. Why? More kids.

When the soon-to-be-village of Glens Falls decided to promote volunteer fire companies in 1835, South Street soon received a firehouse. In 1855, a major firehouse was erected. That pitched-roof building to the right of the old Madden Hotel still stands, one of the oldest structures on the entire 1.6 miles of South Street.

But its creation was never reported then, because it was on South Street. How ironic, for the fire company was the darling of prominent local citizens (males) who vied to be associated with its social joys of camaraderie, parading, and drinking.

Randomly scanning newspapers from the 1850s through the 1880s, I found barely any reference to the whole of South Street. Yet it was there, thriving, growing. As we'll see next week, by 1890 it was on the verge of an economic boom the likes of which it's never seen since.

Next week: Boom times, theater, and 20th century murder on South Street.

"OVER MY SHOULDER" COLUMN FOR OCTOBER 30, 1999
Gangland murder, Prohibition tarnish South Street

It was by the Gay Nineties that South Street in Glens Falls truly emerged as "The Street of Dreams."

The entirety of South Street's 1.6 miles blossomed with homes and businesses after the Civil War. In just that two-block section of South Street between Union Square and Monument Square, the 1868 monument changed that intersection where South Street begins and then a water system in 1873 invited investors' attentions.

Take the building in which Melucci's Restaurant operates today. It began in 1875 as the Union Carriage Works. However, the enterprising Cornelius Corbett and John Callahan converted it to commercial use in 1884, and flush with success built another building in 1890, where Peter's Diner is today.

So, the boom began. That year the streetcar line was extended the full length of South Street, later electrified. Also, an elegant brick school was created at Union Square.

In 1891-92 Dr. Lemon Thomson and partners constructed the building at Elm and South where Dave LaPoint's Sports Bar is now. (Here Thomson established the first "Glens Falls Hospital" to treat workers from the Spier Falls Dam worksite in 1903 – a story for a future column.)

In 1897 Lawrence Dolan had architect E.B. Potter design the building now housing Sandy's Clam Bar. Then in 1899 Potter, "the" architect in town, designed a hotel next to the firehouse. Called the Van Cott House until John E. Madden bought it in 1905, from 1899 on, the Madden Hotel was home to theatre acts playing across the street at the Empire.

For in that crowning year of 1899, the Empire Theatre was built, the product of a local business group that included E. B. Potter. That spurred the Rockwell brothers to refurbish the old American House at South and Glen, rename it the Ruliff Hotel and connect by tunnel the Empire.

With the Empire Theatre, South Street entered a golden age, as did Glens Falls, which became a city in 1908.

The reputation of the "Feeder Dam Road" was gone. But South Street took on a different reputation as a theatre street, with "entertainments" ranging from legitimate theatre with Sarah Bernhardt on the one hand, to dens of booze, gambling and prostitution on the other. All accepted as adult entertainment.

What really sunk South Street's fortunes were the Roaring Twenties and the Depression. When Prohibition began in 1919, Route 9 became the "Bootleg Trail" and South Street its "service corridor." Between Elm and Glen more Canadian booze was transferred than water went over Spier Falls Dam. Gangs emerged and violence erupted. People started to avoid South Street, unless seeking the speakeasies and high stakes gambling.

The Depression that began with the stock market crash of October 1929 brought further degradation. Racketeering, gambling and prostitution increased as people became desperate to survive.

The 1933 the murder of Joey Green showed the depths to which Prohibition, now ending, had plunged South Street – and the City.

The Glens Falls Times described Joseph P. Green of Albany as "a gunman, burglar and `musleman' for liquor interests." Green was an enforcer, a leg-breaker. In March 1930, he had shot up a speakeasy on Park Street. The charge was dropped, but Green was ordered out of the city. He cried all the way out.

Arrested for breaking and entry in Pittsfield in November 1930, he spent a year in prison, then re-emerged on Glens Falls streets around December of 1932. The paper reported that he was involved in "a fracas" and again ordered to leave the city. The judges were tough on Green.

Underworld stories related by the paper said that on February 18, 1933, Green had met with a gunman named Heyson at Jerry Linehan's speakeasy on 28 1/2 South Street to iron out territorial differences. Heyson, no saint, had murdered a man on Park street in 1930, but got off on technicalities. The judges were tough on Heyson.

Green and Heyson argued, then fighting broke out, beginning with knives and broken bottles and progressing to guns. At six in the morning two shots were fired. Responding to the scene, the police found Linehan and another man badly slashed. Green lay dead by the washroom, shot through the chest at such close range that he had powder burns on his suit.

Now read carefully. Overnight *The Glens Falls Times* had gathered enough facts to report at length intimate details of the meeting, fight and murder, plus eyewitness accounts of the high speed getaway cars including a license plate number. And it offered a fair assessment that the killer was Heyson.

But, the paper reported, "although the police and the District Attorney...went to work within a few minutes after the murder..." by the time of publication, they couldn't determine who fired the fatal shot.

Oh, my. But hang on. Right around that time, nationally syndicated columnist Walter Winchell wrote this in his column.: if you want to get away with murder, do it in Warren County.

You don't suppose he was writing about a certain murder investigation taking place in a certain small city on a certain stretch of pavement known as "The Street of Dreams" do you?

Next week South Street heads for the 21st century.

"OVER MY SHOULDER" COLUMN FOR NOVEMBER 6, 1999
New Millennium brings hope for Street of Dreams

We have looked at its highs and its lows, explored its first Golden Age and viewed the depths to which Prohibition and the Depression dragged South Street's reputation into the ground.

But I end this fourth of a series of columns on the history of South Street in Glens Falls with this bold statement of hope. No matter what its problems, South Street brings to the new millennium two things no other major street in Glens Falls has left to offer: a continuity of business history and most of its historic architecture intact.

Over this century on South Street, more businesses have started and remained for generations than nearly any other street in the Greater Glens Falls area. I talked about this with Peter Demas, unofficial mayor of South Street and owner of Peter's Diner in the historic Rae Sims Building.

Peter's Diner began in 1961. When I did my first column on Peter in 1980, I called him "the new kid on the block." His business is now among the oldest there.

In 1961, these were some of the businesses with longevity: The oldest was the NuWay Lunch: in business on South Street since 1916. It actually had begun on Glen before that. There were also K Locksmith, Charlie Kaulfuss' poolroom, since 1916 in the basement of the old Empire Theatre; three generations of MarcAntonios running a barbershop; Sandy's Clam Bar, owned by the Mozelle family; Collotti's Shoes; and businessman Sid Konafsky, who owned several buildings on the street.

Today, four survive: the NuWay Lunch, Collotti's Shoes, formerly in the Empire Theatre Building, is now at 1 Union Square; Sandy's Clam Bar; and Peter's Diner.

There are differences in the kinds of businesses you had in 1961. More than one bus station, with both Greyhound and Trailways present. A pool hall. A taxi company. Newsrooms. A supermarket, the A&P. A taxi, the Globe and Diamond Cab. Garment making shops, such as Clark's and Dennison's Lingerie, an Arrow shirt maker and a glove factory. Tailors.

Yet today business thrives on South Street as it does not on no other city street.

Coupled with this continuity of business, South brings to the millennium its historic architecture. As Peter Demas notes, that was because Urban Renewal, which did so much damage on Glen and Warren Streets, essentially missed South Street. "We were too poor for them to bother with us," Peter said.

Under a government program, South Street did lose the corner of South and Columbia (and the Brick Manor) to make way for the Henry Hudson Townhouses in 1969 and the widening of Hudson Avenue.

The second loss was at Union Square where Rite-Aid Pharmacy is today.

There the former South Street School, which had become a county office building, was demolished in 1964. Finally, the demolition of the A&P made way for the present South Street parking lot.

But by and large, South Street is architecturally intact all along its 1.6 miles, but especially from Monument Square to Union Square. That two block area is also on the National Register of Historic Places, offering the possibility of money to those who would restore their buildings according to certain standards.

I wrote that "South Street is a promise wrapped in a problem wrapped in a dream." The dream is a street filled with businesses and shoppers, its buildings recognized for the architectural treasure they are, and all restored. It's been done in Saratoga Springs.

The problem is that old prejudices against the street, left over from another era, keep people in power from seeing the dream many of us see.

The promise? It's there, if the city will see it. Take the promise, Mayor Regan and Common Council members. South Street is the hope of downtown. Seize it.

I close with some lyrics from sheet music only just sent to me by my friend Bill Richards. Ironically, the lyrics belong to an undated song called the "Street of Dreams," perhaps the source of the street's nickname. These seem to fit the promise:

> "Dreams broken in two
> Can be made like new
> On the Street of Dreams."

Postscript: As of 2019, only two of the four surviving businesses mentioned survive today: NuWay Lunch and Peter's Diner.

"OVER MY SHOULDER" COLUMN FOR JANUARY 15, 2000
Adirondack Pipes and Drums celebrates 50 years

Few all-volunteer organizations can claim to have made it to 50, but Adirondack Pipes and Drums had its start a half century ago and I thought you'd be interested.

Thanks for this column go to my friend Fred Harris of Hudson Falls for his history, "Highland Echoes, a "History of the Adirondack Pipes and Drums[xxxviii]." Unless otherwise noted, I am quoting from it. I hope Fred will publish it in a booklet.

This is only portion, however, as attempting to condense fifty years of any organization's history usually glosses over too much and give too little of substance.

Fred notes that in the fall of 1949, people from Fort Edward, Hudson Falls, and Glens Falls began to form the bagpipe band.

Two names figure prominently in his founding members, Earl Stott of Hudson Falls and Jack Donahue of Fort Edward. Fred describes Earl Stott as "the prime mover and early leader of this new group."

Jack holds the record as the only founding member who played with the band for nearly a half century. Jack, of Irish descent, was permitted by his ancestors' ghosts to march with those of Scottish descent. When you see Jack today, striding the streets of Fort Edward, it's with the same gait as in a marching band.

Earl Stott had a fascination with the Colonial history of the region, in particular the famed 42nd Regiment, the Black Watch. He wrote to the commander of the Black Watch's Second Battalion, headquartered in Montreal, asking permission for the new band to pay tribute to the Black Watch.

Permission came. The band adopted the Black Watch tartans. For the piper there was the "red Royal Stuart tartan," and for the drummers "the dark green regimental Black Watch or `Government' tartan." A full military uniform with tunic and a long plaid was adopted by spring.

In September of 1949, the Village of Fort Edward celebrated its 100th anniversary by holding, among other things, a humongous parade. Marching was the Schenectady Pipe Band, still producing music today.

Two members of that band became intimately associated with the new group: John Bisset of Troy, a long time piper, and Dan Slater of Albany, a drummer.

The remainder of the original members were as follows. "From Glens Falls came William Kirkpatrick, of Scottish ancestry, along with two of his sons, Robert and John." Bill was a snare drummer, the boys pipers. Two Hudson Falls brothers, "Bruce Waite on pipers and Robert Waite, who became the band's first drum major. Also, from Hudson Falls and Kingsbury were beginning pipers Fred Harris and Robert LaCross, bass drummer Frank Vaughn and on the snare drum Wayne Harris." Also joining were "pipers Fred Hamilton and Larry Cashion and drummers John Callahan, Wes Cox, and William Jones. These were the "nucleus of the Adirondack Pipes and Drums." By the spring, piper Bradley Wright had joined.

Four generations of the Kirkpatrick family have played in the band, with the most recent being Dr. Harold Kirkpatrick, for years its pipe major, and his son. What a record.

The band's constitution and by-laws were adopted in January 1950 and Judge Howard Glassbrook of Glens Falls, father-in-law of Fred Hamilton, drew up the charter. The band was official.

Winter practice sessions were held in the basement of the old A&P building in Fort Edward, beneath what is today John Weber's store. Fred notes that most of the pipes were purchased from Highland Industries of Scotland, but when it came to the first uniforms, many were made by the wives of the then all-male band.

Some practices were held at the home of William and Alice Kirkpatrick.

Having learned a set of essential tunes, such as "The Forty-Second" (the regimental march of the Black Watch) and others, the band was ready to go public. Its first event was a parade in Hudson Falls in 1950.

It would march on, and does to this day, bearing a proud and unique history among bagpipe bands. Happy anniversary to the Adirondack Pipes and Drums.

"OVER MY SHOULDER" COLUMN FOR FEBRUARY 26, 2000
Bridging the gap, more than once, over the falls

NOTE: When the four columns on the history of the Hudson River bridge between Glens Falls and South Glens Falls were published, no one knew that a new bridge would be constructed in 2004, replacing the concrete viaduct built in 1915. Anticipating the ending of my last bridge column, in which I ask for a renewal of access to Coopers Cave, the new bridge was built with access and signage.

When is a bridge more than a bridge?

A while ago I spoke to the Glens Falls Lion's Club about the bridge spanning the Hudson River between Glens Falls and South Glens Falls. It's known as the "Route 9 bridge," the "South Glens Falls bridge," and the "Glens Falls bridge." And with a push from *The Post-Star*, it will also be known as the "Cooper's Cave bridge."

If you live within a 15 mile radius of the bridge, very likely you've crossed it. If so, you've been in the company of some pretty historic personages. Let's look at the history of this famed span that has been legally a part of two nations, one province, one state, three counties, three towns, one village and one city.

Although I don't have proof, I surmise that the first bridge was created around 1770, when this whole region was a part of Albany County. Two years later, it would be a part of Charlotte County, which technically was in the Province of New York, and a part of Great Britain.

Why a bridge then? There were other ways to travel in 1770. Near the falls there were sections shallow enough for horses and wagons to ford the river at a diagonal. A ferry was constructed in 1765, two years after Abraham Wing and his fellow Quakers came to settle. It crossed the river to the west of the present bridge starting near the Rice-Folsom House (by McDonald's today) and went diagonally above the falls to the Glens Falls side near Henry Street.

But after the various ferries were completed, Wing's business interest still would have prompted a bridge. After all, Wing had his sawmill where Finch Pruyn is today, and there were settlers across the river.

Also, Hyde's *History of Glens Falls* does state that in 1780 the Marquis de Chastellux had come by sled to visit the falls, breathtakingly set in a deep chasm. It seems sensible that he approached by a road leading to a "string bridge," that is that is a bridge of rope and plank.

Hyde wrote that where the bridge is today a "string bridge" was built in 1786. My surmise is that Wing and his neighbors had already put up a string bridge there around 1770. If true, the 1786 string bridge could possibly have been bridge number 2, but now in Washington County, State of New York, in the United States of America.

But enough speculation. We know a string bridge existed from 1786 to about 1792 and that Abraham Wing was among the movers and shakers to create a new bridge.

Outside of the fact that he had a saw mill there, Wing had another good reason to want a new bridge, according to a story by his granddaughter Amanda, related in *Bridging the Years*. Amanda said that in 1788 Abe Wing had come home from the famed wine supper at which he had sold the rights to the Falls to a man named Glen. The next morning Wing noticed the tracks of his sleigh in the snow on the bridge and saw that one of the runners had passed barely an inch from the edge. An inch more and Wing would have really been in the drink.

Amanda said Abe "took a pledge which was not broken for several months."

Around 1791, Wing and other "subscribers of Washington County," issued a petition asking people to support the creation of a new bridge. He noted that in flood times, the shallow crossings and ferries were useless, and people needed a constant way to cross the river at this spot – logically, over the falls. Vision became reality. Wing used that bridge until his death in 1794.

Oh, by the way, please note that this was a toll bridge. Unlike now when people protest having to pay highway tolls, in 1792 tolls were considered a very natural way to fund highways and bridges.

Besides, you had to have a toll house, right? No toll house, no cookies.

More on this historic span next week.

"OVER MY SHOULDER" COLUMN FOR MARCH 4, 2000
Hudson River's bridge experienced identity crisis

We've come to the next episode of the Bridge Story, the history of the bridge over Glens Falls in the Hudson River.

I say "over Glens Falls" as that's what the falls themselves were named when Colonel John Glen bought the rights to them from Abraham Wing in 1788. This episode could also be called "The Time of the Bridge's Identity Crisis," because in those early years, people changed the governments in this area more than they changed their underwear.

Last week I had theorized that a first bridge had actually been built in the early 1770s and was, like the second one, a "string bridge" of rope and plank. Bridge One linked the Town of Queensbury of Charlotte County with the Town of Saratoga in Albany County. By the time Abraham Wing and his Quakers returned in 1783 to rebuild Queensbury after the Revolution, Bridge

Number One may well have been destroyed along with the rest of Queensbury, torched in 1780.

When Bridge Two, another "string bridge," was built in 1786, it connected the Town of Queensbury of Washington County with the Town of Saratoga in Albany County.

Bridge Three, a toll bridge, was built in 1792. The Town of Saratoga was now in Saratoga County. Are you keeping tally of government changes? It gets worse.

Bridge Three, like its predecessors, was two spans meeting at the island mid-river. It was wider, stronger, and definitely meant to last longer. It only made it ten years. During that time, the land it touched in Saratoga County became part of the Town of Northumberland in 1805 and then part of the Town of Moreau in 1808. (Who has the score sheet?)

Where the bridge crossed was a very deep chasm through which water thundered. It was not yet cut back by quarrying. In 1810 the bridge was swept away by a violent spring flood called a "freshet," which sounds like a deodorant to me. ("Use Freshet and feel fresh all day.") But freshets were lethal and would take more than this bridge.

In 1810 another toll bridge was constructed. In 1813, Warren County was carved from Washington and the bridge entered yet another county. This was not the end of government changes.

During the next 23 years, Bridge Four would make the fame of these falls. By this time, people had begun to travel to our area as tourists. Alvan Fisher was among the first on the long list of famed American artists who would capture the chasm and falls in oil, engraving, and charcoal. European artists came as well: the French Milbert, the Irish Wall, the English Bartlett.[xxxix]

Early engravings from the 1820s and '30s show the Hudson raging between the steep walls of this canyon with Abe Wing's sawmill sitting where Finch Pruyn is today. As the history *Bridging the Years* relates, the river took many lives. Some were miraculously spared. One young woman who lived in the toll house on the island, dipped her bucket in the torrent for water and was swept in. Her billowy clothing acted as a floatation device and she was rescued. Let's hear it for petticoats!

Famed writers came during this period. One, James Fenimore Cooper, stopped at the falls in 1825. He visited Lake George and was enthralled with the history of our region. Cooper could see that only a short time before all this had been frontier, the "wild west" of the mid-to-late 1700s. He fully grasped how the French and Indian War had changed North America and he embodied the war's violence and heroics in his novel, *The Last of the Mohicans*.

He saw a cave in the island beneath the bridge's toll house, and in that cave he set a scene that made the falls world famous. Cooper's Cave became so anchored in the imaginations of people that even when I was at the Chapman Historical Museum in the 1970s and '80s, kids would ask about Hawkeye and the other characters, as if they were real. In the early 1990s, Daniel Day Lewis' movie of Cooper's novel gave renewed life to Cooper's creation.

The falls, and Cooper's Cave, were on the map. Next week we look at more bridges and their impact. Including upon Hawaii.

"OVER MY SHOULDER" COLUMN FOR MARCH 11, 2000
Crossings began to define Glens Falls to the world

We are now at Bridge Four in the saga of The Bridge over Glens Falls. This toll bridge was constructed in 1810 and lasted until 1833. This bridge began its life linking Washington County to Saratoga County and ended by linking Warren County to Saratoga County.

It was during this time that the fame of the falls and Cooper's Cave in the island beneath the tollhouse would be secured across America and across the Atlantic.[xl]

Adirondack tourism really blossomed then. When James Fenimore Cooper had crossed the bridge in 1825 as a tourist, could he know how famous he would make Cooper's Cave? Perhaps, for by the time of his death in 1851 people were taking guided tours of Cooper's Cave. That phenomenon would go on for decades.

Bridge Four gave way to Bridge Five in 1833. Bridge Five was constructed in what I call "an atmosphere of the miraculous," because it was done by a cooperative agreement between two governments, the towns of Queensbury and Moreau. It was called the "Free Bridge," as it had no tolls, which distressed some politicians.

The Free Bridge lasted only 9 years, but the English artist Bartlett immortalized it and the falls in a painting that was so farfetched I think the man was either intensely romantic or had sniffed a little too much paint thinner. His image shows an immensely deep, craggy gorge near which are huge mountains. The image has caused untold confusion among people to this day.

During this time a new government entity was added to the mix, the Village of Glens Falls, incorporated in 1839.

The free bridge needed repair and, in a continuation of the miraculous, the two towns again joined forces to create a new bridge. New York State loaned Warren and Saratoga counties the money to complete the job. Moreau spent its share on putting in a stone foundation for its end of the bridge, plus a stone arch over the gap between the shore and the island. Queensbury paid for a wooden covered bridge that went from Wing's sawmill to the island.

Bridge Six, the covered bridge, was itself immortalized by several famous artists, including Ferguson of the Hudson River School, and one of the most important photographers of the 19th century, Seneca Ray Stoddard. Through his guidebooks and photos Stoddard also continued the promotion of Cooper's Cave, helping to secure its fame well into the 20th century.

Early in his career, Stoddard captured the near-demise of the covered bridge in the freshet of 1869. Only by cables lashed to it was the span saved, and afterwards, a stone pier was put underneath for support.

Most ironically, everything about the bridge, the island, and Cooper's Cave slowly came to become identified with Glens Falls. First it was Cooper's Cave. Then the Glens Falls Insurance Company adopted Moreau's stone as its logo arch. By the early 20th century the company had become nationally famous, as did its logo.[xli] And so by extension were Glens Falls, Queensbury, and Warren County.

The irony? The arch, the island, and Cooper's Cave were all located in Saratoga County. Whoops.

Moreau got some satisfaction in the 1880s when Queensbury sued it for help in repairing covered bridge. Moreau won, as the state ruled the covered bridge was entirely in Queensbury. This marked the end of the miraculous municipal cooperation regarding the bridge for many years.

It was decided the covered bridge would go. But it did not go willingly. Tragically, as workers were disassembling the bridge in 1890, the temporary supports proved too weak and the remains of the covered bridge fell into the Hudson, killing two men.

Its replacement, Bridge Seven, was a cast iron truss work bridge called, appropriately, "The Iron Bridge." It was hailed as a marvel of 19th century technology, and by golly everyone said it would last forever.

It lasted 23 whole years, swept away in 1913, the victim of Mother Nature's worst freshet yet.

Next week we'll conclude with a story of how elephants predicted the end of Bridge Seven, some little known history of Eight, and the story of lucky number Nine.

"OVER MY SHOULDER" COLUMN FOR MARCH 18, 2000
Iron bridge undone by progress and pachyderms

Of all the "Bridges at Glens Falls" only the Iron Bridge had its end predicted by elephants.

It was sabotaged by the same progress that created it and ultimately destroyed by a combination of the industry that built Queensbury and Glens Falls and a force far older than both.

Constructed in 1890, the Iron Bridge was Bridge Seven – that is, allowing for my theory that a bridge existed between 1770 and 1785.

The Iron Bridge's demise actually began in 1891, the year after its completion, when the horse drawn trolley system was electrified. Up to this point, all the bridges had one thing in common: from each side of the river, they joined at the island.

The Iron Bridge kind of went right over the top of the island. The actual iron truss work stopped there, but the connecting roadway from Moreau was built up so that it also flew right over the historic arch Moreau had built. The two famed symbols, Cooper's Cave and the arch, were being ignored.

The level of the whole bridge being higher, the trolley company spotted that straight line from the foot of Glens Street hill to South Glens Falls, incorporated as a village in 1895.

After 1901, huge interurban trolley cars began to cross the bridge, their weight causing it to sag and jounce. According to circus historian James Cotter, of Glens Falls, in 1906 Ringling Bros. Circus rolled into South Glens Falls by train. In grand fashion, the circus would parade across the bridge into Glens Falls.

The elephants would not cross it. Having set foot on the truss portion, not one would cross. Instead, they went to Fenimore, where they crossed the new bridge into Sandy Hill.

Obviously, the Iron Bridge had a problem. By 1910, two things had occurred. In 1908 Glens Falls became a city, marking the 16th government that would have a role in the bridge. Then in 1910 huge supports were placed under the bridge to support the interurban cars. What a mistake.

In late March of 1913, the Hudson River began to flood. Logs being floated downriver to sawmills were caught against those supports. The log jam increased and on March 27, 1913 the Iron Bridge was swept into the drink. Bridge Seven was gone.

In the 1970s, the late Dr. Francis X. Dever of Glens Falls, a wonderful historian with a wry sense of humor, related to me how the bridge spawned many tales of heroism. In spite of the looming danger people continued to cross the bridge, some actually fleeing as it was torn from its moorings. After the crash, many claimed they were "the last on the bridge" and Dr. Dever wryly noted that over the years the number of claimants rose. "Joseph," he said, "therein was the problem. By my reckoning over 2,000 people were on that bridge just before it fell. The structure simply couldn't bear their weight."

In 1913 another political miracle occurred with the agreement by the City of Glens Falls and Town of Moreau, with Warren and Saratoga counties' blessing, to split the $150,000 cost of a new and higher bridge. This one jumped the entire Hudson, island and all.

However, few realize that a temporary bridge, Bridge Eight, loaned by the Delaware and Hudson, was brought from up north and placed across the river. Ironically it was an iron bridge.

By 1915 Bridge Nine was completed, a vaulted concrete viaduct sporting a cantilever stairway down to Cooper's Cave, again receiving its due attention. Eerily, the remains of Bridge Seven could, and can, still be seen on the South Glens Falls side.

Bridge Nine, now officially owned by New York State, has stood for 95 years, longest-lived of all nine bridges. The stairway was closed around 1960, but now a movement is afoot to reopen access to Cooper's Cave, a wonderful project. It deserves the support of every government ever involved with the bridge – 16 in all.

And for the record, that includes, in chronological order, 2 countries (the UK, then the USA), 1 province and 1 state (both New York); 5 counties (Albany, Charlotte, Washington, Saratoga and Warren); 4 towns (Queensbury, Saratoga, Northumberland, and Moreau); 2 villages (Glens Falls and South Glens Falls); and 1 city (Glens Falls).

I say we start the fund drive at the beginning of that list. We'll bury the hatchet and telephone Prime Minister Tony Blair in London and say, "Hey Tony, we're taking up a collection for the Cooper's Cave Bridge Project. You're first!"

"OVER MY SHOULDER" COLUMN FOR APRIL 8, 2000
Column, historian's office mark anniversaries

Anniversaries abound! "Over My Shoulder" is now observing its sixth. My thanks to *The Post-Star* for allowing me to share personal memories and offer opinion as I strive to explore the history of our paper's vast territory, an area about the size of Rhode Island.

Besides this column I have other, totally separate, work that I do. One job is serving as the Washington County Historian. And that provides my not-so-clever lead-in to the fact that the office I inherited from Doris McEachron in 1998 is now observing its 60th anniversary.

In January of 1940, Susan E. Wade began as the first Washington County Historian, a county department. Interestingly, but not at all coincidentally, the Washington County Historical Society is also observing its 60th anniversary. The reason there's nothing coincidental about the two anniversaries is their mutual link, Susan E. Wade, a hero of the local history movement in the county and region.

Sue Wade, as everyone always called her, played a critical role not just in the founding of the Washington County Historian's Department and the Washington County Historical Society, but also in the resuscitation of the Fort Edward Historical Association and in the saving of the Patt Smyth House, now the Old Fort House Museum, among other things. Because of these dual anniversaries, I want to focus upon her and the work she did as the first Washington County Historian.

First, however, let me acknowledge all of my predecessors, who have kept the lamp in the Historian's Department lit these many years. Sue Wade herself would serve as Washington County Historian from 1940 to her death in 1955. As I will be writing extensively about her activities, let me only briefly say that she had begun her career as Historian while an employee of the County Clerk's office, from which she retired in 1948. Up to her death in 1955, she remained Historian, actively promoting preservation, expanding the Historian's archival collection, and in last year of her life, cataloging that collection.

Mary M. "Molly" MacMorris, who had been the Argyle Town Historian, began as the second Historian in 1956 and would serve through 1967. She helped the successful move from the Hudson Falls quarters to the new county building in Fort Edward in 1957. Under her, the present Archives, as they are today, would take shape and more extensive cataloging of the holdings would be done.

In 1968, Molly MacMorris was succeeded by Mildred Southard of Hudson Falls, who served as County Historian the longest of anyone, 19 years. In a conversation the other day, Mildred told me that under her the Historian's Office doubled in size.

Like her predecessors, she depended upon the help of volunteers, including Doris McEachron. Doris, also an Argyle Town Historian, succeeded Mildred in 1987 and served as County Historian until 1997. During her tenure, the office was mapped out for cataloging purposes, new historical archives were acquired, and conservation programs began.

After retirement, Doris graciously came back to train me in 1998. However, her additional "gift" to the office was that she had also trained a volunteer, Loretta Bates[xlii], who has worked in the office since 1990. For me, that "gift" has proven a godsend. Still, we occasionally pester Doris and even have an "Ask Doris" file, into which we slip notes about questions we have.

And now to introduce our main subject, the beginning of the Washington County Historian's department and Susan E. Wade, first Washington County Historian. Born and educated in Fort Edward, Sue Wade began working in the Washington County Clerk's office in 1918. That same year the state passed the law for every town and village to appoint a historian.

Believe me, as you'll see next week those two unrelated incidents in 1918 would combine to provide a force in the late 1930s that would literally make history.

"OVER MY SHOULDER" COLUMN FOR APRIL 15, 2000
Start of county's historic tourism aided by Sue Wade

When Susan E. Wade began as the first Washington County Historian in January of 1940, she had already been deeply involved in preserving the county's documentary history.

Sue Wade, as everyone has always referred to her, had joined the Washington County Clerk's office in 1918. Born October 8, 1878 in Fort Edward, she was 40 years old when she came to the department, having worked for many years as the secretary for the Hon. Edgar Hull, county district attorney and Republican party official. She brought the County Clerk office not only maturity and experience, but also a good education and a historian's inquisitive mind.

Because Sue Wade dedicated so much of her life to preserving the history of others, let us briefly look at her own, taken in part from her personal scrapbooks. Her nephew, V.K. Malcolm Tasker of Fort Edward, kindly let me look through them. Sue Wade was the daughter of Thomas Robert Wade, who emigrated from England in 1867, and of Louise Muir Harsha of Argyle. While she would extensively research her family genealogy, obviously the Harsha line, tracing back to the Rev. Dr. Clark's colony in colonial Salem, New York, was a major factor in her knowledge of county history.

So too was her education at Dr. King's Fort Edward Collegiate Institute, for King and his faculty were active in preserving and teaching the history of this region. She joined the county in 1918 with her interests well defined and she successfully prevailed upon the county clerk to allow her to begin systematically arranging the historical records of that office.

Outside of county government, she was very active in local history. In 1925, she was among the co-founders of the Fort Edward Historical Association, which traces to a motoring club formed around 1920 that sought to promote tourism along the historic sites of Washington County and the region. Their interest focused on upcoming observances in 1927 to commemorate the 150th anniversary of the defeat of Burgoyne at the Battles of Saratoga, including the dedication of the Saratoga Battlefield, now the Saratoga National Historic Park, and a huge pageant in Fort Edward in observance of the massacre of Jane McCrea.

Their efforts bore fruit in 1927 as Route 4, roughly the route of Burgoyne's Campaign, was paved with concrete, dubbed the Burgoyne Trail, and festooned with historic monuments and markers.

Historic tourism was born, and Sue Wade was actively involved in it all.

The onset of the Great Depression stopped much of that effort. However, she continued working at the clerk's office. Although I don't have record of it, I believe that because of her, in 1935, the clerk secured New Deal funding for a survey of the county's historic resources, including public and private records, historic structures, places, routes, monuments, and markers. Sue Wade's vision had truly become county-wide.

While the state enacted a law for towns and villages to appoint historians in 1918, the law apparently went unheeded in many places and 21 years later a new law was enacted for appointment of town, village and county historians. Sue Wade was a leader in the Washington County movement to appoint local historians and became the first town historian for Fort Edward.

Information is sadly sketchy, but it is obvious that she established a strong working relationship with Acting State Historian, Hugh Flick. In 1939, Flick wrote the county supervisors urging that they appoint her as county historian, which they did in November. She began work on January 1, 1940, still maintaining her position in the county clerk's office.

In a year, Sue Wade had become both the Washington County Historian and the Fort Edward Town Historian. But this leader among local historians had only begun her finest work. Next week, we'll see how Sue Wade led the founding of a county historical society. We'll also see how, in the midst of the Second World War, she not only helped save a landmark of the Revolution but insured that World War II's service men and women would be remembered for all times.

"OVER MY SHOULDER" COLUMN FOR APRIL 22, 2000
Sue Wade set standard for future county historians

We conclude the history of Sue Wade.

Few of you would expect to read that the only publicly accessible record of all Washington County service men and women in World War II exists because of Susan E. Wade, the first Washington County Historian.

In a moment, more on that, but let's take Sue Wade's accomplishments chronologically. When she took office in January, 1940, her first achievement was huge: the creation of the Washington County Historical Society. Thanks to Old Fort House Museum librarian Mary Jane Ellis, Washington County Historical Society's director Michael Russert, and Sue Wade's nephew, V. K. Malcolm Tasker, I have been able to learn more about Sue Wade's role.

A naturally shy person who avoided public speaking and the limelight, she preferred to organize behind the scenes. Under her leadership, all appointed town historians organized a meeting at the county clerk's office in June of 1940. As a news clipping stated, "Miss Wade presented the object of the meeting...to organize a Washington County historical society."

The office was jammed with local citizens, politicians, representatives of the New York State Historical Association and the DAR. Acting State Historian Hugh Flick addressed them. The upshot was a second meeting, in July, with Flick attending again. He praised her work at the county archives and urged creation of a county historical society.

At a third meeting, later in July in Cambridge, the Washington County Historical Society was organized and Sue Wade would come to be known as its founder and first curator. In a later column, I'll have more detail on the society's formation and early years.

That would be the first of her accomplishments as county historian. At the June meeting Acting State Historian Hugh Flick prophetically urged municipal historians to compile records about World War I soldiers. Eighteen months later, World War II began and over the next four years, Sue Wade led the town-by-town recording of all service men and women in the war, their names, addresses, parentage and war record. Andrew Cimo, of the Fort Edward Italian History Committee, knows its value. He has spent hours culling from it the names of Italian-American veterans in preparation for the upcoming history of the Fort Edward Italian community.

Ironically, as she was recording the history of World War II, she saved a piece of history from the Revolution. In 1943, the Baldwin House in Fort Edward caught fire. Wade and William Hill, who succeeded her as Fort Edward Town Historian, saved the building from demolition. They knew its value. This was the 1772 home of Justice Patrick Smyth, which also served as the first county municipal building, and served in 1777 as military headquarters for both American and the British generals during Burgoyne's unsuccessful campaign.

They recruited others to help restore the Smyth House. Perhaps because of that, she now turned her attention back to the inactive Fort Edward Historical Association, which, she helped resuscitate. It was 1948. Sue Wade was 70. Over the next few years she prepared the association to receive as a gift the Baldwin House, which it opened in 1953 as the Old Fort House Museum.

She fought for causes. She began the Century Farms program to identify farms which had been in families for a century or more. In name of education and historic tourism, she promoted a campaign to photograph the county, to publish more books on local history, to create more markers and monuments, and to place the date of construction over the doorways of all the county's historic houses.

In 1955, she was reporting to county supervisors that the county now had four historical societies and that she had been cataloging thousands of county records the county clerk had placed in her office for safe keeping. In her historian's office she assembled records on everything from ancient cemeteries to Korean War veterans.

Sue Wade died November 2, 1955 in Fort Edward at age 77. Right up to her death she was a fighter. She fought, unsuccessfully, Cornell University's taking of Salem's historical document collections. And in the July before her death, she was reminding the county supervisors in a rather chastising letter that a certain cemetery should not be made into a children's playground. She pointedly sent them a book on state cemetery law.

Susan E. Wade, a hero of the local history movement: may she be remembered, and emulated, by present and future generations.

"OVER MY SHOULDER" COLUMN FOR AUGUST 26, 2000
Gompers brought eloquence to Washington County

In a few days we shall observe a very important centennial in our region, for on September 1, 1900, the Village of Glens Falls observed its first Labor Day.

Also, the 100th anniversary of another important date in local labor history occurred two days ago, August 24. It directly ties in with that first Labor Day observance and with the Washington County Fair, now celebrating its "Fair Week."

On August 24, 1900, the general public and labor unions from the villages of Glens Falls, Sandy Hill (now Hudson Falls), and Fort Edward gathered at the Washington County Fairgrounds to listen to an address by Samuel Gompers, now a legend in the American labor movement.

Gompers appeared at the old Washington County Fairgrounds in Fort Edward, today the site of the Washington County Municipal Center and General Electric. The August 25th edition of *The Morning Star*, a predecessor of *The Post-Star*, reported that Gompers was "escorted from the fair ground gate to the grand stand by the Fort Edward Band, followed by representatives of every labor union in the three villages."

Gompers had been born in London in 1850, one of five children. Educated at The Jews' Free School, he started working at age 10. He later became a cigarmaker, like his father. The Gompers family moved to New York City 1863.

Working his way up through the fast growing labor movement of the post-Civil War era, Gompers became prominent in joint unionization efforts in Canada and the US. In the 1880s he joined P.J. McGuire's movement, which created the American Federation of Labor – the AF of L. Gompers accepted the American Federation of Labor presidency in 1886.

By the time Gompers came to the fairgrounds, unions had become a powerful force in our region. The earlier ones began in the early 1880s.

Gompers had come to make an address on labor in general but was drawn into talking about a particular "Open Shop" issue that filled the papers. In an open shop the workplace employs people without knowing whether or not they are union members, but more often the assumption is that they are not. A closed shop, by contrast, is specifically closed to unions, while a union shop is totally union.

The day before, *The Morning Star* reported that the "Hon. Daniel Davenport," a member of Congress, had addressed a huge gathering at the fair on the issue of the open shop. Gompers noted that although he hadn't come to specifically address the open shop issue, he opposed it. Both Gompers and Davenport were at the fairgrounds together as Gompers made his remarks.

Gompers said that Davenport had spared his feelings in his speech the day before, but had not been so kind in a talk given before Congress the previous winter, when Gompers was not around and Davenport had characterized certain pro-labor legislation in Congress "as extortion and bribery." *The Morning Star* reported that Gompers said, "'I have courage enough to say in a man's presence what I say to his back.'" The paper noted that Gompers smiled at Davenport and Davenport smiled back.

Gompers said that union people were as patriotic as all other citizens. He also said the New York State circuit court had recognized unions' legality. But he noted that "some acts have been done which are not legal according to the statutes." He went on to cite John Brown's actions as going counter to slavery laws. He also brilliantly used two American icons in his argument. George Washington went against the government in starting the Revolution, he said, and Thomas Jefferson was branded a traitor for drafting the Declaration of Independence.

He concluded by saying that the "union man does not want to control his employer's business. He wants only a livelihood, wholesome food, good clothes, a recreation now and then, good schools for his children, and not a hut to live in."

One hundred years have passed since those comments were made. Other than changing the wording to reflect working women, the sentiments expressed still stand, eloquent testimony to the labor movement, to working people everywhere, and to the notion of what Labor Day means.

"OVER MY SHOULDER" COLUMN FOR SEPTEMBER 2, 2000
City's first Labor Day celebration was huge affair

In last week's column I gave the wrong day for Glens Falls' first Labor Day. It was not September 1, 1900, but Monday, September 3. So tomorrow marks the 100th anniversary of the first Labor Day. I should have labored a little harder on that research.

The newspapers' lead-up to the big day was extensive and universally positive, as was coverage after the event.

The day's events began at 9:30 am with an enormous parade, presided over by Grand Marshall M. F. Nason. Downtown and most of the houses along the main route were festooned with bunting and flags – patriotism was high after the Spanish American War victory.

The occasion was covered by *The Morning Star*, predecessor to *The Post-Star*, which observed strong local support for Labor Day that cut across economic lines. This the newspaper sagely implied when it listed all of the numerous old and well established downtown businesses that closed in support of the day, including DeLong and Sons, P.P. Braley's, The Boston Store, B. B. Fowler's, and others.

The involvement of these old-line establishments told the reader that "those who were" sanctioned this newfangled Labor Day. Labor unions were still recent to the area, having only started around 1882, and were not viewed with love by many large business owners who feared the power of the unions.

But all was harmony on September 3, 1900. The massive parade began at the Rockwell House, a large hotel that stood where Hudson Avenue intersects with Glen Street today. There were two divisions, filled with these unions from the villages of Glens Falls, Sandy Hill, and Fort Edward in full force: Brick Makers International; Brick Masons; Carpenters; Cigar Makers; International Paper Machine Tenders; Painters, Painters and Decorators; Printers; Shirt Collar and Waist Cutters; Machinists; and Stone Cutters.

Division 1 was flanked by two platoons of Glens Falls police and led by the Glens Falls City Band. Marshall Isaac Yarter and the Fort Edward Band, archrival of the Glens Falls Band led division two.

The parade went up Glen to Union over to Bay Street, along Maple then down to Warren. Then along Warren to Park, all the way over to South Street, finally coming back to Glen. It stopped at the Rockwell House. There, Grand Marshall Mason addressed the exhausted marchers on "Architecture past and Present in Its Relationship to Organized Labor."

Not exactly a rousing-sounding speech, but Nason did have a captive audience.

After that, the unions marched to "their respective halls" and disbanded to go on to the next part of the day's events, "the field sports on the mile track, [held] under the auspices of the Knights of Columbus." The sponsorship of the K of C is totally understandable in that as so many union members were Roman Catholic, and in particular Irish, who would have belonged to the Knights.

The Mile Track was where the Broadacres section of Glens Falls and Queensbury is today. The judged events included baseball, Gaelic football, track and field sports, pole-vaulting, gentlemen's carriage driving, and bicycling, among others. So, having warmed up with a two-mile march through Glens Falls, the union members then had a chance to demonstrate their physical prowess.

The get-together at the mile track actually combined two of the world's most potentially explosive events, outside of the meeting of in-laws at a marriage – politics and sports. With the crowd packed into the mile track's huge grandstand to cheer them on, Representative Thomas Carmody, Democrat of Penn Yan, debated E. B. Vreeland, Republican of Chautauqua County, on presidential campaign issues.

In announcing the debate earlier, *The Morning Star* stressed that the issues would be "intelligently discussed" and "the spirit of partisanship" would be "eliminated." It would just be a "good natured presentation of the principles for which the two parties are contending in the presidential campaign."

My reaction was to wonder what planet *The Morning Star*'s writer had just come from. However, it was reported that everyone acted properly and the speakers "commanded the rapt attention of the crowd." Perhaps significantly, it was also reported that only "temperance drinks" were served at the track.

In all Glens Falls' first Labor Day proved a wonderful success. May its spirit of good will and its honoring of good, hard labor be present on this Labor day and the ones to follow.

Happy Labor Day to you.

"OVER MY SHOULDER" COLUMN FOR OCTOBER 28, 2000
Municipal water system boon to firefighters

This is the concluding part on the formation of the Glens Falls Fire Department.

After the disastrous 1864 fire that consumed most of downtown, two more volunteer companies were formed: the Jerome Lapham Engine Company Number Three in 1865 and the M. B. Little Hose Company in 1873. At this point the village, with a population of 4500 people, had 5 volunteer companies, with a total of, conservatively, 150 volunteers.

These companies were also tremendous social organizations that attracted members from all ranks. Outside of the firefighting itself, the camaraderie, the dress uniforms, and the pageantry attracted men of the village. The fire company parades and competitions held locally and state-wide were a large part of being a volunteer fireman.

After the purchase of a pumper and the formation of volunteer fire departments, a third event occurred that was momentous in Glens Falls firefighting history: the creation of a water system in 1873. Water supplied from reservoirs at tremendous pressure throughout the village provided every building equal coverage for the first time.

Between 1873 and 1903, several other advances were made. Technology created a steam pumper, increasing the ability to supply water. Glens Falls bought its first in 1891 and then in 1893 bought its first aerial truck. Now firefighters and water could go higher and closer to the fire. Because of the sheer weight of the machinery, horses replaced people in pulling it, and horses were faster.

Companies began to consolidate. In 1873, the new M. B. Little Hose company merged with the M. B. Little Engine Company and the Defiance Engine Company to form the M. B. Little Engine and Hose Company. There remained three large volunteer companies. All disbanded when the paid department was begun in 1903.

Several things prompted a 24-hour-a-day paid department. First, as Glens Falls grew up and out, large multi-story buildings demanded new equipment and highly skilled fire fighters available around the clock. The huge fire on Warren Street in 1884 was a prime example.

Second, between 1898 and 1900, arson became rampant, the worst in the village's history. Newspapers carried constant stories on it.

Possibly connected to this arson was the 1902 downtown fire that struck by Glen and Exchange Streets, destroying *The Glens Falls Times* building and others. In spite of technology, between 1884 and 1902, three-quarters of a million dollars' worth of property had burned.

The village was in an uproar. Hints of vigilante action could be detected. *The Glens Falls Times* joined the crusade for a totally paid fire department. In 1894

Cornelius Leary had already been hired as the first paid fire department employee. He was to use his team of horses to haul the engines from the South Street Station. Also in 1894, Jeremiah O'Connor was hired for the same purpose at the Ridge Street fire station, which had been built in 1865, just to the south of today's City Hall.

The village put up $10,000 and on June 8, 1903, the paid fire department began, with John Mack as its chief. The volunteer companies were disbanded, the last in the village and the town until 1948, when the Queensbury Volunteer Fire Department began. In 1913, the City of Glens Falls' first new fire station was built on Broad Street to replace the South Street station, which still stands.

However, it was 1915 that marked the second and arguably most important technological event in the department's history: the advent of the motorized fire vehicle, with the conversion of a Buick touring car into a hose-carrying vehicle. Up to that point, horses provided the locomotion. Standing ready in the station, their harnesses would drop down on them from overhead. Firemen would strap them up and the horse drawn pumpers and aerial cars would fly down the street.

With gas and diesel engines, fire trucks moved more quickly and performed more functions. American LaFrance pumpers were purchased. In 1939, the Ridge Street fire station was constructed, the first fire station in Glens Falls specifically designed for motorized vehicles. A second station was built in 1973 on Broad Street, replacing the older one.

The Glens Falls Fire Department is now nearing its 100th anniversary and is one of the older paid forces in the state. Before the department celebrates its centennial in 2003, isn't it time for a formal history to be written? Something longer than just a few columns and a book filled with all the facts and all photos that the department deserves?

I think so. And forgive me for putting it this way, but it's an idea I'm hoping will catch fire.

"OVER MY SHOULDER" COLUMN FOR DECEMBER 9, 2000
Celebrating paintings' homecoming

This last Thursday, David Blow, staff writer for *The Post-Star*, documented a homecoming that ended a mystery that he'd uncovered last February—the mystery of the whereabouts of the Ferris and Yohn collection of the old Glens Falls Insurance Company.

He wrote of how CNA, successor to the Glens Falls Insurance Company, had unexpectedly called Chapman Historical Museum Executive Director Tim Weidner,[xliii] offering to donate the Ferris and Yohn water colors and paintings to the museum.

The collection has come home. Home to the Glens Falls region and, in particular, home to the Chapman.

Dave said that it was quite a sight to see staff and volunteers of the Chapman transporting the individually boxed Ferris and Yohn paintings and watercolors from the CNA building to the museum. That wasn't the first trip that Glens Falls Insurance Company materials made across Glen to the Chapman.

In the museum's first year, 1968, Richard Van Dusen reported on an exhibit of insurance company artifacts in his *Post-Star* column "Historical Museum Notes." Van Dusen was one of the founders of the Glens Falls-Queensbury Historical Association, parent organization of the Chapman. He was also a retired officer of the insurance company. The exhibit was part of the large collection of company history and fire-fighting memorabilia assembled by Rob Carter, also a company officer.

I started as the Chapman's curator in November 1975. By then, part of the Carter exhibition was on display in the front room of the Chapman, including huge, heavy display cases filled with photographs, fire marks, etc. The company had also donated large filing cabinets, which the museum's first curator, Ralph M. Lapham, told me were part of the Carter collection. Ralph began my education on the insurance company's history. It's ongoing.

Shortly after I arrived, it was announced that the old 1912 Glens Falls Insurance Company building at Bay and Glen building was to be razed. I contacted Vice President Robert Morgan and asked if there might be any filing cabinets we could have. He said to go to the old building and select what we needed.

I went and found the same style cabinets as at the museum. All full. I am my mother's child, a profound pack rat. I pawed through the files. Dumbstruck, I pulled out the architect's plans for the building in which I stood. I contacted Mr. Morgan. Could we have both cabinets and contents? There was a long silence. He said he would call.

He did and the Chapman was lucky beyond belief. Excepting current records and employee records, the company allowed the Chapman to have far more than just cabinets and contents. Most of the remainder of the Carter collection came, including books, scrapbooks, photos on the company, firefighting publications and artifacts dating to the 1700s. Beyond that, there were the original handwritten company minutes, financial statements, early policies, and company newsletters right up to 1968 – 119 years of company history. It would take a small booklet to list the thousands of pieces in that collection, representing a major national insurance company that had a profound effect on this region.

It was a bonanza, but it did not contain the Ferris and Yohn collection. Twenty-four years and several museum directors later, that would occur. The last leg of the homecoming began in February with David Blow's article on the search for Ferris and Yohn. He opened the door on the mystery. Then Gene Hinners at CNA solved the whereabouts of the collection.

But Ferris and Yohn weren't home yet.

They were, once Tim Weidner received the call in which CNA offered the Chapman the collection. Tim makes light of his role. I disagree. He was the right person in the right place at the right time. He knew the importance of Ferris and Yohn. Consider if he hadn't.

Are you a former Glens Falls Insurance Company employee or simply someone who appreciates its history? Visit the Chapman. See this collection. Celebrate its homecoming.

Oh, and call David Blow at *The Post-Star,* 792-3131, extension 3222, and say, "Good job, Dave!"

"OVER MY SHOULDER" COLUMN FOR DECEMBER 16, 2000
Empty spaces hold much history

Empty spaces often hold so much history.

I forget that many people don't know the history of empty sites that were once so vital. So, I'm revisiting a story I began in a May column on the intersection of Hudson Avenue and Glen Street in downtown Glens Falls, and Mayor Regan's rather courageous proposal to build on that spot.

Right now the site is, well, nothing. In former times, it was a hot spot. Perhaps the mayor is reflecting upon previous days when the site was occupied by tall buildings in which major events transpired.

Holden's 1874 history of Queensbury relates that the site was occupied from 1802 on, when John A. Ferris erected the first building on it. It would hold buildings for another 173 years.

The site became a major stopover when Peter Threehouse erected Threehouse and Thurston's Inn in 1826. Holden says that Threehouse "built up for the house a deservedly famous reputation among the traveling public. In those days, and right up to the Northway's coming, Glen Street was a part of the great travel route that brought authors, Presidents and princes among the waves of tourists assaulting the Adirondacks.

Threehouse's hotel passed through many hands until 1852, when Wait S. Carpenter purchased it, razed it and built a new structure, the Glens Falls Hotel. His building lasted until the Great Fire of 1864, which burned down the better part of downtown. Sort of an unintended urban renewal.

Actually, the fire started in the huge kitchen stoves of the Glens Falls Hotel. In a previous column I wrote that the fire began on May 31st and in almost two days burned 112 buildings, including three churches, two hotels, sixty stores and two banks.

This was not the last time fire was connected to that site.

Property owners quickly regrouped, building bigger, better, and overall safer buildings, predominantly of brick. The Glens Falls Hotel site was the last to be rebuilt and in that fact lies a lesson in foresight. The site sat empty as rebuilding swiftly happened around it. Fearing this prime site would be filled with nondescript stores, a group raised $15,400 and bought it. They advertised for a hotel developer and brothers H. J. and George H. Rockwell, of the famed hotel family of Luzerne, took up the challenge.

Construction of the elegant and ornate four story Rockwell House began March 26, 1871 and was completed January 31, 1872. Among the first guests was President U. S. Grant.

The Rockwell House became famed as a public meeting spot. In it, decisions were made affecting the public education system, the hospital, town, and city government and even the suffrage movement.

By the 1920s it was considered antiquated and the opening of the Queensbury Hotel in 1926 effectively replaced the aging Rockwell. Extensive renovation was done around that time to modernize it. It was again renovated in 1949 and renamed the Towers Hotel. However, on February 22nd, an arsonist's handiwork burned the hotel to the ground. The hotel site's last moment of fame came when Warren County District Attorney Frederick Bascom prosecuted the case that brought the arsonist to justice.

W. T. Grant Company built a rather characterless building that stood there for the next 25 years, a sad shadow of former glory. But the final indignity came in 1975 when under the "demolishing guidance" of Urban Renewal, Hudson Avenue was extended to Glen and 173 years of something was suddenly made nothing.

Peggy Lee's refrain, "Is that all there is?" comes to mind here. I certainly hope not. The intersection's emptiness is unbearable, but I understand there are those who say the through traffic is essential. So, here's a historian's compromise solution, offered as a Christmas wish: build a multi-story parking structure on the site, with ground level shops facing out onto Glen Street. To keep traffic flowing, make a tunnel beneath it, allowing the tunnel access to the parking structure above.

Perhaps in this way, past glory and current need could both be served.

And perhaps nothing could become something.

SECTION 2: AREA HISTORY

"OVER MY SHOULDER" COLUMN FOR JANUARY 4, 1998
Putting the focus on temperance

The hangover from New Year's eve has begun to wear off and the ghost of Dr. Billy J. Clark smiles ruefully down on the sufferers.

Dr. Billy J. holds the distinction in world history for being the founder of the first temperance society – anywhere, ever. Other societies had included temperance in their mission, but his was the first to focus solely upon temperance.

Previously, I had given a sketch of Dr. Clark's society. Today a fuller history is in order for it is his birthday. He was born in Northampton, Massachusetts, on January 4, 1788.

After apprenticing under a physician in Easton, New York, Dr. Clark settled with his wife at Clark's Corners in Moreau in 1799. As physicians will, Clark saw the best and worst of humankind. In his 1878 "History of Saratoga County" Nathaniel Sylvester wrote: "Daily witnessing in his practice the physical and moral ruin wrought by intemperance, he was aroused by the necessity of making an effort to resist the evil." Despite Sylvester's rhetorical flourish and obvious bias, the truth was the Town of Moreau was full of drunken people – as was most of the country. Our nation had a drinking problem.

From Colonial times alcohol was not just allowed, but condoned. The Puritans drank beer for breakfast. Soldiers were partially paid in rum. Alcohol was considered a blood fortifier and a common substitute for often polluted water. It was nothing for Dr. Clark to see drunken 10 year old boys and girls at home or in taverns. Hard cider was a common "soft drink" in these frontier areas, where alcoholism was rampant not just among lumberjacks, trappers and all their families, but among people of all walks of life.

In very early 1808, Dr. Clark approached Saratoga's County's legal establishment for help to start a county temperance society in Ballston Spa. Sylvester wrote that while Sheriff Bull helped Clark, the rest considered Clark and Bull "visionary enthusiasts."

Clark persevered. On April 13,1808, he called a meeting of friends in Moreau and Northumberland to form a temperance society. The meeting was held in a house, diagonally opposite Clark's own, the Mawney house, which still stands. Ironically, at that time, the Mawney house was also a tavern! What an appropriate cradle for the world's first temperance society.

Clark had gathered an illustrious and powerful group of people, such as Rev. Lebbeus Armstrong, a Congregational minister, James Mott, Nicholas W. Angle and Colonel Sidney Berry, Revolutionary War hero and the first surrogate of Saratoga County. At a subsequent meeting, Berry became the first president of the "Moreau and Northumberland Temperate Society," Ichabod Hawley vice-president and Dr. Billy J. Clark, the secretary. Within no time, hundreds had joined the society.

The society prohibited drinking "any rum, brandy, gin, whiskey or any kind of distilled spirits." Exceptions were physicians' prescriptions, communion wine or wine at "a public dinner." At the society's reorganization in 1843, Clark urged everyone to take the "Total Abstinence" pledge.

Society members formed local temperance societies in Queensbury and other towns. By 1866 when Clark died in Glens Falls – where he had later opened a drugstore and then eventually retired – nationwide there were all manner of temperance organizations, such as the Sons of Temperance, which had a local division named for Clark. By the end of the century, Clark's effort had spawned the Women's Christian Temperance Union and the Prohibition Party, among others. It was a national movement that called for nationwide temperance – if not voluntarily, then at least by legal prohibition.

By 1908, it was a worldwide movement, symbolized by the World Temperance Centennial Congress' erecting a monument that may be seen today near the Mawney House. It honored the 100th anniversary of the "first temperance society in history." Dr. Clark, the "visionary enthusiast," had spawned an incredible force.

Twelve years later, "Prohibition" began in the United States of America.

"OVER MY SHOULDER" COLUMN FOR FEBRUARY 1, 1998
The early days of an IP mill

International Paper Company, "IP," turned 100 this year, growing from an initial union of 20 papermills in 1898. This is the story of one of those firms – and a father and son.

By the Route 9 bridge in South Glens Falls is a brick building with a terra cotta plaque bearing the inscription "Glens Falls Paper Mill Company 1864 - 1890," the last year being the date the building was erected. Today that building is occupied by Encore Paper Company which stands where the "Glens Falls Paper Company" began.

An article in a "Glens Falls Messenger of 1873" (reprinted in Hyde's "History of Glens Falls") states that The Glens Falls Paper Company was actually started in 1862 by a stock company, with Dr. M. A. Cushing the mill's first superintendent. Cushing left in 1864 after two profitless years. Perhaps in revenge the shareholders decided to date the mill's origins from his departure.

By 1872, the superintendent was Solomon A. Parks, a descendant of the Parks family of Revolutionary War fame in Moreau. But he brought more than heritage to the position. In 1872, he moved to Glens Falls, built a home on Park Street, and bought one-quarter of The Glens Falls Paper Company. In addition to money, he brought managerial talent to a company ready for growth.

Its president was now James Morgan, rich and very powerful from Adirondack lumber holdings and enormous sawmills in South Glens Falls and Glens Falls. (In a previous column, I described Morgan's suspicious death in 1873.) The company's excellent treasurer and secretary was Arthur T. Harris, who came in 1866 and stayed for several decades.

Despite Morgan's untimely death, the firm thrived under Parks. It made newsprint for newspapers in New York, Boston, Troy and Glens Falls, initially using locally grown straw, plus rags. It was the first in the area to use chlorine for bleaching, which the local papers described as smelling bad, but having the side effect of helping cure consumption!

In 1876 the firm was building an addition when catastrophe struck. One of the gigantic "bleachers" blew up. Miraculously only one person was killed in this blast that leveled a whole building. Parks continued new construction, expanding the mill to a 292 foot long structure, in some places five stories high.

In 1882, the company was renamed "The Glens Falls Paper Mill Company." It was expanding again by 1884, turning out 10 tons of paper a day compared to 781 tons for the whole year of 1872. In the 1880s, the company, and others, began to switch from straw to far more easily accessible wood pulp. By 1890, a new company headquarters had been built on Main Street and other changes had come about. Parks had brought in his son Frederick Hewitt Parks, who started as the foreman and, in time, assumed more power as his father aged and gradually eased into retirement around 1896. Solomon's last act was to donate his home to become the Glens Falls Hospital.

And Frederick? The "Glens Falls Daily Times" of February 15, 1898 confirmed that Frederick's papermill, the "largest in the country," and 19 other papermills would form the "International Paper Company." Frederick would be the new company's "general manager," third in line after W. A. Russell of Russell Paper, Lawrence, Massachusetts, and Hugh Chisholm of Otis Paper in Livermore Falls, Maine. Russell was actually only "nominally president," with Chisholm the real "power behind the throne."

This made Frederick Parks the second in line of the world's newest and largest papermaking company. Parks moved to Manhattan to live in 1899 and would eventually become company president.

And Parks' own company in South Glens Falls? It would become the first headquarters of the multinational company known as International Paper.

"OVER MY SHOULDER" COLUMN FOR FEBRUARY 15, 1998
Putnam's roots stretch to Scotland

The Town of Putnam is going to celebrate its first Founders' Day on February 18 with a public dinner and ceremony at the Putnam School. The whole event will honor Putnam's Scottish roots.

The Post-Star correspondent Maury Thompson reported that the day was based upon the original deeding of the land in Edinburgh, Scotland, on February 18, 1771. I thought a column was certainly in order and made a dive for my trusty *History of Washington County*.

Putnam's first European settlers date to the end of the French and Indian War. (Part of Putnam was settled by African Americans and I'll have that story shortly.) Veterans, many of them Scottish, were given land "patents" and part of modern Putnam was deeded to a Scot named Hodgson, who sold it to a "William Hutton & Co." in Paisley, Scotland.

William Hutton's two partners bowed out and left Hutton to come to America. He and his wife settled in Skenesborough, now Whitehall, but the Revolution erupted, delaying the Huttons from settling their land. They were too busy protecting their Skenesborough home. A British patrol, probably during Burgoyne's march in 1777, attempted to "appropriate" their cattle. (They'd give IOUs for what they took.) Mrs. Hutton thrust a musket in their faces and said they'd only get the cattle over her body. An aggravated Scots woman is the embodiment of ferocity. Wisely, the British retreated.

The Huttons finally settled in what is now Putnam in 1786, although a squatter named Haskins had settled there around 1782. While he could have bounced Haskins, Hutton simply had him pay for the land – land sales and money being Hutton's aim.

Hutton settled on Lake Champlain "about a mile and a half north of Mill Bay," but his life was complicated by a conflict over Alexander Turner's adjacent land grant. Hutton was sued by a man who said Turner had sold him the land that Hutton was claiming. The plaintiff withdrew and in 1801 Hutton paid off his attorney, Dickinson, and his surveyor, Cockburn, in land.

The settlers who came after Hutton were almost entirely Scottish, many from Hutton's native Paisley, though many had been living in America, such as George Easton and Robert Cummings, both of Cambridge, Massachusetts. Cummings married Hutton's daughter, Hannah, who, before her marriage, showed how much like her mother she was. During her father's land dispute, a man named Lytle arrived saying he bought land from Turner. He became a nuisance. One day, when the men were gone, he hounded Hannah and her sister, who threatened to dunk Lytle in the lake if didn't go. He didn't. So, they grabbed him and held him under water three times until he agreed to go. He agreed and ran!

Today the Huttons and Cummings, and their descendants, are immortalized in Hutton's Square Road and Cummings Road, and founding names, such as Dedrick, can still be found in the region.

After the Revolution, Putnam was a part of Westfield (now Fort Ann), then later of Dresden. Then on February 28, 1806, Hutton's essentially Scottish community formed its own town, named in honor of Revolutionary War hero, General Israel Putnam. The first Town Meeting was held on April 4 at the home of Hutton's nephew, James Burnet, originally a gardener in Paisley, then New York City, before coming to Putnam. John Gourley, a Scottish distiller and gardener, was elected as the first Town Supervisor. Most of the board was Scottish.

So, this Wednesday night, in honor of Putnam's Scottish heritage, bagpipes will wail at the Founder's Day spaghetti dinner.

Wait a minute. Spaghetti? No Scottish tatties? No neeps? No haggis?

No problem. Just get town Supervisor John LaPointe to wear a kilt!

"OVER MY SHOULDER" COLUMN FOR MARCH 1, 1998
Tale of Prince Taylor

A very early landowner in Ticonderoga, who ran one of the first taverns, if not the very first, was a Revolutionary War veteran named Taylor. According to the 1969 history *Ticonderoga Patches and Patterns from Its Past*[xlv], Mr. Taylor was quite an accomplished person. Having served on board a ship and being a tailor by trade, he was also an "excellent cook," dancer, and acknowledged wit. He was a pillar of his church and community.

So, what distinguished Taylor from other citizens, many also Revolutionary War veterans and landowners? Mr. Taylor, whose full name was Prince Taylor, was an African American. Taylor had served onboard the warship "Diligence" as a steward and then in the Continental Army under a Captain Pillsbury.

I have not found when Prince Taylor came to Ticonderoga. Possibly it was with the army during the Revolution. The presence of an African American in Ticonderoga would not have been unique, as both freemen and slaves were to be found throughout the area. A fact noted in histories and in historical fiction, such as Kenneth Roberts' *Rabble in Arms*[xlv], is that African Americans came out of the hills to enlist when the British first offered freedom to slaves in return for their being soldiers. When the Americans quickly countered with the same offer, blacks responded. The First Rhode Regiment, as an example, was two-thirds African American.

In my column on the origins of Putnam, I mentioned that Johnson's 1878 History of Washington County[xlvi] indicated that a part of Putnam had been settled by African Americans. The history states: "Black Point on Lake George, in the extreme north part of the town (of Putnam) is supposed to have received its name from the legend that it was first settled by Black people at a very early day. Tradition says it was owned by one Prince Taylor, also known as Black

Prince."

The Ticonderoga history tells us that Prince Taylor also worked as a surveying assistant to Lodewick Shear, "laying out the roads in the town of Putnam."

Taylor actually owned land in several places, including two pieces in the hamlet of Alexandria, now a part of the Village of Ticonderoga[xlvii]. In fact, a New York State historic marker at the corner of Lake George and Alexandria Avenues indicates Taylor was the first tavern owner. The famed Joseph Cook[xlviii] later wrote of Taylor as a man of wit and piety, and noting his culinary skills, also wrote that few parties were ever held without him as "chief director."

He was more than that. He was a person of standing and presumably some wealth. An early schoolteacher in Ticonderoga wrote that Taylor was a supporter of the Episcopalian church, meaning that Taylor had money to support the church. In fact, Taylor was one of the group who commissioned the teacher to also be a lay reader in the church. Taylor later converted to Congregationalism.

When he could no longer work, Taylor applied for and received a pension for his service as a soldier in the Revolution. He died without any known family in Ticonderoga in 1828.

Much more, I believe, could be known about Prince Taylor. His having been a pensioned soldier from Pillsbury's unit could give us his origins and, possibly, whether he had family. Census records would help, too. I don't believe that he was the sole black person in Ticonderoga, based upon the county history stating that "black people" (that is, more than one person) settled Black Point.

Can you help me find more on Prince Taylor? His is definitely a story that needs expanding. You can contact me through *The Post-Star*. Thanks!

"OVER MY SHOULDER" COLUMN FOR MARCH 22, 1998
Important date for Fort Ann

Tomorrow, March 23, marks the 211th anniversary of the founding of the Town of Fort Ann.
Actually, the Town of Fort Ann began its political life as the Town of Westfield.

But that's confusing things. Let's start with the first name, "Fort Ann," which traces to 1757, when the stockade named "Fort Anne" was built shortly after the outbreak of the French and Indian War. The 1878 "History of Washington County" states Fort Anne was built at the intersection of Wood Creek and Halfway Brook. At about this spot today in the Village of Fort Ann, a branch of the Glens Falls National Bank and Trust Company is located in a modern building constructed in the style of a colonial fort.

I spoke with Fort Ann Town Historian Virginia Parrott about this. She said the original Fort Anne was actually a stockade of massive logs that undoubtedly occupied a great deal of land beyond the bank's present property. In fact, the well for the fort was located where the Portage Restaurant is today, so when you are dining at the Portage, you are sitting around the well of the old fort. That's very appropriate.

The fortress was named "Fort Anne" for Queen Anne, who had died in 1713. As Fort Edward Historian Paul McCarty notes, the "e" in Anne's name was later dropped. Fort Anne itself lasted through to the Revolution, where it was "recycled" for the new war. On July 8, 1777, as General Burgoyne advanced toward Saratoga, he clashed with a group of Americans at a spot just above the present village and there many died. As the Americans retreated, they burned Fort Anne, in order not to give the good general anywhere to sleep that night.

The first subdivision of land in what is now the Town of Fort Ann occurred October 24, 1764, when the British crown granted a patent of land to Joseph Walton and 23 other British officers for their services in the French and Indian War. This was called the Artillery Patent and forms the southern part of the present town. In what is now the town, there was little settlement, except for two families, the Harrisons and Braytons, who settled in 1773. Also, a man named Charles Kane was hired by Whitehall's founder, Philip Skene, to set up grinding mills on some waterfalls – now known as "Kane Falls."

In late 1780, Loyalist raiders burned nearly everything in the region, but within not even a year, ten families had moved into the Artillery Patent. Another 14 families had joined them by 1786, the same year Charlotte County became Washington County.

It was also the year those 24 families founded the Town of Westfield, named for Westfield, Massachusetts, source of many of the original settlers. Present-day Dresden, Hartford, and Putnam were a part of Westfield, too. It seems old "Fort Anne" had been forgotten.

However, there was something about the people in this region that wouldn't let go of names that were part of English colonial rule. True, they switched the county from "Charlotte" to "Washington," but they kept "Lake George," named for George II, and Fort Edward, named for the Duke of Albany. And Kingsbury and Queensbury named for... Well, you figure that one. So, "Westfield" itself was not destined to last long, and 22 years later, in 1808, the townspeople decided it was time to go back to the name they liked best, "Fort Ann."

And, for the sake of fairness, probably just as well, because in all of the places in New York State that begin with the word "Fort," Fort Ann is the only one named for a woman.

Happy anniversary Fort Ann.

"OVER MY SHOULDER" COLUMN FOR APRIL 12, 1998
A girl, a boy and a dunking

Thanks go to my friend Jane Mackintosh[xlix], Assistant Curator at the Adirondack Museum, for supplying me with information about Wevertown "the second of John Thurman's hamlets."

Driving through Wevertown I had always wondered about its name. Were there originally weavers there who didn't how to spell? As it turns out, how Wevertown actually gained its name is a far more interesting story.

In her notes, Jane writes (with credits to Glen Pearsall and Doris Patton) that in 1795 the famed John Thurman owned what is now Wevertown. He wanted this parcel settled and offered to name it for the first family that did so.

Two families, the Paddocks and the Wevers, vied for the trophy and started blazing trails to the area, but joined forces when they realized how much work was involved. Jane writes, "As they approached Mill Creek, the oldest Paddock child, a boy, and the oldest Wever child, a girl, were chosen to cross the creek together. Hand in hand they started out, but about halfway across, the Wever girl pushed the boy into the stream and raced to the other side." The settlement was therefore named for the Andrus Wever family.

That fact beats fiction! But equally incredible is the fact that Wevertown owed its first industry to California, South America and Spain – specifically, to the hides brought to the Adirondacks from those places. Smith's 1886 History of Warren County[l] notes that Wevertown, like the rest of Johnsburg, struggled in its early years because it was on the edge of the "Northern Wilderness," the raw wilderness of the central Adirondacks. Grain and butter produced in Wevertown were traded in Glens Falls for other of life's staples, but the settlers were just existing.

Then, in 1832, William Wasson and James Watson of Blanford, Massachusetts, built the first tannery in Wevertown. This was a year after the county's first tannery was built in Warrensburg and the same year that the feeder canal connecting Glens Falls and Kingsbury was completed.

Now, this region's history of hide tanning is a bit bizarre. Hemlock bark was used for tanning cowhides. With the depletion of hemlock in the Catskills and other forests near the Atlantic, tanners looked inland. They spotted the Adirondacks, loaded with hemlock. The canal made it feasible to bring the hides to Wevertown, and the bizarre aspect is that it was cheaper to bring the hides to the forest, rather than vice versa. It simply was more cost effective to haul hides to Wevertown than to send Wevertown's hemlock bark to Glens Falls or beyond.

So hides from ranches in Spain, as well as Spanish colonial ranches in South America and California, were sent by sailing ship to New York, up the canal to Glens Falls and overland to Wevertown and other tanneries in Warren County. (This wasn't the first time Spain was involved in our region's economy. Farmers in Washington County had already been importing Marino sheep from Spain for decades.)

A tanning mill and a dam for water power were erected on Mill Creek, hemlocks were cut, the bark stripped and boiled to produce a tanning "liquor." Sadly, the wood was left to rot. The dried hides were scraped, tanned and then rolled to an even thickness with a giant brass roller weighted by hardwood beams (more about which next week).

The tannery thrived. The 1850 census reported that there were 22 employees who produced 26,000 sides of sole leather. (A side, by the way, is half of one hide.) Next week, I'll have more history about the mill and Wevertown in general – including the tannery's double connection with Glens Falls and a mystery concerning a Wevertown church and Milan, Italy.

Really.

"OVER MY SHOULDER" COLUMN FOR APRIL 19, 1998
Tales from the tannery

We continue with Wevertown history, thanks to Jane Mackintosh.

After Wasson and Watson built Wevertown's first tannery in 1832, the community grew, thanks to having this constant source of employment. In 1833, Linus Barnes joined the firm and by 1841 was sole proprietor. By 1849, when Barnes took on Jarret Thomas as partner, the mill was really thriving. As I wrote last week, the 1850 census reported 22 employees producing 26,000 sides of sole leather. (Remember, a side is half of one hide.)

It is incredible that it was actually profitable to ship dried sides of leather from ranches in Spain, South America, and California to New York City by sailing vessel, then to Glens Falls via the canal and finally overland to Wevertown for tanning. For 18 years, teamsters hauled the finished sides back to Glens Falls over a rutted dirt road. By 1858 that was "upgraded" to a plank road, half-logs anchored in the mud, but still a bone-jarring ride at best. (And we complain today.)

Another "international" part of the tannery were the French Canadian and southern Irish immigrants, who made up the mill's principle workers. Despite language differences, they were all Roman Catholic. In 1875, they hired A. Gustave LaHaise of Glens Falls to design and build their church (which is today a landmark, housing Beaver Brook Outfitters).

They named it for the Italian St. Charles Borromeo[li], and introduced an unsolved mystery: why select Borromeo, a mid-1500s Milan cardinal and ardent church reformer, canonized in the 1700s? Were the workers subtly signaling for labor reforms?

For the work was backbreaking. (If drinking morning coffee, you may want to go to next paragraph.) In an 18,000 square foot, three-story building, the hides were scraped of fat and gristle on the second and third floors, then placed in huge vats to soak and tan in the basement, where the hemlock bark was also boiled to make the tanning liquor. The tanned hides were hung to dry, then brought to the rolling mill where an enormous brass roller exerted tons of flattening pressure to bring the hides to a uniform thickness. Poisonous fumes, disease from the hides and possible flattening of one's limbs were daily occurrences.

The self-contained tannery also included a carpenter shop, harness shop, and horse barn. By 1870, however, it began to lose ground, producing only 30,000 sides, down from 32,000 in 1860. Perhaps this was because hemlock grew scarce as the Adirondacks were deforested by clear-cutting for lumber and, to a lesser degree, by farming. Also, the depression that started in 1873 lasted most of the decade.

The tannery was purchased in 1883 by Augustus Sherman, the astute Glens Falls lumber baron. If anyone could have saved the tannery's hides, he could have. Unfortunately for the mill's survival, and for him, he died in December of 1884. The mill closed in 1885.

Philip Moston bought the tannery in 1888, built a new dam, dismantled the tannery and used the timber to build a sawmill that his family operated until 1913, when T.C. Murphy bought it. In 1947, the sawmill was removed, because, ironically, the water needed to power the mill decreased as abandoned farmland was reclaimed by the forests, which held back the water as farmland could not. Today, the T.C. Murphy lumber company operates out of the original tannery store.

As to the rest of the tannery, the rolling mill burned in 1911, while other buildings, such as the carpenter shop and schoolhouse, were converted to homes. While the traces of Wevertown's first industry have disappeared, the hamlet that started with a girl shoving a boy into the water has survived and its history has grown.

Let's hope Jane Mackintosh turns her Wevertown history notes into a book.

"OVER MY SHOULDER" COLUMN FOR APRIL 26, 1998
Mystery of a silent film star

My request for history on local women yielded phone calls from Salem Town/Village Historian Al Cormier[lii] and Helen Cackener, a member of "Friends in Council."

We'll begin with Al Cormier's wealth of information, far more than I can relate, so I'll save some for future columns and concentrate upon Jane Gail, an early silent film actress.

Jane Gail was born Ethel Magee on August 16, 1880 in the Village of Salem, the daughter of Charles Magee of West Broadway. Her family was not rich, but Ethel was able to attend the Salem Washington Academy, an excellent school in the village, where, Al Cormier notes, she "participated successfully in numerous speaking contests, a foreshadowing of her future career."

After graduation in 1899, Ethel went to Chicago to attend the Frohman Dramatic School. That she had the talent is apparent, but that she had the drive is the fascinating aspect. A woman in a small village in the late 1800s had only a few "acceptable" careers open to her at that time, with wife and mother being number one. There were some factory positions for women, working as a store clerk or, from the 1890s onward, being a secretary.

But to go to Chicago to a dramatic school? What a leap of incredible proportions. Jane Gail's career started strongly. Soon she was performing in the "legitimate theater" at Bush Temple, Chicago, then with the Shubert Stock Company of Rochester, New York, and later with the Lubin Company.

These would have exposed her to the theatrical hub of New York City and the budding film industry, then centered in Astoria and Long Island City, Queens. The phrase "legitimate theater" suggests that performing outside of it was less than legitimate and few who ventured into motion pictures then were able to continue in both. Once Jane did, she never went back to the stage.

Her first film, "Traffic in Souls," came out in 1913 and catapulted her to immediate fame. The film's credits list her as Jane Gail, although it's not certain when she dropped "Ethel Magee." During her career, Jane worked under contract to Independent Moving Pictures, London Films, and Universal Films. The second is a key to a major change in Jane's life, for she moved to London after her first film, prompting "Moving Picture World" magazine to regret her loss and speak of her "important work."

In London she made a series of movies, including "Who killed Olga Carew?", "The Prisoner of Zenda," and "20,000 Leagues Under the Sea." Interestingly, she also shot the "Jane" series of popular one-reel comedies at Universal Studios in California. Among her London work, Jane Gail was in some high quality silent films, later overshadowed by film masterpieces of the 1920s.

Al Cormier writes that "The Salem Press" announced each of her films whenever they played at the Star Theater. "Local girl makes good!" would have been the fitting cliché of that time.

Jane had returned to the United States briefly in 1915 to marry Edwin C. Hill, later a broadcaster on WJSV-CBS, and then returned to London, where she made films for five more years. As Al writes, her last film was ironically named "Bitter Fruit," made in 1920. English silent film historian Kevin Brownlow wrote to Al that the film was a quick and cheap one, typical of the kind made by film stars on the wane. Jane Gail's film career was finished.

It is a sad mystery as to why her career ended after only seven years. Sadder yet is that the rest of her life remains a mystery as well. Can you help Al Cormier complete the life story of Salem's Ethel Magee, who became the actress and silent film star Jane Gail?

"OVER MY SHOULDER" COLUMN FOR JULY 12, 1998
The early abolition movement in Greenwich

Recently I received a copy of a news clipping, sent by Tom Calarco[liii] who is working on a book on the underground railroad. I thought I'd be interested in the article. Instead I was riveted.

The article, from the April 7, 1854 issue of William Lloyd Garrison's Boston newspaper *The Liberator*,, contained many names so famous that books had been written about them. Yet the article was about this region, its headline reading, "Hiram Corliss notes lecture by Frederick Douglass in Union Village and neighboring communities."

Union Village was the name for today's Village of Greenwich. Frederick Douglass, the freed slave whose pre-Civil War lectures were so powerful and instrumental in firing the Abolitionist movement, had come to Greenwich, one of the hotbeds of Abolitionism in this region.

Since it was Dr. Hiram Corliss who had written for *The Liberator*, let's look at him first. The 1878 *History of Washington County*," itself citing a "Thurston's History," said Corliss moved to Greenwich in 1827, set up medical practice, then immediately became involved in the temperance movement. In 1833, he turned his sights on abolition and became "one of the first abolitionists of the county and of the state."

Corliss enlisted Elder Colver of the Bottskill Baptist Church, established an underground railroad, then the two recruited William Mowry, A.C. Holmes, Leonard Gibbs and many others, many of whom used their homes to hide runaway slaves on their "station." The history states that they were so successful that no slave who reached Greenwich was ever returned to slavery. Breaking the federal fugitive slave law meant imprisonment if caught for whites. For blacks, it meant a return to slavery, often at a plantation designed to curb runaways; possibly even death.

The local law enforcement apparently winked at this wholesale breach, so much so that, in one instance, Corliss even convinced runaway slave John Salter to remain and live openly in Easton, as a farmer. For five years, bounty hunters tried to get Salter, but gave up because of the protection given by Corliss and Salter's neighbors.

By 1854, Corliss had moved in many different directions, not just maintaining and expanding the Underground Railroad, but also pushing for more local education about abolition. Corliss also expanded his connections to William Lloyd Garrison, evidenced by the salutation "My Dear Friend Garrison" in Corliss' letter to "The Liberator." This helps describe Corliss' philosophy, which as a "Garrisonian," was radical.

Indeed, Garrison was radical, though not as vituperative as painted in some histories. When Northern clergy ignored Garrison's call for them to apply their Christianity in demanding freedom for the slaves, his attacks on them and his radical policy caused a split within abolitionist ranks. This policy also included equal rights for women; refusal to take an oath in support of the Constitution, because of its slavery clauses; and pacifism, through which he proposed the free states peaceful dissolving the union with the slave states – and this two decades before southern states seceded! "No Union with Slaveholders" was his cry. (When war erupted, he dropped his pacifism and supported the war with the motto: "Union without Slavery.")

Corliss' letter to *The Liberator* actually began by telling of the lectures given in the area by Sallie Holley of Rochester, NY, a Unitarian affiliated with Garrison who lectured throughout the Northeast and into the Midwest. She had preceded Douglass's arrival from Rochester, spending three weeks in the area lecturing. In the Town of Greenwich, Holley lectured at Battenville and Galesville, and in Saratoga County at Quaker Springs. In the Town of Easton, she held "four meetings, two at the North Quaker meeting-house, and one at the other, and also one at the Methodist church."

Next week, Frederick Douglass speaks to the people of Greenwich.

"OVER MY SHOULDER" COLUMN FOR JULY 19, 1998
Douglass' powerful presence

Last week's column told of Dr. Hiram Corliss of Greenwich, a leader in the abolitionist movement to end slavery, whose letter in April 7, 1854 issue of *The Liberator* newspaper, described lectures given in Greenwich by Frederick Douglass.

The Liberator was published in Boston by his friend William Lloyd Garrison and read by thousands of "Garrisonians," all like-minded, and some incredibly influential.

Corliss wrote that Sallie Holley, an abolitionist speaker from Rochester, had preceded Douglass. She had been invited by Corliss and his abolitionist group, while Douglass had been invited by the Greenwich chapter of the Free Democratic League, an abolitionist society not affiliated with Garrison or Corliss. Douglass' first speech was scheduled for the evening of March 1st, 1854 at the Congregational Church of Greenwich. Corliss noted, "Free Democrats...unanimously requested me, an out-and-out Garrisonian, to taken charge of the meeting."

Douglass' train was late, and Holley stood to speak in his place. Then the audience called for Leonard Gibbs, of Corliss' group, to speak and he did so for an hour. (By now the crowd had sat for three hours. Imagine that today?)

As a black choir sang, Douglass suddenly arrived about 9:00 pm and made a short speech. The evening was a success! He lectured in many spots, again at Greenwich Village, Galesville, Shushan, Cambridge and Lakeville, today known as Cossayuna. That means he spoke at the Lakeville Baptist Church, which with the Easton Quaker meeting house is today one of the existing local structures the great Frederick Douglass spoke in.

And what a speaker he must have been. Corliss states that his talks were "full of great truths, sound logic and enforced by vivid illustrations." Given his life that must have been easy. Douglass was born in 1817 in Maryland, half black, half white, his mother a slave. Badly mistreated, Douglass escaped in 1838 and went to New Bedford, Massachusetts.

He began as an abolitionist in 1841 with a totally off-the-cuff speech at an antislavery convention in Nantucket. He went on to work and speak for the state abolition society and was so eloquent people claimed he was not a slave, prompting him to write his autobiography in 1845.

He went to Great Britain to avoid seizure under the fugitive slave laws, lectured there and won friends for the cause. By 1854, when he was lecturing in Greenwich, the internationally famous Douglass was running the Rochester, NY, station of the Underground Railroad, where he had started the abolitionist newspaper *North Star*.

Douglass did not shy from controversial issues and even explained his conversion from the belief that "the Constitution...was slaveholding," going against the Garrisonians' view. "But, "Corliss added, "he said nothing to offend us who differ from him."

In fact, just the opposite! He packed them in. Corliss related that two of Douglass' meetings filled "the Quaker meeting-house in South Easton...and the Baptist meeting-house" in Greenwich, "to a perfect jam," attributing it to "the Nebraska matter which now agitates the public mind" and which "gave a zest to the abolition truth presented." This was the Congressional debate on the Kansas-Nebraska Bill to allow slavery in those territories. It became law on May 30, 1854, subsequently destroying the Whig Party and setting off the bloody "Border War" in the Kansas Territory between pro-slavery and antislavery settlers, a prelude to the Civil War.

For a brief moment, Corliss and others in Greenwich hosted a living legend, Frederick Douglass, with whom they shared a struggle to abolish the slavery of Douglass' race. I do not know whether Douglass and Corliss ever met again, but I am thankful to Tom Calarco for sending the copy of Corliss' letter in *The Liberator* and giving us an expanded view of the powerful history that occurred in this region

"OVER MY SHOULDER" COLUMN FOR AUGUST 16, 1998
Baroness' mystery of the Red House

This is the mystery of the "Red House."

It began during wartime with a woman. She was thousands of miles from home and English was not her first language. She had followed her husband, a mercenary, bringing their two children into a region so utterly foreign that, ironically, only her own childhood nursery tales could prepare her for the kinds of beasts she would see.

The way had been rough, in spite of the fact that she was from a "privileged" class, with money that allowed her to do what many others could not. Nonetheless, there was first an arduous ocean voyage. Then there was the trip through a pristine wilderness, made more on inland waterways than on land, for the roads were often no more than rutted paths, barely fit for a wagon. And the wilderness was filled with wolves, exterminated in her native land and only remembered in tales. And there were the rattlesnakes.

Yet she managed, with her upbeat spirit and youthful energy, to entertain her children and maintain a diary. Perhaps, some may say, it was because she did not speak the language well that she called it "the Red House," unable to find the name of the true owner. Perhaps, too, she did not identify its exact location because she was too busy to note those details, as she shifted from spot to spot seeking her husband. Or, once they had united, staying near him.

For staying near him was not easy, because he was the Baron Friedrich Adolphus von Riedesel of Lauterbach, Duchy of Brunswick. And she was Frederika Charlotte Luisa von Massow – the Baroness von Riedesel. Today historians owe so much of what they know of the background of the defeat of General John Burgoyne to the diaries kept by the Baroness during her time here in America.

Her husband and his troops had been "rented," as historian Louise Hall Tharp put it, by Duke Ferdinand of Brunswick, Germany, to King George III of England. The indomitable Baroness had decided that no mercenary situation, no rental for war, would keep the family apart, so to America she came. This was not uncommon as many other officers brought along their families. But unlike the others she would be remembered, for her diaries – and for the mystery of the Red House.

It was on August 14th that the Baron came to meet the Baroness and their children on their ship at the head of Lake George. Now, together after months of separation they went to Fort Edward, but sadly had only two days to spend alone. The Baron was reassigned by Burgoyne on August 16. The Baroness stayed on several weeks in Fort Edward, joining the Baron again in September at present-day Schuylerville and the Battle of Saratoga. Her detailed diaries of the Battle of Saratoga and the aftermath of Burgoyne's defeat make for fantastic reading.

The mystery of the Red House began at Fort Edward, for in identifying that first place that the von Riedesels were able to reunite, the Baroness only named it "the Red House," after its color. Nor did she exactly say where it was, only indicating "near Fort Edward." In those days, however, that meant literally near the remains of the fortification called "Fort Edward," which in 1777, was a decaying fort in the lower part of today's Village of Fort Edward.

But what concerns us now is what happened in the years after the Revolution, when our historians began to comb every available source for information on it and to try to pinpoint where such and such a place was according to this report or that diary.

Next, we'll see how the Mystery of the red House was compounded...and then, perhaps, solved.

"OVER MY SHOULDER" COLUMN FOR AUGUST 23, 1998
The Red House mystery solved

We conclude the mystery of the "Red House," the name of the Fort Edward home where the Baroness von Riedesel and her husband were reunited in August 1777.

While the Baroness' fascinating diaries of her family's life with Burgoyne's army may have perpetuated the name "the Red House," we must remember that General Burgoyne himself had also referred to the home as the "Red House," used briefly as his military headquarters in 1777.

Why did the name the "Red House" survive and why did no one ever seem to take the time to identify the actual owner and location of the home where the von Riedesel family stayed? It's simple. For historians in the decades after the Revolution, it was enough to know that they were at Fort Edward. For local people then, resuming normal life was more important.

As time passed, common knowledge of the Red House's owner and location faded as people died. Then in the 1840s, as the last of the generation of the Revolution were dying, interest in the Revolution revived. Histories blossomed, and memoirs and biographies of local people were published. But in the case of the Red House, either their memories were not wholly credited or, more likely, they were ignored by historians. Later, when the Baroness' diaries were translated from German into English and the question "What 'Red House'?" arose, local historians pinpointed the home of George Smyth, brother of Justice Patt Smyth. George Smyth's house, now gone, originally stood about a half a block east of the northeast corner of present day Broadway and State Street in Fort Edward.

His house became fixed in local history as the Red House, culminating, the New York State erecting a cast iron historic marker in 1927, which indicated that the Red House, cited in Madame Riedesel's diaries, had stood nearby.

Yet questions were left begging. If George Smyth's house had been a two room shed-like home that met Madame Riedesel's descriptions for the Red House, what about Burgoyne's "Red House" that he used as headquarters in 1777? The same historians who accepted George's house for Madame Riedesel's Red House claimed that Burgoyne's "Red House" was the larger, more elegant home of George's brother, Patt Smyth, located about an eighth of a mile south on Broadway.

Their reasoning? They said that most homes at that time were painted red! Interestingly, in 1772 Patt Smyth had expanded his shed-like structure (built in

1765, the same year as George's) into a most elegant Colonial home. Could not the original part of Patt's house be what the Baroness had been describing? And it was red. But these facts were ignored.

We fast-forward to 1988. Now Patt Smyth's home is known as "the Old Fort House," the central building of the Old Fort House Museum on lower Broadway. In 1988, the museum's director Paul McCarty commissions historian Field Horne to research the history of Patt Smyth's House.

Previously written autobiographical materials, now re-examined, buttress the claim that the Red House was Patt Smyth's. One especially is convincing: the 1884 memoir of Thomas Adiel Sherwood, whose father bought the Smyth house, had been born in the house in 1791. He states unequivocally that it was occupied by the Baroness.

In 1988, paint scrapings show a brownish-red paint. Then in 1994, archeologist David Starbuck[liv] uncovers the original 1765 cellar of Patt's house and it is appropriate for what the Baroness was describing.

The pieces fit. The Red House must be Patt Smyth's home.

Is the "case solved"? Not 100%, no. But to the degree that Paul McCarty can now take that state marker indicating the location of the Red House and place the marker in front of the Old Fort House Museum, the mystery is over.

"OVER MY SHOULDER" COLUMN FOR SEPTEMBER 13, 1998
Friends, feathers in Easton

Today the Society of Friends will host "Easton Day," remembering an incredible historical incident called the story of the "Feathers of Peace," that took place in the Town of Easton in southern Washington County in September of 1777.

The Society of Friends – Quakers, as they are commonly called by those of us who are not Friends – played a significant, but often little known, role in the settlement of Saratoga, Warren and Washington Counties. Over the next two columns we'll look at that early history, but first the story of the "Feathers of Peace."

The incident of the "Feathers of Peace" occurred at a Friend's mid-week meeting of worship in Easton, somewhere in mid-September of 1777 in the Town of Easton. As it had been reported a few months later by letter, the actual date is not known. However, it is quite certain that it occurred just before the British General John Burgoyne entered into the first Battle of Saratoga on September 19, 1777.

This was one of the most tumultuous times in our region's history. Having advanced south from Canada, Burgoyne was now in Saratoga County with an army of thousands of English regulars, Hessians mercenaries, Colonial Loyalists and Native Americans. Along his route, our frontier communities lay abandoned, many in ruins.

In late July, Burgoyne's Native American scouts had murdered numerous individuals and families, Jane McCrea's murder being among the most infamous as she was a Loyalist. All of them ratcheted up the region's fear quotient from panic to hysteria. And now, only days before, General Stark had killed or captured a major contingent of Burgoyne's forces at the Battle of Bennington. Blood was in the air.

Amidst this the Easton Friends, pacifists all, were at their meeting on the site of the present South Meetinghouse in Easton. Their silent worship was interrupted as a band of 12 Native Americans, presumed to be scouts for Burgoyne, burst in on the meeting with an obvious intent. In spite of the Friends' fear, the meeting leader and others smiled and nodded an invitation to the party to join them. The scouts sat silently. After the worship meeting, a Quaker translated later for the group that the scouts had, as everyone suspected, burst in to kill the Quakers. They had not because of the absence of weapons and the invitation to join the obvious worship of the Great Spirit, which was done silently, in the same manner as the Native Americans worshipped.

The Quakers then invited them to eat, after which the scouts left, but not before placing symbols, some say feathers, around the meetinghouse as a sign that no other Native Americans should disturb that place of peace.

A member of the Easton Friends, Jean Cary, has told me that Easton Day is open to all. It begins with registration at 10:30 at the South Meetinghouse on Meetinghouse Road in Barkers Grove, Easton. Then at 11:00 am the Friends will hold their traditional silent worship meeting at the beginning of which Jeannine Laverty will give a fuller narration of "Feathers of Peace" story. The meeting for worship is followed by a potluck luncheon at noon. All attending are asked to bring food and non-alcoholic beverages to share.

Then in the afternoon there will be two speakers, both dealing with topics of history: one on the history of the Easton Meeting and the other who will debunk myths about the Quaker roots of the Anglo-American anti-slavery movement.

The good fortune that befell the Easton Quakers on that day was not always the rule for other Quakers living in the area, as we'll see next week when we look at the Quaker history of Saratoga, Warren and Washington Counties.

"OVER MY SHOULDER" COLUMN FOR SEPTEMBER 20, 1998
Quakers' impact on our region

The Society of Friends – Quakers – played a vital role in the founding of the Tri-Counties in the 1700s, but we'll see that the Revolutionary War showed no respect for their religious practice of non-violence and their neutrality.

Quakers first settled in today's Warren County in 1762, when a predominantly Quaker group from Dutchess County, led by Abraham Wing, was granted the Queensbury Patent. In 1763, they settled today's Queensbury and Glens Falls.

Presumably their meetings for worship were held at Abraham Wing's house, located near Warren and McDonald Streets in Glens Falls. In 1767, they established a formal "meeting." However, it would not be until after the Revolution that they built their meetinghouse and adjacent burial grounds at today's southwest corner of Bay and Quaker Roads in Queensbury. Ironically, while the recent archeological dig at that site focused attention upon Queensbury's Quaker origins, few today even realize why Quaker Road has that name.

The Revolution brought grief to Queensbury Quakers who, seeking to remain non-violent, supported neither side in the conflict. Both Patriots and Loyalists "conscripted" their crops and cattle, only sometimes stopping to give an "IOU." In 1779, the Quakers were forced to return to Dutchess County. Quaker neutrality meant nothing to the British in 1780 when Carlton's raiders swept out of Canada, burning almost everything to the ground, including all of Queensbury.

Even more personally, while Wing remained, his daughter Deborah, married to Loyalist Daniel Jones, was forced to flee with Jones to Canada. Tragically, she died there in childbirth in 1782 without ever again seeing her father.

The second settlement of Friends occurred in the Town of Saratoga, Saratoga County, in 1765. The earliest meetinghouse was a log structure just south of Quaker Springs, standing on the site of the present meetinghouse of the Monthly Meeting of Friends. The 1878 "History of Saratoga County" lists among the "founders" Isaac Leggett, incorrectly described as the first "minister" since their meetings had no ministers. Before settling at Quaker Springs, Leggett had been taken prisoner by the Iroquois. However, the history states that "he conducted himself with such hilarity and played such pranks with the young Indians, as ...pushing them in the water, that he escaped all severe treatment and was not long after released." I have not found how those Quakers fared during the Revolution.

Quakers first settled in southern Washington County before the Revolution, in the present towns of Easton and White Creek. Easton's first Quakers were Rufus Hall and Zebulon Hoxsie, brothers-in-law who came in 1773 from Dutchess County. The first meeting for worship was held in Hoxsie's house. An unbroken practice of worship continues to this day among the Easton Meeting of the Society of Friends.

In 1775, the first meetinghouse was built on the site of the present South Meetinghouse. This was where the "Feathers of Peace" incident, related in last week's column, took place. Sadly, the Easton Quakers' good fortune incurred during that incident did not continue during the rest of the Revolution. They were persecuted by Patriots and Loyalists and suffered tremendous property loss.

A sad case was that of White Creek tavern-owner Seth Chase, a Quaker who had come from Rhode Island before the Revolution. Chase, a neutral because of his beliefs, was tricked by two Patriots who were drinking in his tavern. Asked if he supported Tories, Chase replied that he did not oppose them. For this, he was arrested, taken to Albany and jailed, and his tavern seized. It was not until much later that he cleared his name and regained his property.

In spite of persecution and personal loss, the early Quaker settlers rebuilt after the Revolution and made an indelible contribution to the history of our region.

"OVER MY SHOULDER" COLUMN FOR SEPTEMBER 27, 1998
A legal case for the books

Between the affairs of state in Washington, DC, and the general discontent over the flood of lawsuits clogging the court system, the legal profession has been taking it on the chin more than it usually has.

But, frankly, lawyer-bashing has been around for centuries. Even Shakespeare had something to say about lawyers, although I think he was a bit excessive when, in "Henry VI," he has Dick say, "The first thing we do, let's kill all the lawyers."

I mean, some of my best friends are lawyers. And one of my heroes is Abraham Lincoln, a lawyer.

It's interesting that, among the traditional professions of medicine, law or teaching, few seem to have inspired as many stories and humorous anecdotes as the legal profession. In fact, I found a marvelous anecdote in the 1878 "History of Washington County."

The incident took place in Easton, possibly in the early 1800s, though no exact date is given. To get into the feel of it, let's examine the facts at hand. One "Mrs. Cook" was the defendant, while the unnamed plaintiff was being represented by Erastus D. Culver, attorney at law. We do not know the name of Mrs. Cook's lawyer.

The history states that the case was being tried before a "referee," who according to my dictionary is "a person appointed by a court to study, take testimony in, judge, and report on, a matter." Maybe that is why things happened the way they did.

During the trial, Erastus Culver did something that outraged Mrs. Cook's attorney, who in turn called Culver a "pettifogging little rascal." Now, I know enough about history and language to presume he said something a tad more vulgar, but in the spirit of legality, I will accept the evidence at face value that "pettifogging little rascal" were his exact words.

As the history notes, Mrs. Cook's lawyer also said to Culver, "by way of emphasis, that were it not for the law, he would `take it out of his hide.'" Here the referee stepped in and, again, one wonders if the following would have occurred had it been a judge at the bench. For the referee suggested that the two lawyers "soothe their lacerated feelings and argue the case by a wrestling match." The winner of the match would win the case!

Well, that suited the two attorneys beautifully, as it apparently did Mrs. Cook and the plaintiff against her. Obviously wishing to ensure that no lawsuit would ensue from the destruction of property, the "room was cleared of its furniture" and the two lawyers "pitched in." Oh, it was a fearsome struggle. However, in the end, attorney Culver threw Mrs. Cook's attorney and beat him fair and square.

(Perhaps this may have led to the phrase "throwing the case," but we'll leave that speculation to linguistic historians.)

Now, please realize that Mrs. Cook had lost the case, and all because her lawyer had lost a wrestling match. Certainly, in the annals of American jurisprudence this must be one for the books. In losing, Mrs. Cook was most gracious, and she paid her fine without complaint.

However, should you think that she really and truly lost, think again. For in paying her fine, she remarked on Culver's winning of the wrestling match, saying "it was the only smart thing I ever saw Rat Culver do." Not only had she insulted attorney Culver, but her insult was recorded for posterity. She lost? I hardly think so.

For those of you who are lawyers now, you should take heart from this anecdote. It proves your professional life could be worse. Because, if that referee had set legal precedent, you could be taking steroids before going into court today.

"OVER MY SHOULDER" COLUMN FOR OCTOBER 11, 1998
The war against the flu

During late September of 1918, the "Spanish Influenza" invaded the United States.

Ultimately the "flu," as it came to be called, killed over 20 million people worldwide, 12.5 million in India alone. In our region, thousands would fall ill, hundreds would die.

The war which began in Europe in 1914 was now a "World War." Having gone "over there" in 1917, the Yanks were suffering terrible losses. The Meuse-Argonne Battle, begun on September 26, 1918, caused 120,000 casualties, 10 percent of the 1.2 million American doughboys in that battle.

Reeling from that, America now dealt with a second killer produced by the war: the flu, a highly contagious viral infection of the respiratory tracts producing fever, chills, muscle weakness, nausea – and often death. The flu had started in 1918 among the armies in northern France. Fueled by ghastly sanitary conditions, its spread was rampant. It lasted into 1919 before subsiding on its own.

The flu was blindingly swift, horribly deadly. In our region, people often literally dropped where they stood. Quarantines were invoked everywhere. *The Post-Star* reported that war plants, already short-handed, were losing workers and casual visitors were "barred." The Warren County Court had ceased functioning. And, even more seriously, the paper said that Glens Falls Country Club pro Ben Lord had reported the cancellation of a match with an Albany country club because of "the grip." (Bear in mind, golfers normally play through hurricanes.)

Whole families came down with it. Nicholas "Chuckie" Cantiello recalls of his boyhood in Fort Edward that "my whole family had the flu" and was in bed, including Chuckie although he did not have it. Whether Chuckie's father had it or not, he kept on working, as the family was too poor to be without his earnings.

The Glens Falls Hospital filled so swiftly with flu sufferers that the Red Cross created a temporary "Emergency Hospital" for flu victims at the armory on Warren Street.

Hospital and Red Cross board members worked hand-in-hand. They also worked as staff, as many victims were regular staff. Hospital minutes recorded that 32 of the 33 student nurses had the flu. Two nurses died. All but two of the entire staff fell ill. On top of that, there were "there were 73 patients in the hospital at one time."

While Red Cross Treasurer, Cutler J. DeLong, coordinated the Emergency Hospital's use of the Glens Falls Hospital's laundry, hospital board member Henry L. Sherman literally worked night and day at the hospital and drove the ambulance as well.

The region mobilized. Over 130 volunteers from 30 miles around worked in either hospital, sometimes both. Their generosity was exemplified by a Mrs. E. R. Winsor of Luzerne, who ran the Glens Falls Hospital kitchen without pay for an entire month. The majority of the volunteers were women, serving as nurses aids, and staffing the dining room, kitchen and laundry.

The Red Cross opened the "Armory Hospital" on October 10. All patients were under the charge of Bertha Hampton, "visiting nurse" of the Woman's Civic Club. Dr. A.W. Chapman was named head of the medical committee and Estelle Palmer, head of the Red Cross, was its administrator. The hospital opened with 100 beds and ran like a wartime field hospital.

By mid-November, relief had arrived. The epidemic had subsided enough that the Armory Hospital was closed and the Glens Falls Hospital had returned to normal. Then on the heels of the flu's waning, the Armistice was announced on November 11, 1918. Death stopped in the battlefields and was slowing its "flu campaign" here and throughout the world.

Thankfully today we have vaccines against influenza, which prompts me to ask: have you had your flu shot?

"Over My Shoulder" column for November 15, 1998
Giving Culver his due

It's sequel time.

Recently, I had written about attorney Erastus Culver who, while representing a client in the Easton town court in the 1830s, was insulted by his brother attorney. The judge recommended the two settle their differences, and the outcome of the trial, by a wrestling match.

With Jesse Ventura's becoming governor in Minnesota, we may see whole pieces of legislation decided in this manner.

But I digress. Culver won the match and the case, inspiring his client to state that it was the only "smart thing" she "ever saw Rat Culver do." Some readers took umbrage with the article, as it showed neither Culver nor his profession in the best light.

Well, this sequel should more than exonerate Culver and his profession. Thanks to William Lee Richards[lv] of Queensbury for sending in biographical information on his distant relative.

Erastus Dean Culver was born "Erastus Dean Culver" in 1803 in Champlain, NY. He took degrees in the classics at the University of Vermont, where, according to his biography, he "carelessly spelled his name Colver."

The biography states that in later years he legally had it changed to Culver because, when living in Brooklyn, he had found "difficulty in the delivery of his then heavy mail." Whether this means that he operated under two different names or that the Brooklynites wouldn't deliver to anyone named "Colver," I'm not sure.

He taught for a while in Fort Ann, but the law called and he studied with Judge Parker in Whitehall. He was admitted to the bar in 1831 and somewhere between then and 1838 he performed his courtroom wrestling.

In 1836, he and his wife moved to Greenwich, from which he won a state assembly seat in 1838. An Albany paper praised his assembly "debut," stating his speech was filled with "pure argument, sound sense and touching eloquence, blended with admirable sarcasm." Obviously, he could think as well as he wrestled.

Culver was in Congress from 1845-1847 and then, in 1850, moved to Brooklyn, where he served as City Court Judge from 1854-1861. But he never lost touch with Greenwich and its people. By the mid-1850s Culver was partners in the Manhattan law firm of Culver, Parker and Arthur. The "Arthur" of the firm was junior partner Chester A. Arthur, in whose father's church Culver had worshipped in Greenwich. Arthur would later be President.

Culver joined the newly formed Republican Party in 1855 and stumped for Abraham Lincoln in 1860. He was rewarded with the ambassadorship to Venezuela from 1862 to 1866.

Culver's friends were in the upper echelon of American politics: Lincoln,

Henry Clay, William H. Seward and Horace Greeley. In fact, when Greeley, a Democrat, ran for President in 1872 against Ulysses S. Grant, Culver crossed party lines to support him, but never suffered politically. Culver's assistance was gladly welcomed in helping elect Hayes President in 1876.

Indeed, he had reached his political zenith in the 1870s. Culver joined fellow Republicans, and Democrats such as Samuel Tilden, in a crusade against the corrupt regime of the infamous Democratic "Boss" Tweed and his Tweed Ring, immortalized by Thomas Nast's political cartooning.

In 1872 at the Broadway Tabernacle, Culver stood with such greats as Henry Ward Beecher in addressing a mass rally against Tweed. Together they broke the Democratic machine.

However, truthfully, Culver's own Republicans were equally as corrupt. Somehow Culver stayed free of it. In spite of Culver's own New York Republican party working with U.S. Grant and other party cronies nationwide to make the post-Civil War United States a sinkhole of corruption, no one ever "pinned" any blame on that country lawyer who once wrestled in a courthouse, Erastus D. Culver.

Indeed, Culver maintained a spotless reputation until his death, in Greenwich, in 1889.

"OVER MY SHOULDER" COLUMN FOR DECEMBER 6, 1998
"Ordinary hero" is honored in Whitehall

When does a cemetery cease to be a cemetery and become a monument in its own right?

In one case, it occurred on a sunny but brisk day in mid-October. A group of us stood in the Kinner Cemetery near Route 4 in the Town of Whitehall. The traffic's roar seemed out of place amidst the many leaning and fallen headstones. Often that roar would drown out the words of praise and honor being spoken over this last resting place of a man named Norton.

None of us knew Joseph Norton, of course. He had died in the 1800s. But, paradoxically, in two ways we did know him. The first way was through the words of praise for an ordinary citizen who became extra-ordinary when he took arms against his government to help create a new government, the United States.

We were at a ceremony being held by the Jane McCrea Chapter of the Daughters of the American Revolution in honor of Captain Joseph Norton, who had started his service in the American Revolution in his native Massachusetts. As we stood near Norton's grave, Kingsbury Town Historian Paul Loding[lvi] spoke of those in the military during that period.

As I heard how Norton served in the Massachusetts Militia from April to November of 1776 and again in 1777, I wondered how men like Norton were able to do so and yet make ends meet, to keep their farms and businesses going, their families fed. Norton did take time out of service in 1778, but from 1779 to 1782 he was again in uniform, this time as a recruiting officer. During this last stint he became a Captain.

After the Revolution, land in this region was offered to the veterans and Norton came to settle, to raise a family and, finally, to die in the Town of Whitehall.

What made the day most special was the second reason why we "knew" Joseph Norton. It was the introduction of a California man, who had come three thousand miles with his wife to stand for a few moments with some public officials and private citizens he had never met. His name is Donald Gumaer, the direct descendant of Joseph Norton. The Gumaers had taken some time out of their life to help make the final resting place of Capt. Norton a bit more special.

I watched him as he placed the flag in the special holder over the grave. While no one would present him with an award for this, this moment indeed was his award.

Near the color guard, made up of members of the Whitehall American Legion Post 83, stood members of a Revolutionary War re-enactment group, Alden's 6th Massachusetts Regiment. Their uniforms were representative of what Americans wore to battle at the time: sometimes just their everyday clothing, sometimes everyday clothing mixed with some military touches. But it was the ordinary citizens, like the Legionnaires standing nearby – and like Joseph Norton who laid at rest near us – it was the ordinary citizens who made up the Continental soldiers and sailors who would defeat an empire.

Captain Joseph Norton stepped out of his life and into a Revolution. His name is not remembered today as is that of General John Stark or other citizen-soldiers who went on to immortality. But without the steadfast Nortons, the Starks could not have shown their brilliance. And there would have been no United States of America. How fundamental.

The Kinner Cemetery has seen a better day and I can only hope that the town and area organizations will pause occasionally to give it a bit of help. For it is, after all, the resting place of many good citizens, among them a very "ordinary hero" named Joseph Norton.

"OVER MY SHOULDER" COLUMN FOR JANUARY 17, 1999
100 years for DAR chapter

On January 27, the Jane McCrea Chapter of the Daughters of the American Revolution will celebrate its 100th anniversary.

Chapter historian, Mary Havens, kindly sent me the chapter's history, which is so full that I could not do it justice here. So, let's look at some history of the highlights of its early years, as written by the chapter's founder and first Regent, Mrs. Josephine Mary Clements King.

The Jane McCrea Chapter was the 462nd chapter of the national DAR It started in 1899 in Mrs. King's home on Seminary Street in Fort Edward. (For those wondering, her husband was Dr. Joseph E. King, founder of the Fort Edward Collegiate Institute. They are not related to me.)

Josephine King was a person of great ability, as were her 13 co-founders. Her chapter history demonstrates the progress women made between 1899 and 1924. With no little irony, she wrote of the founding year that, "the period antedates that of the supremacy of the weaker sex" a reference to women's suffrage being achieved in 1920. She and many of her follow founders were involved in that cause. The DAR was among the many organizations which gave Victorian women a venue to exercise their intellect and organizational skills outside the family.

These are her fellow officers as she listed them: "vice-regent, Mrs. Robert C. Bascom (Mary Platt); recording secretary, Mrs. Augustus K. Clements (Adda Thompson); corresponding secretary, Mrs. E.R. Sawyer (Sarah Lord); treasurer, Mrs. John H. Derby (Margaret Stewart); chaplain, Mrs. Charles D. Kellogg (Mary Baucus); historian, Mrs. Preston Paris (Grace Kellogg)."

The chapter's name comes from the Revolutionary War martyr, Jane McCrea, murdered ("massacred" we say locally) by scouts of the British General Burgoyne. McCrea, King wrote, became "a powerful influence" in Burgoyne's defeat, and McCrea's romance with David Jones was legendary. Yet she confessed that someone, in misunderstanding McCrea's importance, had said to her: "Why, I thought Jane McCrea was an Indian maiden sand-bagged by the English."

King didn't mention it, but Jane McCrea was loyal to the Crown. That she ended up an American martyr, and ultimately as the chapter's namesake, is doubly ironic.

King's history has many details of the chapter's involvement in ceremonies at state and local levels, as well as its first project, which was sewing garments for Spanish American War soldiers. However, to me its most distinguishing early efforts were its work to raise money for preserving nationally historic sites, such as the Schuyler House in Albany, and for education, including the creation of various monuments and markers about local history.

Locally, its first effort was to commemorate the site of the "Massacre of Jane McCrea." In 1905, the chapter erected a monument, a miniature pyramid made of Kingsbury granite, on Broadway near the site. Today it stands surrounded by a wrought iron fence, opposite the Fort Edward Public Schools, a constant reminder that war consumes the innocent, too.

The chapter then decided to mark the site of the 1755 British fortification, "Fort Edward," but waited for a suitable boulder to be found. Several years of patience were rewarded during the digging of the present Barge Canal, when a multi-ton rock was removed and placed on a pedestal at the end of Old Fort Street in Fort Edward. That monument was one of the things that sparked me, as a boy, to become fascinated in local history.

The chapter expanded its scope and, today under Regent Glenna Shanahan, it continues its educational work, now throughout the Tri-Counties. Among other things, it awards substantial scholarships for college students, marks the gravesites of Revolutionary soldiers, donates books to libraries, plants memorial trees, and helps better educate the public about our heritage, including the Revolutionary War and the country created from it.

Happy centenary, Jane McCrea Chapter!

"OVER MY SHOULDER" COLUMN FOR JANUARY 24, 1999
Tracing the roots of Ticonderoga's first high school

Here is the history of a school, courtesy of Ticonderoga Town Historian Theresa Lonergan, that has such similarity to other towns' school histories that it is eerie — for each ends with an absolutely identical problem.

At the junction of Champlain Avenue and The Portage in Ticonderoga, there is a large empty building that until recently was the town office building. Originally, it had been a school, but my memories of it are as the area Youth Center. Like a cat, it's had a lot of lives.

Significantly, the school's founding can be traced to the Rev. Joseph Cook, who would become so famous in Boston of the latter 19th century, that his name was as well known then as Billy Graham's is today.

I'll devote a column to Cook another time. Suffice it to say his brilliance showed early. In 1858, only just graduated from a private academy, Cook began to teach in the Streetroad section of town. He assessed the educational system in Ticonderoga as being desperately in need of what we today know as "high school."

Although recently passed state education laws were promoting the idea, they lacked teeth. Until the 1870s, New York State's public education would remain pretty woeful. So, what transpired in Ticonderoga was a revolt against the status quo of inadequate education.

Cook started a subscription to underwrite a private school. Financing would be through selling shares of stock. There was immediate interest in his proposal. A meeting was held, and a corporation formed. Alas, human nature being involved, all hell broke loose when the members agreed to buy a piece of property on the south slope of Mount Hope. The bank owning the property wanted an arm and a leg for it. A group of citizens countered with an offer of free land near where the National Guard Armory is today. Then another group offered free land just north of that, and even another offered land by the Baptist church. Each site was near the present school.

The three groups battled over their generosity, nearly collapsing the whole venture. However, it says much of Cook that he managed a compromise, helped by Clayton Delano, a rich and progressive mill owner. Very near to all of the other pieces of land offered was a grove of oaks, where the local fair had been held the year before. That land was secured, how my history does not indicate, and for $2,300 a fully furnished two-story frame building constructed on the site. Ticonderoga had its first high school level academy.

Thirteen years later, Ticonderoga formed its first Free School District and by 1875, four of the existing rural school districts in the town worked as one, with the former academy enlarged to serve as their high school. In 1906 the district replaced the 1858 school with the present brick structure. And here's something novel: the old building was cut up and sold in three sections.

In 1930, a new high school was built on Calkins Place. The old school continued as a grade school and, when I moved to Ti in 1962, had a youth center in it. (I'll share some memories another time.) In 1968, a new middle school was constructed on Alexandria Avenue and for the first time in 110 years, school was no longer in session on the old Academy site. For a time, the old school building was used for town offices and other services, but now, like so many other old schools, it sits empty, waiting for someone creative to do something with it.

Similar school histories have occurred in many towns, all ending identically with the empty school building that faces being razed. Can't someone save this one?

Like a cat, it still has more lives left.

Postscript: Sadly, this cat was shy a few lives and the building was razed. This was yet another of the author's columns that tilted at windmills.

"OVER MY SHOULDER" COLUMN FOR FEBRUARY 6, 1999
Old-time obituaries raise intriguing questions

Questions, questions!
National Black History Month is here, and I would like to share with you some history provided by the obituaries of three Black people in Hudson Falls. The obituaries, collected by the late James R. Cronkhite of Hudson Falls, are in a scrapbook now at the Old Fort House Museum in Fort Edward. They were copied from the *Sandy Hill Herald*, a newspaper published in Sandy Hill, now Hudson Falls, in the 19th and 20th century.

The obituaries raise as many questions as they provide answers, as well as demonstrating what has and hasn't changed over a more than a century. Take for the example, the obituary of "Julius – Former Slave" from the June 7, 1883 *Herald*. Of these three Black people, two were born as slaves. However, it was only Julius, who apparently had no last name, who had that fact listed in the obituary's title.

It starts out, "Julius, the well-known gentleman of color, after a divorce from

Sandy Hill for a few years, returned to his first love, to remain for all future time." Was the phrase "gentleman of color" used as a term of respect? Out of the three obituaries, only Julius is referred to in that way. The paper also stated that Julius had been "a waif from the South, who came north with the 'Lincum Sojers' at the close of the war to seek his fortune here. He was born in slavery, as were all his ancestors."

We have code words to decipher. "All of his ancestors" had been slaves? Someone had to have been enslaved somewhere along the line. And the use of "Lincum Sojers" instead of "Lincoln Soldiers," would have implied to the reader then that Julius was viewed as a slightly childish man. My understanding of the phrase "gentleman of color" is that it had much the same connotations in 1883 as it did when I was a boy in the 1950s. Which was only a step above the stupid phrase, "of the colored persuasion." In the 1950s, incidentally, the proper word to use was "Negro."

I didn't like the phrase "people of color" as a boy, because of the implied disrespect. "He is a ... (here the speaker paused meaningfully) ... 'person of color.'" Nor do I like its reemergence now, because it is not logical. "People of color" necessitates that there are "people of no color." To me, as a historian, the phrase smacks of something being reintroduced to segregate people, rather than describe a simple difference in skin color. It is like the difference between "He is a mulatto" versus "he is black, a very rich brown color, like coffee with cream." The first sentence is a pejorative racial label. The second is a description.

The questions surrounding the second obituary, of Atticus Siddell James, are more of the "who, what, when" type, but so intriguing. Here are the facts, reported in the obituary, first published in the "Brooklyn Times," then in the "Sandy Hill Herald." James died in the Bedford district of Brooklyn in November 1908. He had lived in Brooklyn since 1868, had been a portrait artist and an umbrella manufacturer, was a Quaker and a Republican.

Born in Salisbury, Indiana in 1861, the paper stated that, "his father was one of leaders in the 'Underground' movement...He is survived by his wife Alice M. Messinger and daughter, Ethel Van Alstyne James. The interment will be made in Union Cemetery, Sandy Hill."

Questions leap to mind. Who was his father? Was he being buried in Sandy Hill (actually Fort Edward's Union Cemetery) because his wife was from there? Are there descendants here today? Who was Atticus Siddell James?

Next week, the third obituary – and so many more questions.

"OVER MY SHOULDER" COLUMN FOR FEBRUARY 13, 1999
Born as property, slave emerged as free person

Last week I was discussing the obituaries of three Black people, whose deaths were reported in the "Sandy Hill Herald," published in Sandy Hill, now Hudson Falls, in the 19th and 20th century. The obituaries, collected by the late James R. Cronkhite, are in a scrapbook now at the Old Fort House Museum in Fort Edward.

The obituaries' fascination is that they provide a wealth of information, but still leave so many questions. Last week's column covered the obituaries of two of the three people, a "Julius – Former Slave" and an "Atticus Siddell James." However, their information was meager compared to the obituary of Mrs. Matilda Johnson, carried in the "Herald" of March 20, 1884.

Her obituary began: "The death of Mrs. Matilda Johnson, age 83, at Dunham's Basin, removes one the few remaining landmarks of the days of Slavery in the Empire State. Lewis Johnson, a prominent citizen here in those times, owned Matilda and her husband." (The word "Slavery" was capitalized.)

In the same paper, another article ran about her, demonstrating her importance in the community. This stated that "after the abolishment of Slavery in the this state, Mrs. Johnson was for a time, the housekeeper of the late Governor Pitcher[lvii], of this village, and subsequently a valuable servant of Dr. William K. Scott and his family." She was so "esteemed" by the family that "they annually remembered her with valuable presents."

The article also reported that when Mrs. Johnson died, she was "the eldest member of the Presbyterian church," was "much esteemed by that congregation," and that "her funeral was attended by a "large number of neighbors and friends."

Let's look behind the facts. Compared to the obituary last week for Julius, this obituary is showing Matilda Johnson respect as a person. Her birthplace was not listed, probably because a record does not exist. I have found none yet. In the census then, wives, children and slaves were only listed as a number.

We can assume she was born a slave in New York State, possibly even born to a slave owned by Lewis Johnson in the Town of Kingsbury. Importation of slaves into the state had been prohibited in 1785. In 1799, legislation provided that every child of a slave born after July 4, 1799 would be "bond servants," all to be freed, females at 25 and males at 28. In 1817, it was finally enacted that all who were slaves would be totally free by 1827. (Compare this to Vermont, which had outlawed slavery from its inception in 1777.) As she was born in 1801, Mrs. Johnson's own freedom must have come in 1826, at age 25. Nothing indicates she was freed before that.

Thanks to Kingsbury Town Clerk Holly Mabb, we have some additional information from Matilda Johnson's death certificate, but only a little bit more, as it lists no mother, father or birth date. Her race was listed by the letter "B."

She died on March 17, 1884, and is buried in the Moss Street Cemetery. In trying to research Lewis Johnson, I found a man by that name living in Dunham Basin in the 1880s. I assume that she died at his home and that he was the son of her owner, as nothing indicates she had children.

If only we knew more. Still, this brief sketch of Matilda Johnson shows a person having been born as property, a horrible thought, but emerging as a full and free human being, such a wonderful thought. Though born a slave without a surname, Matilda Johnson took the name of her owner, making that name her own, and bringing it dignity and respect through her life as a free person. In doing so, she carved the name "Matilda Johnson" into Kingsbury history.

"OVER MY SHOULDER" COLUMN FOR MARCH 20, 1999
Pigs nowhere to be found on modern Bolton streets

Bolton is turning 200! No, not singer Michael Bolton. The Town of Bolton in Warren County. On Thursday, March 25, 1999, the Town celebrates what occurred 200 years ago – the creation of Bolton.

Technically, Bolton has a twin, for the Town of Chester was created on the same day, March 25, 1799, by the same act of the New York State legislature that created Bolton.

Let's take them alphabetically, Bolton, then Chester. Not to sound too biblical, but in the beginning, there were two towns before Bolton, Queensbury, then Thurman. And from Thurman was begat....

Sorry, I did get too biblical. From Thurman, Bolton and Chester were created in 1799. In terms of today, the newly created Town of Bolton took in most of the Town of Lake George and all of the Town of Hague. Bolton's eastern boundary ran from just north of present-day Lake George Village to the border of Essex County.

In 1807 Bolton's borders were reduced by the formation of Hague (at first called Rochester) and then again in 1810 by the creation of the Town of Lake George (at first called Caldwell). The last change was in 1838 with the creation of Horicon. From thereon, Bolton stayed its present size.

Bolton is a town of mystery. Its name's origin is unknown. Brown's 1963 county history[lviii] states that it was "thought that people from the Boltons in New England came to the area and named their new town for their former ones." Brown notes that there was "no discussion concerning the town's name when it was organized."

Genealogists can help here. In New England most towns named Bolton will usually be found to have a nearby town named Manchester, harkening back to "Olde England," where Bolton and Manchester sit in close proximity.

If genealogists could trace the early settlers of Bolton to either a Bolton or a Manchester in New England...or even in England itself, I think it would conclusively prove Brown's theory.

Bolton will have to wait until April 2 to observe the 200th anniversary of the first town meeting. And talk about popular! So many people wanted to attend it that they moved it from the home of John Clawson to Captain Stow's grist mill.

The first person to fill the role Deanne Rehm does today, Town Supervisor, was Asa Brown. At that first meeting Asa and his fellow town board members got right down to business and voted that "swine shall not run at large." And they were effective in their lawmaking, for even 200 years later, you cannot find a pig on the streets of Bolton.

They were also brisk about building some decent roads. The Iroquois trail which led along the west side of the lake was expanded in 1800 and called the Great Road. It was widened out by Bolton's early settlers and milestones placed alongside it all the way to Albany. The great Road through Bolton is now called Route 9N.

In the northern part of the town, the Great Road originally ran more northward to get to Sabbath Day Point. However, in the 1930s the state, exercising a macabre sense of humor, bent Route 9N east over Tongue Mountain, thereby creating the world's only ski jump for cars.

Water defines Bolton, with the Schroon River making up much of its western boundary and Lake George on the east, and Trout Lake and various streams in between. Bolton's first industry used that waterpower for sawmills, but as early as the 1820s another business began to emerge, tourism.

What began with a tavern in the 1820s would see the birth of an internationally renowned resort – and home to some of our greatest musicians and artists.

Next week, our 200th anniversary salute to Bolton continues.

"OVER MY SHOULDER" COLUMN FOR MARCH 27, 1999
Bolton offers summer cottages, museums, arts

We continue with the history of the Town of Bolton, founded on March 25, 1799.

While the origin of Bolton's name is a mystery, the name "Bolton" can cause confusion. In the 1880s, Seneca Ray Stoddard wrote in his guidebooks, "Strangers are sometimes at a loss to locate `Bolton' properly." He referred to the hamlets of Bolton, Bolton Landing and North Bolton, all within the Town of Bolton.

The three original hamlets of Bolton were "The Huddle," North Bolton and Federal Hill, with a substantial settlement on Trout Lake. The confusion emerged when the Postal Service named The Huddle's post office as Bolton and put post offices in North Bolton and Bolton Landing. The last started as a steamboat landing that became prominent after the Civil War, but especially with the creation of the first Sagamore Hotel on Green Island in 1883.

In fact, the key to the Town of Bolton's future success, tourism, began with the creation of a tavern. Bolton's earliest industries were tree-related, including lumbering, sawmills and the making of potash. Before 1820, the forests were gone. The industries disappeared.

Just as well. For the beauty of Lake George, always appreciated, now offered commercial advantage. The history of Bolton's tourism occupies many books, but we can visit some of the high points, beginning with Roger Edgecomb.

Around 1807, in southern Bolton Landing, Edgecomb started a tavern. Nearby Samuel Brown started a store. (A secret room in their dock hid smuggled goods from Canada. Hmmmm.) By the 1850s Edgecomb's tavern had changed hands three times and had become a good-sized lodge called the Mohican House. Owner Capt. Gilbert Gale entertained visitors from Manhattan and beyond. By the 1880s it had added guest cottages and survived into the 20th century.

Other inns, guest houses and hotels emerged up and down Bolton's shore, including the famed Algonquin, the Lake View, and the Marion, to name a few. By the mid-1850s, "summer people" had become a fixture. These folks, and locals, began buying up Bolton's 125 Lake George islands to build summer homes. (The lake has 162 altogether.)

In the post-Civil War boom, many of these islands, as well as the land along the Bolton Road (Route 9N) became the wealthy's place of choice.

And a place for practical jokes. As Stoddard wrote, Recluse Island off Bolton Landing "was subject of the `earthquake hoax' of 1868," when New York City papers reported that the island had sunk "80 feet below the surface." Oh, those Boltonians!

From the 1880s through 1920s, the Town of Bolton became a tourist mecca. Its reputation was enhanced in the `80s and `90s by the Sagamore Hotel, where steamboats brought parasoled women and straw-hatted men "to summer" in elegance. The Sagamore burned twice. Today's, built in 1915, carries on a tradition of elegance.

Perhaps more important for Bolton was the "summer cottage" craze, in which the wealthy built huge homes dubbed "cottages." By the 1920s, these "piles" along the Bolton Road became known as Millionaires Row. These and other Bolton areas attracted not just the rich, but artists of renown, such as Louise and Sidney Homer and the Metropolitan Opera's Mme Marcella Sembrich, whose studio is today a museum.

The list later expanded to include, among others, sculptor David Smith, writer/naturalist William Roden, and historian Wallace Lamb. Today musician/conductor Hugh Allen Wilson lives in Bolton, continuing Bolton's tradition as what I would call "the Adirondack home of the arts."

So much, so little space to do it justice. Let these two columns be your introduction to Bolton's rich history. Read more about it and celebrate with

Boltonians their town's 200th anniversary.

Next week, our 200th anniversary salute to the Town of Chester.

"OVER MY SHOULDER" COLUMN FOR APRIL 3, 1999
Chester's bicentennial chance to reflect on history

This week, a 200th anniversary salute to the Town of Chester, founded on March 25, 1799.

Because the town's earliest records were lost in a fire around 1876, mystery surrounds the exact origins of the town.

Ever since the state legislature split Chester from Thurman, Chester's boundaries have not changed, although things around those boundaries have. For example, in 1799, Chester was part of Washington County. Its northern border was Clinton County. Its southern border was Thurman, until Warrensburgh was created in 1813. Its west boundary, the Hudson, and its east boundary, Schroon Lake and Schroon River, have remained the same.

Published histories have vague or conflicting information on the town's first settlers. The 1886 "History of Warren County" states that the most heavily settled areas in the town were originally around Friends Lake and Loon Lake and claims the town's first settlers were the Meads, on Loon Lake. Apparently not too long after, others settled on Friends Lake, and to the east the Starbucks founded Starbuckville.

Chestertown and Pottersville, the two main villages in the town today, were supposed to have been settled after that, Chestertown around 1805 and Pottersville a few years later. However, the 1886 history states that documents support preaching being done by Methodists in Pottersville in 1796. We'll have Pottersville and Chestertown residents do a tug of war to settle this controversy.

Chestertown was originally called "Chester" because the Postal Service changed the hamlet's name, as a "Chestertown" post office already existed in Orange County. Chestertown's first settler was Baptist minister Jehial Fox, who established the town's first industry, a gristmill, around 1800, and the first church in 1810. (Harvey Powers rounded out that community's needs in 1810 when he built a distillery.)

Chestertown's second settler, Joseph Collins, a blacksmith and farmer from Massachusetts, came around 1805. Then came brothers Norman and Alanson Fox, who then moved into Chestertown proper in 1809, and opened a store and tavern.

The Fox brothers' lumbering, however, earned them fortune and fame – and generated a long-standing controversy. They became partners with Queensbury lumberman Abe Wing II and floated logs downriver to Wing's Glens Falls sawmill. Because of this, Chester credits the Fox brothers with inventing the log drive, Glens Falls and Queensbury credit Wing – and everybody from the state of Maine says it's none of them. I love controversy.

Chestertown's 19th century industries – tanneries, lumber mills, milliners, and such – began to fade by 1900, and tourism took over.

The second largest settlement, Pottersville, took off in 1839 when Joel Potter built a store and post office. The Postal Service named him postmaster and the hamlet "Pottersville." Immortality was Joel's. Pottersville had a tannery and sawmill, though nothing as extensive as Chestertown's.

By 1910, Chester's larger industries were gone, and tourism reigned, growing since before the Civil War. Stoddard's 1873 Adirondacks guidebook shows Chestertown and Pottersville on a long-established route into the High Peaks.

Visitors paused at the Downs Hotel in Chestertown, possibly as early as the 1820s, and Hotchkiss and Collar built the first hotel in Pottersville around 1845. Tourists, and artists, flocked to the town to visit the Stone Bridge and caves, and take steamer trips on Schroon Lake.

In the 20th century, the car brought more summer residents, who built camps on the rivers, lakes and ponds. Motor courts, later motels, flourished. On Schroon Lake, the internationally famous Scaroon Manor attracted the rich and famous – and even Hollywood came in 1956 to make "Marjorie Morningstar" with Natalie Wood.

We've only touched upon the Town of Chester's rich history. In a future column, I'll share a surprising story about Chester's connection to the world of poetry.

In the meantime, a happy 200th anniversary to the Town of Chester.

"OVER MY SHOULDER" COLUMN FOR MAY 1, 1999
Pember museum, library honor 90 years of history

Happy First of May and happy 90th anniversary to the Pember Museum of Natural History and the Pember Library – together, called "the Pember" – in the Village of Granville.

Whether you're a longtime supporter or have never been, today is the perfect day to visit the Pember. There will be special events throughout the day from 10 am to 3 pm. There's no admission, the Pember will have refreshments, so consider yourself invited.

The Pember is a rare hybrid, a combination public library and museum of natural history. The distinctive coupling owes its origin to Franklin Pember, who was born on a farm just south of the Village of Granville in 1858.

Pember was a typical self-made entrepreneur of the 19th century. I saw a document relating to the founding of the Red Cross that Pember had signed in 1918. Next to his name where he was to indicate his profession, Pember wrote the word "Capitalist," in large script reminiscent of the defiant John Hancock on the Declaration. I'm just theorizing, but in the light of the Russian Revolution, I think Pember was stating his conviction to capitalism.

It certainly did him well. After attending the Fort Edward Collegiate Institute, Pember started a career in trapping and in a few years got into the business of fur trading. He traveled extensively and, as was common in that era, hunted big and small game. Most of those trophies, however, Pember himself stuffed and mounted, as he was a taxidermist of considerable ability. He collected mammal, reptile and bird, and in no small quantity.

By the beginning of this century, Franklin Pember's business interests had greatly diversified and he was rich. He built an opera house and was very civic minded. And he had married and he and his wife, Ellen, were among the movers and shakers in Granville.

In March of 1902, the Granville Free Library was formed. The library grew like Topsy and by 1905 was already in its third home, the Pember Opera House Block. Franklin and Ellen offered to donate the land and a new building for a library and museum, on condition that either the town or village vote a $1,000 a year tax to support the institution and that the name Pember be placed on it.

The beautiful stone structure housing the Pember Library and Museum was formally dedicated on March 2, 1909 and received its New York State Regents charter on April 1, 1909. The Library occupied the first floor and Franklin's museum of natural history the second.

Franklin Pember acted as the museum's first curator until his death in 1924. His museum was filled with his life's passion. Pember had huge glass cases with stuffed animals and more than 1,200 specimens of birds. There was also what was among the largest collections of birds' eggs in the state, over 3,000 in all.

It was, and is, unique. Franklin and Ellen had both left bequests for the Pember. However, after Franklin died, the museum did not hire another curator. In time the collection and museum were forgotten.

Forty years later, things began to change. A friends of the library group was formed in 1966. Then one was formed for the museum in 1971, followed by the hiring of a museum curator. In 1979 the Porter District Schoolhouse and adjacent land in the Town of Hebron were donated and converted to a nature preserve and education center.

Now, 20 years later, the Pember Museum of Natural History and the Pember Library will celebrate their 90th anniversary and they invite you to visit and become a part of the celebration.

Happy anniversary, Pember – and many more.

"OVER MY SHOULDER" COLUMN FOR MAY 8, 1999
How bad circumstances dumped on Sarah Fraser

When I began compiling this column, I couldn't know, as you will, the sad link it would have to today's news.

Two columns ago, I noted that in his new book, "The Argyle Patent and Its Early Settlers," James MacNaughton had made some wonderful discoveries. One concerned a lady named Sarah, whose tumultuous life reads like fiction, except that it was real and made history.

"Sarah" was born Sarah Gordon Fraser in Inverness, Scotland in the early 1700s. Of a good family and well-connected (her first cousin Simon Fraser was an officer in the British Army), Sarah married the wealthy Archibald Campbell. They moved to Argyll, Scotland, where they raised two children, Catherine and Archibald. Catherine married and had a daughter, Polly.

It was after Catherine's husband died that Sarah's life changed course. Sarah sailed for New York in 1758, with Archibald, Archy, Catherine and Polly, to retrieve the body of her husband's cousin, Duncan, who had died serving with the Black Watch Regiment during the July, 1758 battle at Fort Ticonderoga.

Indeed, now you know Sarah's first claim to fame. For this was the same Duncan Campbell of Inverness whose death at Ticonderoga that author Robert Louis Stevenson would later immortalize.

Sadly, death became the theme of Sarah's trip. During the Atlantic crossing, Sarah's husband died. She settled in what is now New York City, where within a year her daughter Catherine died, too.

Still, Sarah was left a wealthy widow, and her son Archy did become a prosperous merchant and tavern owner. He married Ann, the daughter of a man coincidentally named Duncan Campbell, the first Supervisor of the Town of Argyle, New York.

Archy became a trustee for the Argyle Patent and before the Revolution, he moved with Ann to Fort Edward, then a part of Argyle.

Sarah's life seemed to be changing for the better. Her granddaughter Polly met her future husband, while Sarah met and married James McNeil.

Then, tragedy again. McNeil drowned in the Hudson River. Sarah and Polly decided to move to Fort Edward, to be near Archy.

Just as the "Widow McNeil" readied herself for a quiet finale to her life, the American Revolution began. And Sarah entered American history because of her cousin, Simon, and Polly's friend, Jane.

It was July, 1777 and General Simon Fraser was with Burgoyne's army, marching to Albany. Polly wasn't at the McNeil home when her friend Jane McCrea stole away from the house of her brother, John McCrea, to join with Polly and Sarah. A British scouting party came to escort Sarah and Jane into the safety of General Fraser's British Camp, where Jane was also to unite with her fiancé, David, a Loyalist.

Of course, Jane, a Loyalist, was instead murdered by those scouts and, ironically, her death spurred Americans to defeat Burgoyne at Saratoga, insuring that there would be a "United States of America."

Sarah lived out her life in this region and has since been a part of Jane McCrea's story in American history. Today Sarah's homestead, a sacred place in America, is identified as the "Jane McCrea House" in Fort Edward.

Which brings me to that "sad link" I mentioned above. Jane's brother, John

McCrea, was not a Loyalist, in fact was a Patriot hero who led troops against the British. Today, his home stands on West River Road in the Town of Northumberland, commemorated by a New York State historic marker.

We recently learned that my native county, Saratoga, will proceed with opening its planned new landfill directly in back of John McCrea's house and has told the McCrea house owners, "Tough luck."

Patriot John McCrea, who fought for America, whose sister was martyred for America, now has a dump in his honor.

And you wonder why kids don't give a damn about history anymore?

"OVER MY SHOULDER" COLUMN FOR JUNE 5, 1999
History washes up on shores of Lake Champlain

What follows is some wonderful archeological history that at the same time is the poignant story of two cultures' religions coming to face to face.

It centers upon the west shore of Lake Champlain just north of present-day Fort Ticonderoga. My thanks go to my friend Stephen Pell Dechame[lix] of Somerville, Massachusetts and of Ticonderoga. Steve's family, the Pells, has a long history in association with Fort Ticonderoga.

Steve found this story in a 1669 French publication, entitled *Relation of What Occurred Most Remarkable in the Missions of the Fathers of the Society of Jesus in New France in the years 1667 and 1668*. The book, compiled by Fr. Etienne Dechamps, is an account of the Jesuit missions in the territory they called New France.

In July 1667, three Jesuit priests, Frs. Fremin, Pierron, and Bruyas, had set out to restore the Iroquois missions that had been abandoned because of war. They kept a journal, which Fr. Dechamps quoted. They said they traveled by canoe on Lake Champlain with three Iroquois. The priests noted the three Iroquois were Christian and that, immediately after embarking, the three "had to pray to God...although they had been present at Holy Mass."

They arrived at a cove "within three-quarters of a league of the Falls by which Lake St. Sacrement [Lake George] empties..." into Lake Champlain. The priests were puzzled as to why they stopped until they saw the Mohawks on the shore, gathering up "flints, which were almost all cut into shape." The flints were precious as they could be struck to make sparks and start fire. They were also used in early European firearms.

Precut flints were an oddity and when questioned, the Iroquois replied that everyone stopped at the spot "to pay homage to the invisible men who dwell there at the bottom of the lake." These men spend their lives "preparing the flints, nearly all cut, for the passersby, provided" that tobacco was spread on the lake's surface as an offering. The more tobacco they give, the Iroquois said, the more generous the invisible men are.

These invisible men traveled by canoe and, when their "great Captain" threw himself in the water to enter his Palace, the noise was so great it caused fear among those who did not know of "this great Spirit" and the little men.

The priests described this as a "fable," less charitably as a "ridiculous story" to explain how the lake, "often agitated by very frightful tempests," caused winds which drove the flints up on the beach. Of course, this made no more sense than the Iroquois' explanation.

Today, thanks to archeology, we know that the cove where they landed is just north of Fort Ticonderoga where prehistoric artifacts have continually been found. These flints were created by human beings, who had migrated into the area thousands of years ago. The spot where the Iroquois found their flints was an archeological trove of prehistoric materials.

This is because the entire area that embraces the Fort Ticonderoga property, as well as the surrounding land, is among the oldest sites of human habitation in the Northeast, dating back, according the materials Steve sent, around 10,000 years.

These people came after the ice cap had receded and the area had warmed sufficiently to allow plants to grow, animals to flourish, and humans to follow. Humans did not live in the area on a constant basis. So, the creation of these flints by one group was forgotten over thousands of years and was gradually transformed into a religious belief, a process equally as fascinating as the prehistoric peoples who made the flints.

Next week we'll look at the prehistoric peoples who inhabited a site that in modern times figured so intimately in the formation of this country.

"OVER MY SHOULDER" COLUMN FOR JUNE 12, 1999
Researchers gain knowledge of early occupants

The west side of Lake Champlain surrounding present-day Fort Ticonderoga has seen human beings tramping on its shores for the last 10,000 years. Information sent to me by Stephen Pell Dechame helps to paint a picture of real people, rather than archeological statistics.

Steve writes that human habitation here has been proven by documented cases of Paleolithic points – shaped pieces of stone – from 10,000 years ago having been found in several places in this region. The sites were on the peninsula occupied by Fort Ticonderoga, on a farm on the Baldwin Road on upper Lake George, on a farm in Crown Point, and at the "Harrisena site on southern Lake George." By the last I am assuming Steve means the hamlet of Harrisena in the Town of Queensbury.

Related to that, I believe that at the rate archeologist Dr. David Starbuck is digging in Fort Edward, he will eventually uncover sites that show prehistoric humans lived in that area around that same time period. He already has proven that 8,000 years ago human beings lived where the Old Fort House Museum is today, what is called the "Little Wood Creek Site."

Of course, we don't have written memoirs of these ancient people. However, between the discoveries in natural history and archeology, we can tell what the land went through and what these ancient people left as evidence to be combined into one story. After the Wisconsin Ice Cap, that two mile thick sheet of ice that once covered this whole region, had receded, the land was so depressed from its weight, seawater from the Atlantic rushed in, bringing sea life, in particular salmon.

Over time, the land rose again and cut off the sea. Fresh water replaced salt water and the lakes of today were formed. It wouldn't be any time at all before stores selling sailboats and jet skis would arrive, but I'm slightly ahead of my story.

Around 8000 BC, or 10,000 years ago, plants were flourishing in the Champlain Valley. It was colder then and the land was like land near the tundra today, with vast areas of grass punctuated mostly by spruce and fir trees, with some dwarf willow. In this land roamed now-extinct moose-elk, mastodon, wooly mammoth and giant beaver. And I mean giant – seven feet long.

Now humans arrived, following the trail of these creatures, upon which they depended for food, as well as fishing in the ancient sea for huge salmon. It is generally accepted that prehistoric humans in this period were a major cause of the extinction of so many of these animals. As I have seen what today's beaver can do to the trees on the pond by my house, I hate to admit it, but I am just as happy that their seven-foot ancestors didn't survive.

Steve notes that at other sites occupied by people of that era, it was found these people had developed ceremonies for their dead that included cremation and making offerings of projectile points and bone tools. They also used red ocher. These and other traits were found to exist in among Paleolithic people in central Europe as early as 25,000 years ago.

Steve states that when Samuel de Champlain encountered the Iroquois in 1609, the descendants of these two branches of the same Paleolithic family were meeting. I'm not sure of that, as there is no conclusive proof of an unbroken link between the Champlain people of 8000 BC and the Iroquois.

However, we do know that discovering and understanding the history of the Champlain Valley's first people of 10,000 years ago has serious supporters, including Stephen Pell Dechame. I am delighted that so much research is being done in Ticonderoga and the Champlain basin and hope that it will lead to even more.

"OVER MY SHOULDER" COLUMN FOR JULY 10, 1999
Village of Fort Edward celebrates long, historic past

The Village of Fort Edward is celebrating the 150th anniversary of its incorporation in 1849.

This weekend in particular my old village will be "whoopin' it up" from Hillview Avenue to Frederick Drive and everywhere in between.

People have occupied the village's site on and off over the last 8,000 years. By the time Europeans settled in 1731, Native Americans had already lived there periodically since 6000 BC. The most recent, the Iroquois, were newcomers, having only settled in the late 1500s or early 1600s.

The acknowledged founder of modern-day Fort Edward was a Dutchman named Lydius. He first plunked down on the spot in 1732 and created a combination home, fortress, and trading post. Burned out by the French in 1745, poor Lydius left for good for England. However, when the French and Indian War started in 1755, the British military roared in, built a fort there and christened it for the King's son, Prince Edward. So was born the name "Fort Edward." Captain Robert Rogers of Rogers Rangers built a military hospital on the island in the Hudson and between the two military installations, Fort Edward would play a role in the French and Indian War that gave it a permanent place in history.

When the American Revolution erupted, the fortification called Fort Edward was pretty well gone as a structure. Yet, in the summer of 1777, the place that had become known as Fort Edward again made history. Justice Patrick Smyth's house, the county's first courthouse and today the Old Fort House Museum, served both British and the American generals as their headquarters for operations during Burgoyne's campaign. Also, tragically, the murder in July 1777 of Jane McCrea would create a martyr that helped hasten Burgoyne's defeat.

Through its role in that hot summer, Fort Edward had again entered history books.

At war's end, previous settlers returned to rebuild in Fort Edward and new settlers joined them. At this time, both the present Town and Village of Fort Edward were actually a part of the Town of Argyle. By the 1780s there were several prosperous merchants and landowners. Patt Smyth's house became a tavern for a while under Adiel Sherwood's ownership. Sherwood then helped to found a Masonic lodge, Washington Lodge, No. 11, in 1787. Here was a sure sign that stability and prosperity had returned.

Smyth's frame house had spared during the British "burning" of 1780. Between 1783 and the turn of the century, dozens of other structures were built. Many were combination home and business. Where the Fort Edward Art Center stands today, William Finn had his home and store. Finn was a large landowner in the lower in end of the village.

John Eddy owned much of what is now the upper half of the village. He opened a tavern at the corner of today's Broadway and Eddy Street, named for the Eddy family. James Rogers – whose family was so intrinsic to the history of this whole region that a book could be written on them – opened a store diagonally across from the present post office.

Local manufacturing and farming were important. In the early 1800s,

Timothy Eddy established the first water-powered mill, to make clothing.

In all, by 1818, Fort Edward was large enough to support at least two physicians and a lawyer, plus numerous taverns, demonstrating which profession had the most demand. That year of 1818 was important for several things. First, the Town of Fort Edward separated from Argyle. The second was for the coming of the canal.

Next week we'll look at how that waterway – and its successor, the railroad – changed a hamlet built on a historic military post to a village called Fort Edward.

"OVER MY SHOULDER" COLUMN FOR JULY 17, 1999
Railroad key to creation of Fort Edward village

By 1818 the hamlet, or district, of "Fort Edward," which had grown up around the site of the old military outpost of that name, had achieved a fairly respectable size.

The year 1818 is significant because the Champlain Canal was finally getting started and in that year the Town of Fort Edward was created from the Town of Argyle. While it took the name Fort Edward, that district was not actually the center of the Town's activities nor population, according to Paul McCarty, the historian for the Village and the Town of Fort Edward.

He said the hamlet was primarily large farm holdings, such as that of James Rogers, whose homestead is now known as the "Jane McCrea House" on Broadway.

In 1818, the town's population was concentrated in Fort Miller, which had agitated for the town's creation. For many years, the town business was conducted in nearby Fort Edward Center, approximately the geographic center of the town.

As Paul notes, the canal was significant for the building of the town, the railroad for the village. The canal helped the future Village of Fort Edward with the building of the feeder canal. A dam was built on the Hudson just above today's yacht basin to "feed" water to the Champlain Canal running from Whitehall to Fort Edward, where it connected with the Hudson.

A sawmill was built at the dam in 1822, the year the canal opened. Other mills sprung up along the feeder canal including a paper mill, an industry which continues there to this day.

The canal was extended to Fort Miller in 1828 and in 1832 the feeder canal between Hudson Falls and Glens Falls was enlarged to provide more water. This also allowed boat traffic on it and Glens Falls began to boom. By contrast Fort Edward did not and the canal's importance for it began to diminish.

Business still grew in the future village of Fort Edward. In 1845, E. B. Nash, H. W. Bennett, D. W. Wing, James Cheesman, Morrill Grace, Lansing Taylor, Abraham Fort, and John Doty bought the feeder dam and canal from the state.

Where Irving Tissue and Decora are today, they and others, including Frederick D. Hodgeman, started the Fort Edward Manufacturing Company. According to the 1878 history of Washington County, it "was to promote...manufacturing industries in the...village, by furnishing sites and power." The 19th century version of the Industrial Development Agency.

Meanwhile, a second attempt was being made at bringing in a railroad, the first attempt having gone under in the Panic of 1837. Some of those Fort Edward investors backed the new railroad, but its placement was not a "done deal." To Fort Edward's good fortune, in 1848 the Saratoga and Washington Railroad opened, bridging the Hudson just below the road bridge built in 1828.

Industry exploded. And the Village of Fort Edward was created, incorporated by the legislature on August 28, 1849. On September 28th, that was ratified in Fort Edward, where, interestingly, the votes were 81 for and 67 against.

Most of the new village's elected officials were the same people who created the Fort Edward Manufacturing Company. Frederick D. Hodgeman was the first village president.

For whatever reason, while the village economy boomed with new paper mills and iron foundries, political activity dwindled. No elections were held between 1854 and 1856 and the state had to restore the village's corporate powers.

That was done in 1857. Political life revived and in 1859 the village boundaries were expanded. (And you thought politics unnecessary!) The 1850s and '60s were a boom time and the town's political center shifted to the Village of Fort Edward.

We'll come back to the history the village, now celebrating the 150th anniversary of its beginning.

Congratulations, Fort Edward!

"OVER MY SHOULDER" COLUMN FOR AUGUST 7, 1999
Crown Point Bridge, first one for cars, turns 70

NOTE: Little could anyone dream that the bridge described in the following series of columns would be demolished a decade later. In the mid-2000s, New York State and Vermont had initially planned to replace it. As work began, it was suddenly found to be just too unsafe to repair. It was closed to all traffic on October 16, 2009 and demolished December 28. The new bridge opened November 7, 2011. The two years without any bridge caused incredible economic distress for businesses and residents in both states.

This month the Crown Point Bridge spanning Lake Champlain turns 70. Over the next two columns, we'll look at the history of this bridge. My deep appreciation for much of the following information goes to historian Janice Robbins of Crown Point and to Maury Thompson, business editor of *The Post-Star*, as well as to those whom I interviewed.

The official dedication of the Crown Point Bridge was held at 2:00 p.m. on Sunday, August 26, 1929. In this week's column, we'll look at the background of the bridge and see how it came to be. Then next week, we'll look at the ceremony and celebration that took place on that dedication day. And we'll hear from a couple of people who have personal memories of that hot day in August of 1929.

Spanning Lake Champlain by bridge had been done in various places over the previous century and a half. There had been a pontoon-style bridge, for example, between Fort Ticonderoga, New York, and Mount Independence, Vermont, in 1776. When the train arrived in the next century, the lake was spanned again, and in several places.

A bridge between Crown Point, New York, and Chimney Point, Vermont was logical. On a map you can see that this is a narrow part in the lake, with the New York State side being the Crown Point peninsula. Near the New York site where the bridge would begin were the ruins of Fort Crown Point. Both that and Vermont's Chimney Point site were already of intense historic interest. Then in 1909 the peninsula had come into national prominence when the two states celebrated the 300th anniversary of Samuel de Champlain's arrival. Huge monuments were built, and ceremonial dedications included President Taft, who also attended other ceremonies at Fort Ticonderoga.

But if a bridge seemed logical in 1909, twenty years later it was a necessity, made so by the automobile. From 1909 to 1929, the North Country went from a handful of cars to cars everywhere, causing the building of better roads, and this bridge, solely for car traffic.

Vermont and New York State agreed to a joint project to create the Crown Point Bridge. Having lived in both New York and Vermont, I know when Adirondackers and Vermonters finally decide to do something, it gets done fast. That bridge was completed in record time.

Construction had begun on the Crown Point Bridge in 1928. In fact, it was 15 months from the time the contracts were awarded to the completion of the bridge in July of 1929.

This is a credit to many people, not the least of whom was New York State Senator Mortimer Ferris, the chairman of the bridge commission. Ferris, of Ticonderoga, would have worked intimately with people in both states, including Vermont's Governor, John E. Weeks, who was in on the planning stages, and two New York governors, Al Smith and his successor, Franklin D. Roosevelt.

Roosevelt was only newly Governor of New York when the contracts were let out on the bridge, but he would have pushed to see it completed, as he liked construction projects. Other state projects in our region that date from that same time period were the building of the road up Whiteface Mountain and the construction of buildings at the Spa State Park in Saratoga Springs.

The cost of the bridge was $1 million and was split between New York and Vermont with New York taking on 60% of the share. New York contributed $120,000 and Vermont put up $80,000. The rest was raised in bonding.

There was an initial inspection on July 29 by Governor Roosevelt and Governor Weeks. And then the two came back in August to do a formal dedication that would be astounding even today.

Next week: the dedication that set a standard.

"OVER MY SHOULDER" COLUMN FOR AUGUST 14, 1999
Residents recall dedication of Crown Point Bridge

Last week's column about the dedication of the Crown Point Bridge on August 26, 1929, brought so many calls from all over that I've had to make this a three-part history. Here's part two.

Everyone I've interviewed who was actually at the event recalls that the celebrations outdid anything they'd seen before or since.

Their memories have played no tricks. Crown Point historian Janice Robbins, to whom I am indebted for so much of this information, forwarded me a tape made from a black and white silent film of the day. There were thousands of people, plus floats and boats galore, and even a future President.

But let's begin at the beginning. The states of New York and Vermont had gone 60/40 respectively in building the million dollar bridge to span Lake Champlain between Crown Point and Chimney Point. Having duly inspected the bridge in late July, now Bridge Commissioner Mortimer Ferris, a New York State Senator, would arrange dedication festivities that would be extraordinary even today. Governor Weeks of Vermont and the jaunty Franklin D. Roosevelt, Governor of New York, would meet at the middle of the bridge.

Gov. Roosevelt had canceled all engagements the previous week due to a pulled muscle but was now ready for the dedication. He arrived by special train.

The official ribbon cutting was at 2:00 p.m. The Green Mountain Chorus, 125 all-Welsh singers sang. The Governors approached the center of the bridge from opposite sides. They halted a few feet from the center of the bridge, very near the ribbon.

Roosevelt was assisted from the car, but in the film that was tactfully omitted. He greeted Governor Weeks and they clasped hands over the ribbon. Governor Roosevelt said, "I am so glad to see you Governor Weeks. How is my neighbor?"

The ribbon cutting came next. Ticonderoga resident Karl J. LaPointe recalls it well, though at the time it took place, he was at a very different vantage point. Karl had driven his future wife, Elizabeth Ferris, to the bridge for her to cut the ribbon. Bess, as he calls his late wife, was the youngest daughter of Commissioner Ferris.

"I drove her out in a Model A convertible," Karl said. "I was down at the bottom, of course." That is to say, he was under the bridge. "I stayed out of the picture."

Though she played such a prominent part, in subsequent years she was very modest about her role. Karl noted, "Bess didn't make much out of it. She wasn't that way."

The newspapers certainly made a fuss of her, as they reported on Miss Ferris attractively dressed in a pink chiffon dress with matching hat and carrying a large bouquet of American Beauty roses. In cutting the ribbon, she said: "In cutting this ribbon, I open the Champlain Bridge to traffic between the state of Vermont and New York, with the hope that it may serve to strengthen the friendship between these two already friendly states."

Karl, who described the day as "hotter than hell," had quite a wait under that bridge. After the ribbon cutting, the Warrensburg band rendered a concert for the spectators, then the parades followed. There were more than 30 floats and the parade went far longer than expected, lasting about two and a half hours.

It was 4:30 before the governors moved to the speakers' stand, but Janice Robbin's film of the event shows that both governors survived the wait and were fully capable of speaking.

Next week we'll look at the parade from the viewpoint of a participant, Dr. G. Peter Cook of Ticonderoga, and a bystander, Pearl Peoples of Saratoga Springs. And we'll share an anecdote from *Post-Star* business writer Maury Thompson.

And for this week's column, thanks for the memories, K. J.!

"OVER MY SHOULDER" COLUMN FOR AUGUST 21, 1999
Simultaneous parades complete bridge's dedication

Dr. G. Peter Cook of Ticonderoga recalls well the parade held after the ribbon cutting for the opening of the Crown Point Bridge on August 26, 1929. Just turned 14 that August, he was a bugler in the Fort Ticonderoga Drum and Bugle Corps. He vividly recalls his band riding and playing off the back of a truck. Thankfully, they didn't have to march because of the intense heat. Corps members wore a colonial-style uniform, with blue coats with buff trim, buff pants and tri-corner hats with a plume.

Two parades ran simultaneously. The New York parade started across the bridge first. After the bugle corps arrived on the Vermont side, Dr. Cook said they turned around and followed the Vermont parade over the bridge to New York.

Prizes were awarded for best of more than 30 floats. New York's first prize of $50 went to Fort Ticonderoga for Samuel de Champlain fully attired in breast plate and accompanied by Hurons. The second prize of $25 went to Mineville for the Witherbee Sherman Company float depicting small boys dressed as miners.

First prize for Vermont was won by Brandon. Floats came from everywhere. In Janice Robbins's tape I saw floats from as far north in New York as Plattsburgh, and from all over western Vermont, including Burlington in the north to Bennington in the south.

Speaking of tapes, Janice needs to talk with William Lee Richards of Queensbury. Bill's mother took 16 mm home movies with some great shots of Bill's Dad decked out in a colonial outfit. His father was a co-founder of the New York State Historical Association, headquartered at that time in Ticonderoga.

Now, catch these statistics. In all, 40,000 people attended the opening ceremonies! A detail of 25 state troopers from Malone was on hand, but the day went perfectly. Beneath the bridge, a flotilla of sleek wooden-hulled yachts and race boats crowded the lake.

An estimated 7,000 cars crossed that day and tolls were waived. One of those viewing the parade and remembering that toll-free crossing is Pearl Torrey Peoples of Saratoga Springs. Ten year old Pearl was with her family, visiting relatives in West Ferrisburg and Bristol, Vermont.

The Torreys sat on the Chimney Point side "looking right on the bridge," she said. "We watched the ceremony." Then the family drove over in their Model T.

A 10 stanza poem was written by an unknown author for the opening. Here is first stanza: "Hands across the Chasm! / No longer need we wait / To unite our varied interests / With our sister state / Hands across the chasm / While the shining waters flow, / Subdued, but not impeded, / On their steady course below!"

In 1987 the tolls and the bridge commission were abolished. Vermont gave its share of the bridge to New York, which is responsible for its upkeep.

Post-Star business writer Maury Thompson related this bridge anecdote, told to him by the late Clayton Wright of Chilson. A New York minister on his way to preach a revival service in Vermont lacked money to pay the toll. He prayed and asked for guidance. When he came to the bridge the toll taker was sleeping. So, he drove on across and preached his revival meeting, at which they took an offering. On his way home he told the toll taker that since he was asleep earlier, he would pay him double.

Maury, who had originally interviewed Janice Robbins for an article on the bridge's anniversary, noted he was "sorry they stopped charging tolls. It always seemed nice to have a friendly face halfway on the ride home from Vermont. Also, it seems a great way to welcome tourists to the state."

Thanks to Maury, Janice, and everyone I interviewed for memories of the Crown Point Bridge, another link in the long history shared by New York and Vermont.

"OVER MY SHOULDER" COLUMN FOR DECEMBER 11, 1999
Washington County to mark namesake's death

On the evening of Tuesday, December 14, Washington County will pause to acknowledge the 200th anniversary of George Washington, for whom Washington County was named.

At 5:00 p.m. in the Supervisors Chambers of the Washington County Municipal Center, there will be a ceremony, brief and totally fitting to the occasion, to note the death of Washington on December 14, 1799. I hope everyone, not only citizens of Washington County will be there, for a ceremony about Washington is a ceremony for every American.

Tuesday evening's event culminates the "George Washington Bicentennial," a year of observances that has been sponsored by George Washington's Mount Vernon, the association that runs Washington's home. Our county's George Washington Bicentennial committee was headed by Kingsbury/Hudson Falls municipal historian Paul Loding.

His committee has sponsored, among other things, the placement of markers to commemorate the three stops George Washington made in present day Washington County, in the towns of Greenwich, Fort Edward and Kingsbury.

It surprises people to learn that George Washington came through this area in the summer of 1783. I think we forget he was real. Washington was touring the northern battlefields in 1783 and what surprises me is how it is forgotten today that we were still technically at war with Great Britain at that time. British troops and ships still occupied New York City and harbors (and would until December). Although no battles were being fought, the Treaty of Paris would not be signed until September 1783. In signing it, Britain officially ended the war and recognized "the said United States" as the treaty read.

So, Washington was on a triumphal tour when technically we were still at war. His visit here, as everywhere, electrified people, inspiring the kind of trust and awe that I haven't seen today. At the height of power, he resigned his military commission to go home. He could have been the king of America, in fact his officers suggested he should, but Washington turned it down.

He so inspired New Yorkers that on April 2, 1784, the state legislature renamed Charlotte County "Washington County" in his honor.

At that time, Washington County included most of the present counties of Warren, Essex, Clinton, part of Hamilton County, and of course, Washington County (except lands south of the Battenkill). The new county also claimed most of western Vermont.

I had thought that our Washington County was the first to be named after him. Not so according to John Frye, Historian of the Western Maryland Room of the Washington County Library in Hagerstown, Maryland. Washington County, Maryland, was the first. Our Washington County was among the first.

He agreed me with that Washington County, New York, appears to be the first county to have been formed after the Treaty of Paris, with which the United States officially became "The United States of America." Thus, our county has the distinction of being the first (that I know of) to be formed after the USA legally became the USA to the world.

He said there are 31 counties in the country named for George Washington, plus numerous towns and villages, and of course one state. I had found Washington County, Maryland on the Internet, but only found some of the others. As John noted, to his knowledge no one had listed them all in one place.

On the day of December 14, the 200th anniversary of the death of George Washington, all flags across America will be lowered to half-mast in those places named for Washington and in every place, in accordance with Senate Resolution 83. It is suggested that all bells ring for a minute beginning at 12 noon central standard time.

And I hope you can take a few minutes Tuesday evening to attend the ceremony at the Washington County Municipal Center, Building B, second floor, in the Supervisors Chambers

I think it will be something you'll always remember.

"OVER MY SHOULDER" COLUMN FOR JANUARY 29, 2000
Recalling coincidental childhood memories with pal

Here's a story that contains a coincidence that did not start a friendship, but certainly deepened it.

Gladys Lapham has honored our family with her friendship for several decades now. I first met her when I moved to Glens Falls to become the director of the Chapman Historical Museum in 1975.

Gladys, or Gladdie as many call her, was one of what I have come to think of as "The Ladies of the Chapman," a group of extremely talented and energetic women who helped make the museum the success it is today.

Gladys volunteered at the museum and over time our friendship developed, and we got to know one another better. Gladys told me that she had been born in Fort Edward March 6, 1903, the daughter of Loie Rogers Contryman and Ora Contryman. Her father, Ora, was a pharmacist in Contryman and Donnell's in Fort Edward. She grew up in Fort Edward and attended all grades of school in the large brick schoolhouse that still stands near the intersection of Broadway and Bridge Street. She worked in her father's store. Later, she married and moved to Glens Falls.

How much we had in common! My parents moved to Fort Edward when I was little, and I spent a good part of my childhood there. My father, also a pharmacist, started his store in what had been Contryman and Donnell's. I went to elementary school in what had been Gladys' school. We both had lived in the lower end of the village. I had worked in a pharmacy in the same building as she. I later moved to Glens Falls, where I married.

Gladys recently sent some written memories to the Old Fort House Museum. These next few columns are based upon those memories, my memories, and a call I gave her just a few days ago.

Gladys' father Ora Contryman, also known as "Orie," had come to Fort Edward around 1890. His uncle Amos Contryman was co-owner of Contryman and Donnell, a store that had started Contryman and Wing. Gladys said that "Amos wrote his brother Wilson" in Watertown and "said that if he sent his son to Fort Edward, he'd do right by him."

Ora left school and came to work for Amos at 14. Gladys noted that this was the end of his formal schooling. However, as we'll see, his education never ended.

Ora and his wife, Loie, were living on Fort Street when Gladys was born in the family home. About a month later, the family moved to a house they bought on lower Broadway, which still stands today across from the present Old Fort House Museum.

Gladys said the house cost $1,500 and had no electricity, no indoor plumbing, no furnace, and no cellar to put one in. Her father "dug the cellar out by hand."

At that time, the house backed up to the old Champlain Canal and the canal boats were pulled by mules. Gladys recalled watching them intently and she said, "I learned to swear from the mule drivers." Neither of her parents swore and she kept her newfound skill a secret from them.

When she was old enough, she went to work in her father's store and that forms a special bond between us. You may recall Suzanne Seay's excellent article on Gladys in *The Post-Star* last October, with a photo of Gladys as a girl, seated at a table in the store. She has vivid memories of that store, and many of mine are nearly identical.

Next week, I'll relate how Gladys and I matched memories on what our families' pharmacies looked like and how similar things were. And, I'll continue with some other history of my friend, including a stint as a model for a famous illustrator.

"OVER MY SHOULDER" COLUMN FOR FEBRUARY 5, 2000
Recollections of growing up, working in the pharmacy

In last week's column I was telling you about my friend Gladys Lapham, whose early life in Fort Edward was centered around the family pharmacy, Contryman and Donnell's.

This was the same store my in which father would have his pharmacy from 1952 to 1962. What fascinates me is what remained in the drugstore that allowed us to have such similar memories. Gladys wrote that her father would "let me wait on customers...selling cigars, cough syrup, candy" even bath towels. She has a photo of the new cash register that her father had put in. That machine was still in the store when we arrived in 1952. When I was older, I also worked in the store, selling cigarettes, cough syrup, candy, and even Mickey Mouse watches.

We shared memories of the soda fountain. Contryman and Donnell's first "mechanical" soda fountain probably was bought around 1900 from her description of it. Gladys still has the mirror from that first fountain. These soda fountains of steel and marble had spigots for dispensing plain and carbonated water, and stainless steel wells for holding sundae toppings, some with pumps to dispense syrups.

They also held large containers of ice cream, which Ora made in the house of his uncle Amos Contryman, the store's co-owner. Ora brought the ice cream to the store to freeze.

She said her father made his own chocolate syrup on a small gas burner, and "never burned it." That burner was still in the store when we came.

A second fountain was installed in 1918 and still there in 1952. It was made of nickel-plated steel and marble and had a refrigeration unit, but we still had ice delivered for the attached Coke dispenser. We bought our ice cream in 5 gallon tubs from Borden's. Gladys and I share identical memories of making sundaes and sodas. Some things are forever.

We both remembered the 2-story wooden structure that had been attached to the store's brick front portion, which still stands. She said the ground floor was open, allowing customers with horses and buggies to park underneath. (The first drive-in?) On its second floor, at the same level as the store's first floor, her father would cut window glass to order. I said my father did too. "We sold Devoe house paint," she said. We did too. It was on the shelves near the glass. We stored it there as well, and also sold paint out front.

The store depended upon her help as she grew older, but obviously her parents decided against it being her career, as they provided her with a college education to become a teacher. However, when another career beckoned, her father said no.

Bradshaw Crandall was a famous American illustrator at that time, the mid-1920s. He was, also, a Glens Falls native, who owned a summer camp near that of Glady's family, on Dunham's Bay, Lake George. Crandall stopped by the camp one day to ask Ora Contryman if he would allow his daughter to pose for him. He painted Gladys for a calendar he was doing, although, as she told me, he made her a blonde!

He must have been impressed with her for he offered her a job modeling in New York City that summer. However, Gladys said that her father had said "he couldn't let her off" her job in the store. The reality was that he actually didn't want her to be a model.

Instead, Gladys continued her college studies at Elmira and went on to become a teacher. However, she still has the portrait that Crandall did of her those many summers ago.

In next week's column, I'll conclude my series on Gladys Contryman Lapham by sharing her memories of village life in the first three decades of the 20th century, then comparing them with the mid-20th century and now.

"OVER MY SHOULDER" COLUMN FOR FEBRUARY 12, 2000
Changes came slowly during the "good old days"

Here is the last of three columns about my friend Gladys Lapham, who has been graciously sharing her memories of growing up in Fort Edward in the first three decades of the 1900s.

I'd written that her father, Ora Contryman, had come to Fort Edward around 1890, at age 14, to work for his uncle Amos in the Contryman and Donnell drugstore. Ora's formal education stopped then, but he never stopped learning, eventually becoming a pharmacist. In his day, there were druggists and pharmacists. Both took a state test to be licensed to dispense medicine, but to be a pharmacist position required far more advanced training. Ora began as a druggist, then asked permission of Amos and his partner William Donnell, a druggist, to study for the state pharmacy exams.

They doubted the utility of it, but granted permission. Ora studied chemistry and the appropriate science courses with a professor Wolf of the Fort Edward Institute and took his pharmacist's exam in Albany.

On the personal side, he married Loie Viola Rogers, daughter of George Henry and Sarah Libby Downs Rogers. The couple had one child, Gladys, born March 6, 1903.

In a letter she sent to the Old Fort House Museum recently, Gladys recalled growing up in Fort Edward. Forty-some years later, I was there and the similarities in our memories are striking.

Her home was on lower Broadway, directly across from the Old Fort House known then only as "the house where George Washington slept after the Revolutionary War." The Champlain Canal was to the rear of her house. The trolley ran past her house along Broadway, "on their way to Glens Falls from Troy. We called them Troy cars." The family would take the trolley to Glens Falls to shop for "coats and cloth to make underwear, nightgowns...etc." Forty years later, we'd go to Glens Falls on the bus.

Gladys said that her mother made her "dresses to wear to college" on a foot-powered sewing machine. "I'd come home and there in the clothes closet would be a new dress."

For all that, she was of the automobile generation. She wrote that she "learned to drive in the driveway...We had cars from the start. They were like carriages..." with a hand crank for starting. "I learned to do that," she wrote. Their Maxwell had "lights hanging on the outside and [it] carried fuel...on the running board."

Their Maxwell cars built muscles as they "didn't have much power. I recall having to get out and push them over the canal bridge." And they changed life:

"We let the poultry run free all over the road until cars came into being...Ultimately we kept the hens and roosters in coops."

Housekeeping was different. To clean clothes, "we used rubbing boards" of rippled metal and boiled the clothes "to get them white. No Clorox." Clothes hung to dry in the winter were brought inside frozen to finish drying in the cellar.

Here's a thought to make you cherish modern plumbing: "There was no plumbing in our house when I was little. We used outhouses and ``slop' jars," ceramic vessels kept under the bed. "We had real toilet paper in the outhouses, but it was customary to use catalogues." Originally, the "man of the house" had to clean out the outhouse periodically, but "that was solved in the `20s by building the outhouse so it hung over the" canal.

In Fort Edward of the 1950s our raw sewage was carried directly by pipes to the Hudson, in which we swam. Ah, those good old days.

That being said, I think there were some aspects of "those good old days" that may have been better. Perhaps one practice that could stand to be revived was the chaperoned date in the parlor. Gladys' grandmother's house on nearby Cortland Street had a parlor, filled with horse-hair covered furniture and an organ. Gladys wrote, "The girls brought their dates and they all sang together. My aunt Ede played that organ. That was before movies."

In the 1950s we inherited a Victorian couch with an underlayer of horse hair. You never really knew torture until you sat on that.

The parlor date could eventually lead to marriage – in the parlor. "My Aunt Ede had her wedding in the parlor," she wrote.

And the parlor was the place of the ultimate departure. Gladys notes that the parlor served as funeral parlor and church: "We had family funeral services in that room, too. The body was kept in that room until the funeral service, which always happened at home."

When my cousin died in 1965, his wake and funeral were held out of my grandmother's home. I don't know of anyone who does that now.

In the almost 50 years that passed from her childhood in Fort Edward a century ago, to my childhood in Fort Edward in the 1950s, there were some changes. The trolley, the movie house, the steam locomotive disappeared. The radio and television appeared.

Yet it was more similar than different. Gladys' school for grades K to 12 was my school for grades 1 to 4. The pharmacy she grew up in, I grew up in. And comparing photos of downtown in 1910 and in 1960, most of the buildings she knew as a child were still there 50 years later. Physically, the changes to Fort Edward in the last 50 years are far more dramatic than those of the previous 50.

But Gladys' friendship has helped me to learn that you accept these changes and move on. Her life, of which we've only covered a smidgen, is a testament to one who looks to the future, including a 97th birthday on March 6.

Thanks for sharing your memories, Gladdie. It's been fun. We'll do it again, okay?

"OVER MY SHOULDER" COLUMN FOR FEBRUARY 19, 2000
Reese, Rebel flag boosters have skewed view of history

I have waited to respond to a Charley Reese[lx] column concerning the Confederate flag flying over South Carolina's state capitol. I wanted to attempt a reasoned response to an unreasoning topic, which is history. For when Charley Reese writes of "The Confederate Flag" or "The Sovereign Rights of the States" or even "What the Founding Fathers Really Intended" – he interprets history.

That can be dangerous, for history is unreasoning, by which I mean this: when you use history to buttress your arguments, you better damn well be ready for facts you didn't expect and truths you may not want.

Some facts concerning the Confederate flag: it was the flag of 11 renegade states, which tried to secede to form the Confederate States of America. Our country, The United States of America, considered the states' action illegal, along with the constitution they drafted and the flag they waved. In all, 660,000 human beings died because of that confederacy, that constitution – and that flag.

That flag, that constitution, and that confederacy were borne of one institution: slavery. The Confederate constitution was filled with numerous articles concerned with slavery. Just as was, not coincidentally, the original 1789 Constitution of the United States, upon which the Confederate constitution was closely modeled.

And there's a fact that has brought us today to a truth some may not have wanted to have faced before: many people in 1789 viewed slavery with less horror than we do now, even as natural, and the Framers of the Constitution judged the evil of keeping slavery the price for unity. So, now we face the truth that not everything the Constitution's Framers thought then is desirable today and we must be careful to separate their good from their bad.

We know to be true that, although the states in 1861, and subsequently, said the Civil War centered on the issue of "states' rights," the reality was, and is, that slavery was the only real issue. I don't believe Charley Reese has accepted this as a fact, because I feel he has not accepted slavery as a disgusting horror, a loathsome depravity, a universal insult to every human.

I say this because he once blithely described a particular slave-owning plantation owner as living in the "paradise" that was the Antebellum South. Paradise to whom? The slaves?

If Charley had had a great-great grandmother who had been stripped naked, chained to an auction block, prodded and examined in every private part, bought, used, and then thrown away like an old shoe, would he think it paradise? If someone came today and sought to sell Charley Reese or his family into bondage, would he be fighting to his dying breath or saying, "I submit, master"? We know that answer.

History isn't pleasant. It is fact. If we know that slavery and not state's rights led to the Civil War, paradoxically, we know too that the North didn't enter the war because of a fit of conscience over slavery. We know that Union generals owned slaves, too. We know that many Northern whites loathed Black people and many Southern whites did not. Paradoxes? Perhaps. But fact.

And as true, we do know what the leaders of the Confederacy fought for and what its constitution and flag stood for. Slavery. And, on the good side, we know that whatever is said of the Civil War, slavery ended because of it.

So, Charley, I just don't know what the mystery is. Here's the past, learn it, live with it. For God's sake man, the past is complicated enough without re-inventing it. Let the dead be dead and let the truth stand.

The soldiers of the Confederacy are dead. Their actions are history. The cause for which they fought is dead. It is history. The Confederacy is dead, its constitution is dead and its flag a soulless rag that should not grace the halls of any government.

But if those things are not dead for some people, and if they live on in their minds as symbols of a righteous cause, then those people should well take stock of their lives and wonder aloud what it is like to live a lie, for that is what they have come to.

"OVER MY SHOULDER" COLUMN FOR MAY 6, 2000
Honoring a radical endorsed by Civil war history

NOTE: Though this is now dated, as it announced the portrayal of Frederick Douglass by the late actor Ossie Davis in 2000, my Editor agreed that it contains enough good history to be reprinted. Moreover, it is now old enough for the event itself to be called historical.

If you are reading this early in the morning, you still have time to get in your car and drive to Lake Placid.

There you can participate in the momentous event taking place today at the John Brown Farm State Historic Site near Lake Placid. A group of marchers are reviving a tradition of a yearly pilgrimage to the grave of abolitionist John Brown, the death of whom, many said, caused the Civil War.

Among those at this event will be the noted actor, director, and writer Ossie Davis, who will portray anti-slavery leader Frederick Douglass and read from Douglass' 1881 address concerning John Brown.

The event's timing is perfect, as the 200th anniversary of Brown's birth in Connecticut is nearly here, May 9th to be precise. The focus today will be a one-mile walk to the John Brown Farm from the Trinity Chapel on the Old

Military Road. At the farm there will be a wreath-laying ceremony at the gravesite with prominent guest speakers and performers.

From the Glens Falls area, the easiest way there is to take the Northway to exit 30, then go west on Route 73 to Lake Placid. Be at the John Brown Farm State Historic Site by 10:30 a.m. at the very latest. Shuttle busses will take you to the Trinity Chapel on Old Military Road, where the celebration begins with period music. From there will be the march back to the Brown Homestead.

The celebration is important to the region served by *The Post-Star*, for it is another reminder that our region was one of the nation's pathways to freedom along the Underground Railroad for fugitive slaves.

The reason Brown, who was born in Connecticut, came to the Adirondacks with his family was because he was following the example of free black families, who had come to the Adirondacks in the late 1840s. They created the African American settlements of "Timbuctoo" and "Blackville," in Essex and Franklin Counties in an effort to spur independent farm ownership and voter rights for blacks. The movement had deep roots in the Greater Glens Falls area, about which I'll write in a later column.

Brown ultimately gave up peaceful methods for abolition, becoming a radical. A deeply religious man, he believed God had tapped him on the shoulder and appointed him to help eradicate slavery. If it meant shedding blood, so be it. Brown's legacy spread from bloody Kansas to his last act, the raid on the arsenal at Harper's Ferry, Virginia, October 16, 1859.

His execution on December 2, 1859 made him a martyr. Many have said it caused the Civil War. Brown was buried at his farm in North Elba, near Lake Placid. After the Civil War, which claimed over 660,000 lives, thousands made the almost religious pilgrimage to Brown's farm. Guidebooks of the Adirondacks took pains to locate the place. (However, some writers were less than complimentary. In his early guidebooks, S. R. Stoddard credited Brown with precipitating the Civil war and eradicating slavery, while disparaging those formerly enslaved.)

In 1895, Brown's Farm was declared a state historic site. Information furnished me by Martha Swan and Amy Godine[lxi] notes that in 1922, the NAACP founded a John Brown Memorial Association and organized annual pilgrimages to Brown's farm. In that first year, area school children were released from school and joined members of the local chamber of commerce to watch the NAACP's J. Max Barber lay a wreath on Brown's grave. He made an impassioned speech calling for another Brown to combat segregation, lynchings, and the Ku Klux Klan. The Klan had a very strong following in northern New York State at that time.

Today, at 11:00 am, the annual pilgrimage will be revived and Brown's memory renewed at the John Brown Farm State Historic Site near Lake Placid. The song's refrain is true, "John Brown's body lies a-mouldering in the grave." But his memory goes marching on.

You can call the John Brown Farm at 518-523-3900 for more information.

"OVER MY SHOULDER" COLUMN FOR JUNE 24, 2000
Appreciate monuments for the stories they hold

It may be serendipity, but have you noticed the increased interest in the subject of monuments and markers and statues and commemorative structures?

For example, in *The Post-Star* this past week there were two separate articles on monuments. Marie Bucciferro reported June 19 on the proposed monument to list the names of all 1,200 Saratoga County veterans killed in battle since the Revolution.

Then a series on monuments by *Post-Star* staff intern began June 21 with an article on the Civil War monument in Hudson Falls. I think both articles indicate a renewed interest in our effort as human beings to commemorate and memorialize people and events.

Certainly, the new series on markers will have so many lovely monuments to feature. The Civil War monuments alone are so numerous and different that to name some without naming all is to risk a raft of rotten letters. But there are four that come immediately into mind. One, in the Village of Greenwich has simple but majestic lines that are pure elegance. The Hudson Falls and Glens Falls Civil War monuments are obelisks embellished with sculpted images of soldiers. Those three are stone. The fourth in Ticonderoga is a bronze of a soldier. All four are majestic and lovely.

Most area monuments are related to past wars. Some are simple, unimposing pieces, created by artists now forgotten. Others are magnificent works by famous artists, such as Daniel Chester French at the Crown Point Reservation. Regardless of the artist, many had been overlooked. Recent restorations of the monuments in Glens Falls, Ticonderoga, and Saratoga Springs, are examples of a renewed interest in this public art.

There is a monument that I've liked for a long time for the story it holds. It sits on Route 9, slightly north of the intersection of 9 and NYS 149. Tourists whiz by the Colonel Williams monument, but they might stop if they knew the story of its tragic connection with Williams College in Williamstown, Massachusetts.

The tale of how Ephraim Williams' name became synonymous with one of America's finest colleges is due to chance happenings in the life of an otherwise lucky man.

Holden's history of Queensbury tells us Williams' life story. Born in 1714 in Newton, Massachusetts, Williams had settled in Stockbridge by 1755, when the French and Indian War began. Through valorous action in skirmishes with the French before the war had actually broken out, Williams had been promoted to Colonel.

Stationed in Albany at the start of the war in the fall of 1755, Williams took time to draw up his will, as Holden notes, "with what foreboding or prescience of his impending fate none can say." He made provision for the creation of both a school and a town to be called Williamstown. He then rode to fight the French – and to meet his death.

Near the site of today's monument, Williams was killed while leading his troops in battle. His body, at first hidden, was subsequently buried beneath a small stone with the initials E.W.

The money from Williams' will was invested and in 1785 the Town of Williamstown was created. The bequest, now grown to almost $6,000, was combined with other funds to build the school, which opened in 1791. It became Williams College in 1793. Ironically, the hero who died for King George II, funded a school that opened under the Presidency of George Washington.

In 1854, three Williams College alumni, one of whom was E.H. Rosecrans of Glens Falls, built a monument in Williams' memory. All the Colonel's remains were transferred to Williamstown and reburied. Well, almost all. In 1795, the colonel's nephew had gone to the gravesite and taken the Colonel's skull. One can only wonder.

Subsequent markers and such were put up by the stone. However, the monument is slowly being forgotten, and not many people think about it nor Williams.

Yet when I see that monument, I can't help but appreciate what an accident of war can do. The stray bullet that could just as easily have missed Williams instead set into motion the founding of a town and the creation of a college that has played so important a role in American education.

Think about that the that the next time you drive up that way or happen to hear the name of Williams College.

"OVER MY SHOULDER" COLUMN FOR JULY 1, 2000
Martha Barnes showed what country is all about

July Fourth is around the corner and life has just shown me what America is about.

There is a proud, determined, hard-working, well-respected, and very much loved woman who is about to take what many would consider a well-deserved retirement. Although in my heart of hearts I think Martha Barnes[lxii] of Salem, New York, would rather go right on delivering mail on her rural route as she has since 1944, until the "final retirement call" was made.

In offering this story to you now I hesitate. Not because it is not a truly wonderful slice of history about a remarkable woman, but because it is better told by the people who have known her for longer than the brief time I've had the privilege of her acquaintance. But circumstances – that funny thing called life poking its head in again — circumstances dictated that this morning, as I write, Martha Barnes will stand at a retirement ceremony that few of the thousands of her friends will even know is taking place.

Oh, the community has known that Martha — you needn't say her last name, Martha is sufficient — they've known that Martha was to retire June 30th. But then suddenly that retirement was so near and then suddenly it was here — and now a quiet little ceremony with a few dignitaries will mark the end of a 56 year career. And that is the just way that Martha Barnes specifically wished it to be. Quiet, unostentatious.

So, I hope that Martha will forgive me if I say that that just didn't seem right to me and that something that momentous must be noted. While I will ask my newspaper to do a longer, fuller, better story than this, I could not let this moment go by without offering you a bit of the story of Martha.

You have to have an image of Martha Barnes in your mind to carry through this story. Before I'd met her, I had heard her described as a short, feisty elderly woman, having a great sense humor, not taking a lot of nonsense and knowing intimately every person on her route. When I first met her, I saw this short woman with wiry gray hair and a cap like the kids wear today, standing in front of the Cossayuna Post office, unloading huge sacks of mail from a "vintage" AMC station wagon. People were coming up and saying, "Hi, Martha," and she was smiling back with eyes that have the most incredible sparkle you'd ever want to see.

To give you a bit of history, Martha Sears Barnes was born in New Brunswick, Canada, in 1914. Her family moved from there to Vermont in the 1920s, and then to our region, where she's spent most of her life. And to be accurate about things, it has to be said that while Martha Barnes has had the contract to deliver the mail on the Salem Post Office's rural delivery route since 1944, she actually began in 1937. Martha began delivering with her husband, Earl Barnes, in 1937.

Her daughter, Janie, told me that she and her siblings would ride the route with her parents, her father hanging on to Janie so she wouldn't fall out of the window. The Barnes raised their kids on that route. In fact, in these later years, Janie has driven the route with her mother.

In 1944, Earl was called into the US Navy and Martha took over the contract, renewing it every year. Until now. On June 30, 2000, her last contract ended without being renewed.

What took place in the interim was more than simply 56 years of delivering mail — which is not to imply in any way that 56 years of rural mail delivery to hundreds of people is anything simple. But Martha extended herself beyond the work for which she contracted. As she went from house to house, she came to know every person on her route as a person. She has seen the birth of three generations since 1944 and more than just her own children have known of her caring. She has built deep and lasting friendships.

One of those on her route is Betty Muhlig, recently retired correspondent for *The Post-Star*. Betty told me yesterday that when each of the Muhlig boys graduated, there was a card and present in the mailbox from Martha. A baby born, a christening, a birthday, a graduation, a marriage...these were things Martha knew and these were things Martha remembered.

With each family on her route, she has shared the soaring heights of those joys of life. And she has taken into her own heart, as her own, the utter devastation that occurs with death, such as the tragic death on a Salem farm last year. She had known that boy, she said, since the time of his birth fifty some years ago. That was all she had said at the post office that day. But those who knew her, knew that the grief was as deep as that of a parent.

To see Martha's car coming down Route 29 on a golden day, she so short behind the wheel that it looked as if the car were driving itself, the car slowly pulling in by the mail box, a brief pause and then out on to the highway again – that was to know that there was a constant in your life. It was to know more than just the fact that the mail had come. It was to know that the person behind the wheel was someone whom you knew, and who knew you. Was a friend. Would be a friend for years to come.

The mail had come. Martha was here. The two sentences meant the same thing.

Martha has delivered the mail on her route longer than many of those on her route have been alive. To think of her retired has been the unthinkable. And now it's happened. As Betty Muhlig said, Martha is as much a part of southern Washington County as the mountains and the rivers. It is surely is going to be a different landscape without her.

I mentioned that July Fourth is around the corner and that life has shown me what America is about. To me, Martha's story is what America is about: individuals who work hard and by their efforts, leave a lasting imprint for future times.

If there is a saving grace in all this, it is that Martha's grandson will be taking over her route. So, in the best way possible, a part of Martha will still be out there every day, delivering that mail, along that rural route out of Salem.

"OVER MY SHOULDER" COLUMN FOR JULY 22, 2000
Call Mel: Battle of Saratoga would make a great movie

On July 8, when I first cheered for "The Battle of Saratoga" design for the quarter, I also referred to "The Patriot," Mel Gibson's movie about the Revolution.

Over the intervening time, the thought has occurred to me that "The Patriot," should be serving to inspire a movie about the two battles of Saratoga and events that, over the months from June to September 1777, led to it.

It would be awesome.

Critics complain "The Patriot" is too bloody, too emotional, too inflammatory. What are they talking about? The Revolution was. Its violence was most horrid, its tragedies inutterably sad, its heroism of the finest.

Saratoga was the Turning Point of our Revolution and, forgive my stating it this way, Mel Gibson could not ask for a hotter movie property.

Look at the script for "The Battle of Saratoga." It's June 1777 on the frontier where the English had only recently defeated the French to take control of the better part of North America. Many colonial settlers here are veterans of that French and Indian War.

Now the English Army, the world's most incredible fighting machine, is preparing to steamroll over the same region, but this time many of the colonists are fighting against the Crown. They are Rebels. They will call themselves Patriots.

Some colonists stay loyal – the Loyalists – and some will try to stay out of it. This Revolution is a civil war, too.

This drama has the perfect villain, the pompous and yet very complicated British General John Burgoyne, loathed by the rebellious colonists and loathing them in return. There are families torn apart by this civil war. We have romance, rivers of blood, sickeningly violent death, traitors as heroes, heroes as traitors. And all set in America's most exquisite scenery.

There's broad drama and individual personal drama in the June to September lead-up to the final battle. An opening shot shows Burgoyne reading his arrogant proclamation to the colonists, threatening to unleash the "devastation, famine and every concomitant horror" of his Indian allies. Yet, he states he can "control" them.

We cut to a wide-screen panorama of the huge flotilla of Burgoyne's army heading south on Lake Champlain to Crown Point and from there, swarming south by land to besiege Fort Ticonderoga. The Patriots abandon the fort by night and flee east to Vermont, as Burgoyne's army pursues. In Hubbardton, the American's give heroic battle.

Meanwhile Burgoyne is advancing by ship on Whitehall – then Skenesborough – taking it in a fiery naval battle on July 6. The land is soaked in blood. Nothing is sacred to either side. With Burgoyne is ally Phillip Skene, Skenesborough's founder, who finds the rebels have broken into his house, stripped the lead from his wife's coffin and even stolen the jewelry from her body.

People flee. Burgoyne's troops discover Castleton, Vermont abandoned, as if the people had left only with their clothes.

July 8 at Fort Ann. Patriots slow his march, but they lose people and two regimental flags. Some historians say one flag is the first American flag adopted by Congress to fall in battle. Camera zooms in on flag.

Shifting scenes, Patriot John McCrea musters his troops near Fort Edward. His sister, Jane, disagreeing with his political stand, is on her way to meet her

Loyalist fiancé, who serves in Burgoyne's army. She is killed by the Indian scouts sent to escort her. The scouts scalp her dead body and bring the scalp to the fiance, who recognizes her by her hair.

In the two days before her death, some of these same scouts had already slaughtered whole families in Argyle.

The countryside goes wild. Patriot and Loyalist alike are stunned. Burgoyne cannot control his Indian allies. Patriots fleeing in disarray before Burgoyne now turn in rage and Rebel volunteers pour into the region.

It is late July 1777, two months since Burgoyne began. The countryside is ablaze, slaughter and destruction are taking place everywhere. Families have been torn apart by divided loyalties and those who are neutral are being attacked by both sides.

Next week, a pregnant woman takes on the British army and a traitor becomes a hero in the final act of the movie drama called "The Battle of Saratoga."

"OVER MY SHOULDER" COLUMN FOR JULY 29, 2000
Local battle would make great climax for movie

The Battle of Saratoga, the movie script concludes — with a few choice comments at the end of the column.

For those of you who may have just joined us, I have been visualizing some scenes for a film script for the Battle of Saratoga. My idea is based upon the idea that, if Mel Gibson can popularize the Revolutionary story of Francis Marion the Swamp Fox, then the Battles of Saratoga, as there were actually two, would be extraordinary.

It was, after all, the Battle of Saratoga that was the "Turning Point of the Revolution," ensuring its success, ensuring that our country would be.

Scenes of enormous complexity, difficult to describe adequately in words, could be done such justice with film. We would see the death and destruction, to be sure, but the religious persecution and the racial conflict would be there as well. Quakers in Queensbury and Easton, attempting to maintain their religious pacifism, would be attacked by both sides. Black people, responding to a promise of freedom, would swarm down from the hills of Whitehall to join Burgoyne's army, only to end up prisoners of war.

It is difficult to pinpoint the exact moment in the film script where things went wrong for Burgoyne, but it would probably focus upon that hot day of July 27, 1777, when Jane McCrea was so brutally murdered by Burgoyne's own scouts.

The delays Burgoyne suffered on his way to Albany, his original destination, had sapped his army's strength. But the deaths of so many people before Jane McCrea had served the purpose of causing the rebel army to retreat and the countryside to panic. Now, galvanized by McCrea's death, the people begin to mobilize by the thousands around Saratoga, today the Schuylerville-Stillwater region.

In August of 1777, as Burgoyne's weakened army approached Saratoga, he dispatched a force of 1,000 German mercenaries, Loyalists, and Indians to capture supplies at Bennington, Vermont. It would lead to their total defeat. My film script would show that through the eyes of Hannah Coon.

In Greenwich, Hannah Coon's husband, a Patriot, was off fighting. Pregnant, she tended the farm. British force captured her and force-marched her to Walloomsac. She actually taunted her captors – and suffered for it. She gave birth on the way and arrived at Walloomsac with a baby in her arms.

While John Stark's forces decimated the British forces there, at what is called the Battle of Bennington, Hannah escaped and returned home to her ransacked home. Living off the few plants left, she and her baby were captured again three weeks later, ending up at the first Battle of Saratoga.

She was reunited with her husband and eventually lived to be 101.

I would have the film's conclusion, Burgoyne's defeat at Saratoga, concentrate on the most ironic event, Benedict Arnold's heroism. The lead-up would show the tension mounting with the failure of Burgoyne's plan to have three British forces meet at Albany. His fellow general St Regis is defeated in the Mohawk Valley and his other partner, Lord Howe, fails to come up the Hudson to his aid. Foolishly Burgoyne moves his now dwindled army to Saratoga, where twenty thousand American patriots gather. Defeat is imminent.

Meanwhile Benedict Arnold, just returning from having helped defeat St Regis, is caught in a political maneuver, where General Gates replaces General Schuyler. Gates hates Arnold and strips him of command. Yet at the first Battle of Saratoga, Arnold defies him, rides into battle and arguably helps turn the tide against Burgoyne, making Saratoga a victory. Benedict Arnold, America's most infamous traitor, the hero of Saratoga. Quite a scene.

The second Battle of Saratoga occurs in October, 1777 and the closing shot is the surrender, with Burgoyne passing his sword to Gates. That was the design that Governor Pataki decided against [*for the license plate design*].

To the many of you who called, sent letters and e-mailed me expressing your indignation that the design for the Battle of Saratoga was dumped in favor of the Statue of Liberty, I am with you. By dumping the Battle of Saratoga design, New York State lost a chance to showcase its most important gift to America – America itself.

Writing in favor of the design, Matt Rozell[lxiii], a history teacher in Hudson Falls stated that he teaches students to value the past. He favored Saratoga because it showed the "vital role New York State history played in the founding of our nation."

I agree, Matt. But teaching must begin with the example set by our leaders. If they don't teach a nation about Saratoga how will a nation care about it?

Has our state become so complacent about its past that it means little or nothing?

And the question is, do you care? Do you care that the place responsible for giving America its start got passed over as a second rate choice? A would be? An almost ran? A ho-hum? A "who gives a damn"?

Because that is exactly what it meant when the Battle of Saratoga design was not chosen as a national symbol, which is what it would have been.

The Battle of Saratoga, the very thing that made America possible, is second rate.

Marvelous.

Postscript: Apparently actor Mel Gibson missed reading *The Post-Star* when these columns were published, as he did not seize upon my suggestion.

"OVER MY SHOULDER" COLUMN FOR AUGUST 5, 2000
County Historical Society has rich 60-year history

The Washington County Historical Society is marking its 60th anniversary this month.

In *The Post-Star* region, the Washington County Historical Society is among the "ancients" in the world of historical societies and museums. I think only two surpass it, Fort Ticonderoga, founded in 1909, and the Fort Edward Historical Association, founded in November 1925.

Previously I had written that Susan E. Wade, the first Washington County Historian, was the true founder of the Washington County Historical Society in 1940. Upon taking office in January 1940, she drew upon the power of that office to help complete a task I am sure she initiated years before. Sue Wade worked with others, preferring to organize behind the scenes and to avoid the limelight. She organized a meeting of all the appointed town historians at the county clerk's office in June of 1940 to organize a Washington County historical society.

The town historians present were: Elizabeth McWhorter, Argyle; Adelaide Cooper, Dresden; Paul Crumley, Fort Ann; William H. Hill, Fort Edward; Helen Morey, Greenwich; Herman Churchill, Hampton; Isabella Brayton[lxiv], Hartford; Beatrice Wilson, Hebron; Frank Dobbin; Jackson; Frank Cronkhite, Kingsbury; Margaret Simpson, Putnam; Gordon Dillon, Salem. Five towns had not yet appointed their historians, as was mandated then by the education law and is still today.

Acting State Historian Hugh Flick addressed that first gathering of historians, as well as politicians and citizens, urging them to form a historical society. Edna Shannon's 1960 history of the society notes that a planning meeting was held July 2, 1940 at the headquarters of the Cambridge Historical Society. Flick was there, too.

Shannon listed the names of some of the people present. In addition to Sue

Wade, Hugh Flick and Shannon herself, there were Ernest Tilford of Smiths Basin, Mrs. Robert McClellan of Cambridge, Gordon Dillon, Salem town historian, Mr. and Mrs. John MacMorris of Corinth, and F. J. Fahrenholz, Superintendent of the Argyle Schools. Mrs. Mary MacMorris, later the second Washington County Historian, became temporary chair. Ernest Tilford was temporary secretary.

The first organizational meeting of the Washington County Historical Society was held August 17, 1940. Its first slate of officers was: L. R. Lewis of Hudson Falls was president, Mrs. Robert McClellan of Cambridge, first vice president; Islay V. H. Gill of Greenwich second vice president; Ernest Tilford of Smiths Basin, Secretary; and Mrs. Roscoe Wilson of Salem, Treasurer.

The WCHS, as it came to be also called, focused on many areas, including the preservation of cemeteries and early records, and the teaching of history to our children. Historic homes, covered bridges, early industry – all were of interest. One of the first, and still visible, tasks the WCHS undertook was creating historic markers throughout the county. Today, most survive, each bearing the initials, "WCHS."

World War II curtailed the society's activities, but they resumed gung ho after the war. Evidence of that was a 1948 meeting held at the Society of Friends South Meeting House in Easton that featured the legendary Grandma Moses.

Over the decades the WCHS would create a healthy publications program and become a county force for the preservation of everything from historic records to historic buildings, although, until 1982, it would not have a permanent home of its own. In 1949, Mrs. Helen McClellan had willed her Cambridge home, "Meikleknox," to the society, but it was decided that the society could not maintain it and it was sold in 1950. It is now the Meikleknox Home.

In 1982 the WCHS acquired historic the Wing-Northup House in Fort Edward, its present headquarters.

As it approached its 60th anniversary, the all-volunteer WCHS took a step which I know Sue Wade and the other founders would have applauded. The society hired its first director, Michael Russert[lxv], who is a retired teacher with a deep interest in history and who is a capable administrator. In an age where change is occurring more rapidly than ever before, and where history is vital for the nourishment of perspective, the Washington County Historical Society has positioned itself well for the 21st Century.

Happy 60th anniversary WCHS.

"OVER MY SHOULDER" COLUMN FOR AUGUST 12, 2000
Club celebrates 100 years of leisurely pursuits

Recently Charles Mullen gave me *The Idle Hour Club*[lxvi], a history he has compiled on the of the Idle Hour Club in Fort Edward, which is observing the centennial of its "first founding" in 1900.

The Idle Hour Club is an organization that is purely social in origin. Social organizations boomed in the post-Civil War decades. Industrialization shifted Americans away from a farming society and Americans moved into towns and cities. The expanding economy allowed people leisure time and social organizations solely for men, solely for women or for the family blossomed.

For years Engineer George H. Mead used to give friends a Sunday ride in his steamboat the "Mary Jane." The group would meet in various places, staging the beginnings of the Idle Hour Club. In 1900, an organization for men was started on Rogers Island in Fort Edward. In the booklet, Lawrence Corbett writes that the Idle Hour Club was built on the southern end of the island, which was at one time a separate island itself.

At first, it was informal, reflecting the casualness of the words "Idle Hour." But my guess is that when the Idle Hour Club leased land from George Mead in 1906, it probably spurred some of the members to think in terms of things more legal and permanent, especially when the club constructed a "large building on a concrete foundation."

On October 19, 1907, the club was incorporated under state law. That being done, the gentlemen got back to the serious business of having a good time. In his history, Charles Mullen included many reprints of newspaper articles about the club and the one with the information on the incorporation vividly portrays a group of people dedicated to fun, festivities and frolic.

The *Fort Edward Advertiser* of November 14th carried a reprint of a rapturous article from the Greenwich Journal. The *Advertiser* described the writer of the article as being someone "apparently full of venison and gratitude...regarding his entertainment at the club's annual feast."

The article reported at length about the "annual eat-fest," with venison provided by club members who "can put the kibosh on Robin Hood or William Tell." Thank goodness those William Tells had no children with them on one Adirondack hunting excursion. One of the party saw movement in the bushes near their camp and shot, only to kill the cow the club members "had hired so as to have fresh milk during their stay in camp." Oops.

Feasting was a major part of the club's exercises and with it went all sorts of other hearty exercise, including card playing and singing. One article describes a banquet that was "fit for royalty." In addition to food there was music from "Tidmarsh's Orchestra," and Master of Ceremonies "Charles Thebo and his colleagues...were put to sleep by the superior dexterity of John M. Stoughton's warriors in a series of pool games." As one article defined the banquets, "nothing was left that the inner man might crave or desire, and good fellowship, speeches, song and story followed these royal banquets."

The club had its ups and downs. While the disastrous flood of April 1913 was unable to wash the club away, ironically a July fire that year leveled the original clubhouse. The present clubhouse was built to replace the charred one. Also that year, the club obtained ownership of its lands from George, Walter, and Minnie Mead.

At the end of World War II, the world had changed, as had people's interests. Membership declined, the club ended, and the property was sold in 1947. It was sold again in 1955, this time to the Vagabond drum corps, and once again, in 1962.

The last sale was to the Fort Edward Idle Hour Club, a brand new corporation started in 1962, the year of the club's "second founding."

Now in 2000, it is celebrating the 100th anniversary of the Idle Hour Club's "first founding."

May the festivities and clam bakes "fit for royalty" last for centuries to come, but on their future hunting expeditions, may the club members remember to stay clear of any rented cows.

"OVER MY SHOULDER" COLUMN FOR OCTOBER 14, 2000
Founding fathers weren't always honorable

Did you ever get sick of hearing how wonderful, how perfect and all-wise the older generations were?

It especially happens during campaigns, when the Founding Fathers are rolled out for their "appearance" in American politics. We get a smidgen of Hamilton here and a dab of Jefferson there, with the quotes from their works tailored into fashionable sound bites to give authenticity to whatever leanings the politician has.

We have to be careful not to lead our children into thinking that the "Founding Fathers and Mothers," whether of the nation or our local towns, were temples of perfection.

Here's a case in point. The other day Loretta Bates was leafing through Brayton and Norton's 1929 history of Hartford[lxvii], when she found a story about one of the town's founder's, Col. John Buck that astounded her. It did me as well.

The history rather matter-of-factly presents a bit of oral history concerning one Colonel John Buck, a Revolutionary War hero, who had been at the Battle of Bunker Hill. The Colonel, his wife and child were out in the woods in Hartford in the late 1700s, when suddenly they confronted a bear in the tree. Let me tell you the story, with facts from the book in quotes and with my comments and interpretations following.

The three were riding through the forest on horseback when "his dog treed a bear." Now, to me this says: Danger! Time to put the horse in reverse and step on the oats, so to speak.

But, the authors write: "Leaving his wife to prevent the escape of the bear, the Colonel hastened home to procure his rifle." Yes. Let me get this straight. We're in frontier Hartford, with the woods full of bears and panthers, and the colonel has taken his wife and baby out for a Sunday ride without his gun. Okay, got that. I'm also thinking he may have left his brains in his other hat at home, as well.

The authors continue: "Meanwhile Mrs. Buck had deposited the infant Abigail at the foot of a neighboring tree, so as to be better able to watch the bear." Now from this, we can infer that the baby must have been at best only a few months old, as the mother was not concerned about the child crawling or walking away. But that ignores the larger issue: what in the name of God was this woman thinking about? Her husband, in essence, has said, darling, stay by the tree and make sure the bear doesn't come down and I'll go for my gun. And she, all gooey-eyed with love and her sense of wifely duty, says, okay John, whatever you say, honey.

Hoo-boy.

The authors then go on to state, "The barking of the dog warned Bruin to beat a retreat and he descended from the tree in great haste, so thoroughly frightening Mrs. Buck that she ran away, and on his return the Colonel could find neither wife nor child." I had two immediate reactions to that sentence. My first reaction was that the bear could as likely have scurried down and made hash out of Fido and then out of the Mrs.

My second reaction that the wife had finally done a return to land of the thinking and had grabbed the kid and made a run for it.

But, no, for the authors state: "Having found the alarmed wife, search was made for the child, who was found cozily nestled against the tree…" Wait a minute! She ran off without baby snookums? Lord. So much for motherly instinct.

The authors continue: the baby was "none the worse off for being left alone in the woods." I'm pretty sure the baby wasn't polled for her opinion on that statement.

And the story concludes, "The bear was found in another tree and was duly shot." Somehow my heart goes out to the bear.

The authors make an observation with which I wholeheartedly concur: The story showed "that the…inhabitants were in no great personal danger from wild animals." Absolutely true. The greatest danger in that forest, at least as far as little Abigail and the bear went, came from the colonel and his wife. The couple could be thankful there was no child protection agency in the land at that time.

So, there you have it. A tale of pioneer daring do. Overall, the more I read that anecdote, the more I believe the dog was the strongest character in it.

"OVER MY SHOULDER" COLUMN FOR NOVEMBER 11, 2000
Historical association celebrates long history

This is being written a few days before members and friends of the Fort Edward Historical Association will gather to celebrate the association's 75th anniversary at a dinner held in the facilities of the Fort Hudson Adult Home.

The main speaker of the night will be the Hon. John Austin, Warren County judge, and one of the foremost historians in this area.[lxviii] Awards will be presented, and everyone will reflect upon the fact that an organization that began with the purpose of preserving area history had now accumulated a history of its own.

I was discussing this with Paul McCarty, director of the association's Old Fort House Museum, that John Austin's presence will demonstrate the interweaving connections that generations of people have had with the association, sometimes through family, sometimes not.

Many think of John Austin in connection with Warren County as, for example, a founder of the Glens Falls-Queensbury Historical Association or of the Warren County Historical Society. But his grandfather, Washington County judge Wyman Bascom, was a founding member of the association. Wyman's father was R. O. Bascom, author of an authoritative history of Fort Edward, published in 1903.

Before we consider some other connections, let's look at some basic history. The association came to be through efforts of a group interested in local history. Their focus was upon the 150th anniversary of the Battle of Saratoga, to be held in 1927. The Historical Association would observe the massacre of Jane McCrea.

Dr. Silas Banker led the group. He was the second village historian, and a collector of Fort Edward antiquities that would make up the original collection of the new association and later in 1953, the nucleus of the Old Fort House Museum. The formation of an "Historical Association" took place at a public meeting on November 5, 1925. Banker was elected president; Willard Robinson, 1st vice president; Asa R. Wing, 2nd vice president; Jay Vaughn, 3rd vice president; Robert Savage, treasurer; and Sue E. Wade, secretary. Important names, added to which were the membership committee: Mrs. Monroe Oppenheim, chair; Dorothy Wing; Mrs. Charles Caswell; Mrs. A. P. Hill; and Mrs. Ferdinand (Blanche) Turney.

There are charter members, listed in the 1926 minutes, who have interesting connections to the association's own history as well as to area history at large.

For example, Dorothy Wing would give the Town of Queensbury her family's heirloom, the original 1762 Queensbury patent.

Frank Cronkhite was the association's first lawyer. Much later his son James, as association president in 1992, would lead the capital campaign that has done so much to improve the museum. The Cronkhite Pavilion is named in Jim's memory.

My previous columns covered how in 1940 Susan E. Wade became the first Washington County Historian and creator of the Washington County Historical Society. In 1943 she and William Hill were instrumental in saving the 1772 Smyth house. In 1948, Wade resuscitated the then-dormant Fort Edward Historical association to which the Smyth House was given in 1952. In 1953 it opened as the Old Fort House Museum, with Wade as its first curator.

William Hill, a noted author of local history, was also an association charter member in 1926. In 1952, Hill and another 1926 charter member, Dr. Byron Tillotson, were among the "Founders" of the Old Fort House Museum. And here's one of those wonderful coincidences that make life fun. Another of the museum's Founders in 1952 was also a physician, Dr. Joseph Feingold[lxix]. When he established his practice in Fort Edward, it was in Dr. Silas Banker's former office on East Street.

Two charter members in 1926 were Mr. and Mrs. Edward Blackall. Their daughter Mary Blackall Robson would be a leader in the creation of the 1935 Washington County Historic Resources Survey and later Fort Edward historian.

Here's yet another wonderful coincidence. A 1926 charter member was Alex Hilfinger. Today, the Hilfinger family is represented by descendant R. Paul McCarty, the museum's director.

I've mentioned the museum several times. Interestingly two of the first orders of business had to do with creating a museum. At a 1926 association meeting, Wyman Bascom and State Historian Robert Flick proposed restoring a portion of the original 1755 fortification called "Fort Edward." I think the presence of many homes precluded that.

Soon after, the association proposed creation of a museum and on December 1, 1926, William Hill reported that the State would provide $1,500 for that. The "Brodie Lot" on lower Broadway in the village and "an old block house on the Taylor farm, Moreau" were considered.

It would not come to be. With the Depression's onset the association nearly expired, not to revive until 1948 and take on a new life with the opening of the museum, as I noted above. In the 52 years since 1948 wonderful things have occurred.

Today, Dr. John Matochik fills Banker's role of association president. I think Dr. Banker and the other charter members are looking down to say, "Good job, John. You and the others keep up that good work and we'll check back with you in 2025 for the 100th anniversary."

"OVER MY SHOULDER" COLUMN FOR NOVEMBER 25, 2000
Revisiting Henry Knox's 1775 trek

Two hundred twenty-five years ago, Henry Knox started a mission that would bring him relatively little fame at that time. Subsequent years would diminish even that. In fact, Knox was more often cited later in American histories for being the first Secretary of War. But the importance of his 1775 mission will be alive as long as there is an America.

In November of 1775, George Washington charged Henry Knox to go to Fort Ticonderoga and haul its cannon all the way to Boston. Washington used the cannon to fortify Dorchester Heights against the British, who subsequently evacuated Boston in March of 1776.

If you recall the Bicentennial of 1976 you may well remember the reenactment of Knox's Trek, that began in December 1975. The reenactors started at Fort Ti and went to Boston recreating Knox's winter ordeal.

Knox's original trek was mind-boggling in complexity, as several published histories have helped me understand. One, William L. Bowne's 1975 "Ye Cohorn Caravan," gets into such minute detail that is fascinating for local historians.

To give a bit of background, Knox was a self-made bookstore owner in pre-Revolutionary Boston. Having started as a bookseller's apprentice, he educated himself through reading. He was somewhat of a social climber, starting his rise by joining First Lodge, Boston's upper crust Masonic lodge. Still, he was a rebel at heart and his bookstore became one of many spots where revolutionaries met.

After the British "invasion" of Boston in 1775, Knox actively joined the rebels and helped build entrenchments, a heavy job suited to the tall and muscular Knox. Knox met Washington during this time. Later, through the influence of friends and fellow-Masons such as John Adams or Benedict Arnold, Knox was commissioned an officer, but interestingly, not until he had already started his mission for Washington.

The central issue for 1775 Boston was its lack of heavy armament. Any number of Washington's officers, including Schuyler, Arnold and others, knew of the imposing array of cannon at Fort Ticonderoga. Knox later wrote that he removed 42 cannon of different sizes and 16 mortars and howitzers. How many tons of metal this represents is beyond me, but we'll get to that in a minute.

Washington got the Continental Congress to issue its famous currency to cover the cost of the mission. Starting from Boston around November 15 on orders from Washington, Knox went to New York to see what that province's assembly could offer. He went to New York City and then headed up the Hudson to Fort Ti. As Bowne notes, he was to go "even to Quebec, if Arnold had captured that city by then."

He progressed northward, passing through Albany, Schuylerville (then Saratoga), and arriving at Fort George in today's Lake George Village on December 4, where he conferred briefly with General Schuyler.

Our mental picture of that time is so romantic, we have no idea of the nature of this area and the state of travel back then. Knox wasn't driving an SUV on well-paved roads like I-87, Route 4, or Route 9 to get to Lake George, remember. The area was primeval forest and the roads were rutted trails that to us would look like glorified hiking trails or logging roads.

And then those cannon! By the time he reached Lake George, he had already assessed the size of the cargo he and his fellow haulers would have. One large cannon alone could weigh a ton! And they didn't have a Mayflower van or a Fed Ex truck to roll up and take it away. Instead, Knox hired oxen and sleds. Unlike us, Knox would have prayed for snow on his highways, in order to slide, rather than drag through ruts and mud, those massive cannon to Boston.

Now you have the picture: rotten roads, tons of cannon, only oxen-power for hauling, and it's winter. I now understand why histories describe Knox as an optimist.

Next week, we we'll look at the trek itself.

"OVER MY SHOULDER" COLUMN FOR DECEMBER 2, 2000
Knox trek highlights region's role in history

In only months, large-framed Boston bookseller Henry Knox had gone from entrenchment-digger, helping fortify a 1775 Boston besieged by British, to commissioned colonel sent by Washington to find artillery for Boston's defense.

Washington said, if necessary, go to Canada to find cannon. But Knox needed only go as far as Fort Ticonderoga, where he arrived December 5, 1775. By January 24, 1776, Knox would deliver Fort Ti's cannon to Cambridge, Massachusetts – 300 miles of traveling wretched roads, fording raging rivers, and all in the middle of winter.

Interestingly, of the 60 granite historical markers installed by New York and Massachusetts in the late 1920s along Knox's route, four are in Ticonderoga. The first is at Fort Ticonderoga's Place d'Armes. Fort Ti Director Nick Westbrook has written that when Knox arrived at Ticonderoga on 5 December, he "immediately selected the best cannon for Washington: 43 cannon, 2 howitzers, and 14 mortars. Knox calculated that these 59 guns, including 13" mortars and brass and iron 18- and 24-pounders, would weigh almost 60 tons."

Knox would encounter three adversities all along his route: weight, weather, and people.

His first "labor of Hercules" was moving 60 tons of cannon 3 miles from Fort Ti up to a landing on Lake George. I mean "up." From the fort, Knox got the cannon by boat to the Lower Falls in the village of Ticonderoga, along the

LaChute River, which is 96 feet above sea level, Lake Champlain's level. There the cannon were transferred to sleds. Knox spent 26 dollars to hire a teamster with sled and oxen to haul the cannon uphill to Lake George, 325 feet above sea level.

A granite marker notes that Knox loaded "the scow, Pettianger, and a Battoe" at Lake George's Mossey Point on December 9. But William Bowne, in "Ye Cohorn Caravan," estimates it occurred where the lake narrows into the LaChute River, "between the intersection of Water Street and The Portage, and the lower end of Water Street."

Knox's crew broke ice for a mile to make a channel into open water. They sailed south, the winds whipping against all 60 tons. Near Sabbath Day Point one ship sank. Exhausted from rescue operations, they camped overnight, doing so again by either Shelving Rock or Tongue Mountain, before reaching Fort George on December 17.

Money plays into the Knox saga. Bowne suggests Knox was too loose with the purse around those too ready to overcharge. Knox's payment of 26 dollars was extraordinary, possibly equaling one person's yearly income.

Then Knox ordered 42 sleds from a Schuylerville man named Palmer. They were to go to Fort George. General Schuyler found Palmer's price far too high and told Knox to hold off. Knox had trusted Palmer too much, perhaps because he was a fellow Mason. But Palmer was gouging. He even showed a darker side in a letter that intimated a threat to the safety of the expedition. Palmer was fired.

Knox did have sleds built and hired 124 pair of oxen and horses. They hauled the cannon from Lake George though today's Queensbury, Kingsbury, Hudson Falls, Fort Edward, Fort Miller, and Greenwich. Around Thomson they crossed to Northumberland down through Schuylerville and south. They crossed the Hudson four times in all, falling through the ice once, forcing them to backtrack and cross the Mohawk.

However, Knox brought most of that sixty tons of Fort Ti cannon through. On March 4, the eve of the sixth anniversary of the Boston Massacre, it was placed on Dorchester Heights overlooking British lines. The British departed March 17.

I'll close my history of Knox's expedition with these thoughts. Isn't it interesting that so much of the American Revolution's success traces to this region between Fort Ticonderoga and the Saratoga National Historical Park?

Wouldn't it be fascinating to see what could happen if the same money the US now puts into rescuing other countries' economies were invested in promoting this region's heritage?

In promoting the very land where the US was born?

SECTION 3: PERSONAL AND FAMILY MEMORIES

"OVER MY SHOULDER" COLUMN FOR FEBRUARY 8, 1998
Sweet sales pitch of George A.

Valentine's Day sparks unique memories to anyone having worked in a pharmacy, but this one is peculiar to me and the small band of people who, at some time in their lives, worked with my father, George A. King.

In pharmacies that sold candy – and I mean fancy boxed candy, produced by Whitman's, Russell Stover, or Fanny Farmer, for example – Valentine's Day could be a BIG day, because of which one small pharmacy could literally sell thousands of dollars of candy. At least, a pharmacy that had George A. King.

Our family firmly understood that as a pharmacist, George A., (as we'd refer to him when not in his presence), had three major attributes. First, he had a computer for a memory, recalling medications you'd taken in infancy, a plus if you were about to take a drug that could kill you. Second, he could diagnose with the best of them, and we agreed he should have become a physician, as he had intended.

Third, Dad could sell ice to Eskimos – sand to Egyptians, etc., etc. He was a phenomenon, due in part to his native gift, an art for selling, and in part for honing that art like a knife. Developed over the years, it was razor sharp because of his secret weapon: Guilt.

Valentine's Day was a big leagues sales day and Dad was the pitcher. He'd start his warm-up on his kids. Shaving in the morning, he'd leave the bathroom door strategically ajar to catch us passing. "Get your mother something for Valentine's Day?" he'd ask, a combination of paternal concern and slight sternness in his tone. (In other words, guilt.) As I aged, I watched this at work in the store.

Incidentally, a card did not count. "Something" meant "candy," like the massive ten-pound Whitman sampler he got Mom. How she, and my father, loved those samplers! There, too, was a key to his selling. He loved his product.

He had two approaches, "subtle" and "atomic bomb." In Fort Edward I watched the subtle approach perfected. During this, he could be, say, ringing up a prescription for "Ed" and, while looking down in the change drawer, he'd whisper, supposedly confidentially, but so everyone could hear: "Get your wife something for Valentine's Day?" Guiltily, Ed would gasp and frantically grab a strategically placed box (huge, of course) with a "Thanks, George!" I stood in awe.

At Burleigh Pharmacy in Ti, while he used both approaches, he mastered "the atomic bomb." Just as you entered the store, there'd be this huge display of boxed candy wrapped in cellophane, some with price tags that defined "sticker shock." As people entered, George A. would magically appear, smile, and personally address each one, especially men, VERY LOUDLY, for the benefit of everyone at the counter. This was baseball. Dad was pitching guilt.

Here's an encounter I actually saw. "Teddy" had just come in. On the mound, George A. with the wind up: "Hey, Teddy!" "Get SOMETHING for your wife?" All eyes shot to Teddy, who started to say, "Now, come on, George..." then, feeling the stabbing glances, guiltily shook his head no. Silence now hung in the store. Grasping, Teddy offered weakly, "A card?"

Now the pitch: with a smile of pity, Dad did his "one-two," shaking his head with paternal concern and saying, with slight sternness in his tone, "Can I wrap you up one of these?" Ashamed, Teddy took it.

STEEE-rike! A twenty dollar sale of a giant sampler was concluded. Everyone cheered. Except Teddy.

So, let me to wish all of you a Happy Valentine's Day and ask just this one thing in memory of George A.: did you remember to "get something"?

"OVER MY SHOULDER" COLUMN FOR JUNE 7, 1998
A baby and a circus

Ringling Bros. Barnum and Bailey Circus doesn't play Glens Falls anymore, but when it did come to town in the spring of 1981, it played a role in my memories of a most special time.

As it was, that year my wife, Sara, and I did not go to the circus as we usually did. Instead, we were spending our first wedding anniversary, May 31, in the Glens Falls Hospital, waiting for our baby to arrive.

We knew it was not going to be an "ordinary" birth. Sara's blood pressure had skyrocketed, and the doctor had (finally) gotten his way and hospitalized her. The due day, then several more days, came and went. This baby was staying put. Being the typically useless father-to-be, I didn't help by mentioning that we (note the "we") were ready, having done our Lamaze training. I got a blast from the patient.

Missing the circus heightened her anxiety. Normally not an issue for Sara, in the context of birth and blood pressure it had become one. Adding to that was that our friend, Bob[lxx], was in the hospital with a coronary. Bob, coincidentally, was a circus freak and frantic about missing the circus, as it meant missing his yearly reunion with friends, performers with Ringling Brothers.

My uselessness was redeemed when I was asked to go to the circus highwire artist to let him know what was happening. With mother-to-be and Bob happy, I shot down to the Civic Center and sat in the artist's quarters discussing the conditions of Bob, and my wife, as the artist graciously autographed posters of himself in thanks for my mission. I thought to myself, "This is as close as we'll get to the circus this year." Silly notion.

The doctor advised a cesarean and on the morning of June 4, I waited with

Sara's mom[lxxi] while Sara gave birth to a healthy baby girl, Julia Cornelia. The nurse wheeled Julia out and I thought, "My God, what have we done?" (Thankfully, in post-op, I had the sense not to say that to my wife.) Then a little later, while rocking our baby to sleep, my question was beautifully answered.

That would have been the ending of the story, except for the circus. My mother[lxxii] had broken all land speed records coming down that day from Ticonderoga. The next day, both she and Dad[lxxiii] came to the hospital. Later they offered to take me to supper at the Queensbury Hotel, where they were spending the night. Supper led to a trip to the Queensbury's bar, where dad convinced me to have a Manhattan, his drink of choice.

The evening blurred, accentuated by the raucous talk and laughter of the entertainers from the circus coming in for a post-performance toddy. The bartender set a drink in front of me and I heard a voice behind me ask, "Could you hand me my drink?"

I looked around, saw no one and turned away, when I heard again, "Could you hand me my drink?" I felt a tug on my belt. I turned, this time looking down – into the face of a Ringling Brothers' little person, one of the ones who climbs out of the tiny car. "My drink, PLEASE?" I handed it down with apologies. Everyone roared. The rest of the evening was insane.

Among my cherished photos is one Sara took of me the next day, asleep in a hospital chair next to Julia in her bassinet. It will always remind me of our first anniversary, Julia's birth and little people.

Happy anniversary, Sara. Happy birthday, Julia. And thanks. For every day has been a "circus day" since that time in 1981 when Ringling Brothers came to town.

"OVER MY SHOULDER" COLUMN FOR JUNE 14, 1998
Memories of Bobby Kennedy

This is being written on the 30th anniversary of the death of Bobby Kennedy, June 6, 1968.

In the early hours of June 6, I had heard the news of his death at my dormitory at Fordham College in the Bronx. I was a senior, only two days from my graduation.

That spring of 1968 was a bizarre ending to a bizarre senior year. The '67 "summer of love" had faded, with many classmates "tuning in" and "turning on" and more than a few "dropping out" to live in communes, join carnivals, or disappear. Those who stayed split into three camps: conservatives, liberals, and those who wanted last summer to go on forever. Hair grew longer. The smell of "burning hemp" flavored the non-stop music from "Hair," Motown, "Sgt. Peppers" and Dylan. Anti-war protests, more common at other city campuses, became more so at traditionally conservative Fordham, especially in late fall after President Lyndon Johnson suspended all graduate deferments from the draft. As a class, we waited for our 1-A draft cards to arrive.

That crazy Spring of 1968 really began with President Johnson taking himself out of the presidential race on March 31st, and with the assassination of Martin Luther King on April 4th. It seemed impossible that after President Kennedy there could be another assassination. But now there was King, whose presence and greatness was solidified for us by television and whose day of death I recall so vividly because it was also my father's birthday.

Now more race riots broke out. Anti-war rallies kept increasing in number. In Paris students marched with laborers and rioted in the streets. In Czechoslovakia, the Prague Spring began, a gentle revolution against the Soviets. What little tolerance I had for the far left disappeared in my arguing about Prague with an acquaintance in the SDS,[lxxiv] who always name-dropped ad nauseam about "being with Che."[lxxv] When he argued that the Soviets needed to invade Prague to preserve the worker state, I realized my SDS friend was like every other fanatic, willing to kill me for his beliefs.

And into all of this rode Bobby Kennedy. Despite Fordham's being Roman Catholic, students had jeered Kennedy as a "carpetbagger" in 1965, because he had moved from Massachusetts to challenge Senator Keating. Now to supporters of presidential hopeful Eugene McCarthy, Kennedy was again the spoiler. Others, myself especially, felt more simply that he was just in it for the politics.

Yet he had his supporters and, that night of June 5, they cheered the news of his California primary victory. People, even those of us who would not admit it, liked Bobby because he had that "Kennedy something" that so appealed to us (to me), whether we (I) wanted to yield to it or not. It spoke to our hearts. To my heart. It does now.

That night of June 5, actually early morning of June 6, we had returned from the senior ball. I think it was that. Funny I can't recall. What I so vividly remember is that my roommate rushed up to me and said that Bobby Kennedy had been killed. Certainly, other emotions fed it, but the overwhelming grief at a third assassination overtook me. I put my head in my hands and cried.

On June 8th, my parents and my grandmother came to my graduation ceremony. It was incredibly hot and incredibly sad, as we sat through a solemn high mass and a ceremony edged with black, tears of grief running down the cheeks of graduates and families alike.

You see, our commencement speaker was to have been Bobby Kennedy, who would speak to us of dreams and hope. Instead, we received our diplomas amidst eulogies and anger.

"OVER MY SHOULDER" COLUMN FOR AUGUST 2, 1998
Cruising your way through summer

There is a serious lack of study on cultural history, such as the way people acted out their passage through adolescence into adulthood. A good example of cultural history, almost a "ritual," that was popular when I was a kid and is still being played out on the main streets of America, is "cruising."

Although "cruising" has other meanings now, I refer specifically to the custom of getting in a car and cruising up and down a main street, parading oneself like a preening chicken or rooster. Notice I referred to chicken or rooster. That is, female or male. Then, as now, cruising belonged to both genders, although more males had access to cars when I was a kid, so you saw more guys cruising.

For those of you who spent your childhood at a mall and need an example of cruising, the movie "American Graffiti," set in a small American town in the early 1960s, is a perfect one of this seemingly mindless waste of gas. Locally, and in the present, a summer night in Lake George Village is another, because it's small, doesn't have a mall where people can "foot cruise," and in the summer when you're out looking to look and looking to be seen, Lake George was and is the place to be.

Of course, when I was younger getting to Lake George from Fort Edward was hard and when we moved to Ticonderoga almost impossible. So, we cruised up and down the streets of Ti.

Well, I didn't as often as I wanted to, because I didn't have access to a car. So I was one of those guys who would try to bum a ride, often left to be a "sidewalk person," walking along the street, watching enviously as the cars rode by, but pretending that it didn't matter. Unless offered a ride, at which time I would nearly break my neck getting into the car.

There was a certain set of unwritten rules then that probably hold true today. First of all, cruising was to be seen by grownups as what I called before a "seemingly mindless waste of gas," while seen by their young as essential for mating. To enhance that notion, cruising was usually only best when done at night, when darkness offered an excuse for anything.

There were rules governing the people in the cars and on the sidewalk. Car rules predominate. A very big rule was that if you were in a hardtop, then really there were only two seats that were cool: the driver's (of course) and the front right seat, the "shotgun" seat. A driver could cruise alone, but it made the driver seem too much a loner, and the fun of being seen is being seen with someone equally as cool as yourself.

Sitting in the middle of the front was okay, but awkward. In that seat it's impossible to assume that position of casual authority given to the driver and the shotgun, who rest one arm out of the window, tapping a finger in time to the music, suavely disposing of a cigarette ash (except in front of their parents' home or place of business), or hitting the side of the door in a booming noise to attract attention.

Being in the middle, a person could be nearly be decapitated by the rear view mirror if the driver suddenly jammed on the brakes to invite a member of the opposite sex for a ride. However, the middle could control the music choice and volume, critical for the proper atmosphere, and could provide humor, a topic I'll get to next week.

In next week's column, the conclusion of our "study" on this important American institution. Be prepared for a pop quiz.

"OVER MY SHOULDER" COLUMN FOR AUGUST 9, 1998
A cool dude's guide to cruising

We conclude last week's study of an American cultural ritual, "cruising" – the custom of getting in a car and cruising up and down a main street, parading oneself like a preening chicken or rooster.

Continuing the rules regarding cruising, a big one concerned those riding in the front seat of hardtops and their maintaining their "cool": constant and unbridled whistling, hooting, hollering and making of rude noises was definitely uncool. It could result in the car's occupants receiving jeers, insults and equally rude remarks from the sidewalk, even having sidewalk people of the opposite sex turning their backs to the car. (About the only "sidewalk rule.")

The last was not to be mistaken for the sidewalk person of the opposite sex's pretended "turning the back to the car," in which one eye of the sidewalk person is strategically revealed to be watching the car intensely.

Another standard rule, that no one and everyone accepted, was: riding in the back seat of a hardtop was not cool. There's no simpler way to put it. Here you were, in your mid-teens, still looking very childlike, with the seats just about swallowing most of you, so that the effect to the sidewalk people was that of seeing a small face desperately peering out from the back. Definitely not cool.

Everyone accepted that rule if they were walking on the sidewalk but did not if they were riding in the back seat of a hardtop. The back seat was preferable to the sidewalk.

But if riding in a convertible, which necessitated summer-like weather of course, then every seat was equally cool. A convertible was Mt. Olympus on wheels. You could even incessantly make dumb faces and catcalls and the sidewalk people accepted you as a god. Or so you thought.

Where did one cruise? Larger place like downtown Glens Falls offered a whole range of opportunities. True resort villages, such as Lake George Village, did as well: Canada Street, Beach Road, Shore Drive. Choice cruising.

In any other place the size of Ticonderoga, it was the main street alone, which in Ti was Montcalm Street. Regardless of the town's size, side streets were solely meant for turning around or stopping to alter seat placement – who sat where – an issue even settled with some pushing and shoving, and sometimes though rarely a punch. No blood was allowed, as it could get on the car seats.

Last week I had mentioned humor. Humorous cruising could include the eye-catching effect of "mambo-ing" a car, alternately gunning then braking, so the car jerked forward. The tedium of stopping at a red-light could be relieved by the fire drill, in which the car was put in neutral, everyone got out, ran around the car and got back in by the green light. Or stalled long enough to make the car in back of you miss the green light. (Uproarious laughter would ensue.)

A teenage driver adept at humor could provide, for adults, heart-stopping pranks, which to the teenagers in the car and on the sidewalk were hysterically humorous. My friends Cy, Dick, and Noel (sorry, no last names) would drive down Montcalm Street in the front seat, Cy at the wheel with either Noel or Dick strategically placed in the middle. The middle rider would actually steer the car and control the gas, while Cy hung out of the driver's side, pretending to fix something on the door. Oncoming adults would practically drive up on the sidewalk. Uproarious laughter would ensue.

We're out of space and never even got to cover topics like rude gestures or going on to the "submarine races." Perhaps in a future column. In the meantime, it's summertime. So, happy cruising!

"OVER MY SHOULDER" COLUMN FOR AUGUST 30, 1998
All the marbles

The fine art of playing marbles is, sadly, losing ground.

My friend Florence McIlvaine wrote recently, and in passing mentioned the marble tournaments held during the 1930s at the various playgrounds in Glens Falls. She wondered if kids played marbles[lxxvi] anymore.

I assume so, as I still see marbles for sale now. But the passion with which the little hunks of glass were shot around the play-yard at school is a thing of yesterday.

The same is true for Jacks, although I didn't get into jacks. I'm the "can't chew gum and walk at the same time" kind of game player. Bouncing a rubber ball so perfectly that it remained suspended in mid-air over a circle, while grabbing a fistful of jacks out of that circle? Simply not my forte.

We played marbles at grade school, and even up into junior high, by which time the hormones were kicking in and marbles inexplicably lost their allure.

I recall the end of summer as being a freight train ride in which the slow moving freight of mid-summer suddenly picked up speed in the last days before school, hurling one at sickening speed toward the inevitable post-Labor Day torture. (This sense of speed was spurred on by Mother's frantic, and all-too-gleeful, store-to-store dash for school clothes and tablets of paper, the smell of which only in late August stills triggers a peculiar nausea.)

The last few swims at the beach only heightened the awareness that summer was over. Marbles were the transitional medicine. They were played all summer long, but as Fall approached the competitive intensity increased and was transferred to the schoolyard. Before the bell rang in the morning, during recess, and then after school, marbles were played with fervor, expertise and the cut-throat competition seen only on Wall Street.

You could buy a bag of marbles. Often had to, as losing was a part of the game. But to carry in a bag of marbles that had been won was to walk with a slight swagger, the bag budging with booty of others' defeats. Slowly the "booty" marbles, scraped and dulled from previous games, would be taken from the little drawstring bag. Those whetted the appetites of the others, greedy to fill their bags.

We played by digging a small hole. Later I learned that others played marbles by shooting into a circle drawn into the dirt or chalked upon a sidewalk. And let's get the terminology right. We called them "marbles" in general, usually referring to the smaller marbles as "alleys" or "aggies" and the big ones as "shooters."

"Alleys" got their name from abbreviating the word "alabaster," a white gypsum used in making statues that looked like sculpted marble. They were only surpassed in quality by "aggies," short for "agates," made from agate stone.

By the mid-20th century, we only played with cats eyes: clear glass marbles with stripes running through it, resembling cats eyes. Squatting or kneeling we held the shooter in our cupped index finger and shot it out with our thumb, attempting to knock alleys sitting on the edge into the hole.

The game taught us life's lessons: how to win (grab the marbles and say "nah, nah-nah, NAH nah!") and how to lose (say, "You lousy cheat!"). Also, the hand-to-eye dexterity we developed would prove priceless in later life when learning how to play pool.

I'm kidding. Well, half-kidding. Overall, it was a good healthy game and I'll match the physical dexterity I developed playing marbles against that developed by a person playing a computer game any day.

Just let me dig out my bag of alleys. I'll show ya!

"OVER MY SHOULDER" COLUMN FOR OCTOBER 18, 1998
Leopard Girl finally sees the candy light

Halloween's delights come again in adulthood in watching the fun a child can have.

In the early 1980s, my family was living on Harrison Avenue in Glens Falls. In our neighborhood the tradition was still to trick'r'treat from house to house. A visit to the mall was possible, but not the expected event that it is now. Possibly, the class of 1999 may be the last never to have thought of the mall as "the place" to trick'r'treat.

My daughter, Julia, was three and a half when the idea of what Halloween could yield struck home. My wife, Sara, ever the creator, had labored each year over elaborate costumes and our daughter was, successively, a bumblebee, a chicken, a clown, and now a leopard.

The costumes, frankly, had more meaning for Sara and me, as Julia had developed early as, what I would call, a "self-costumer." At one point in her career as self-costumer, she came to look like a bag-lady on a Manhattan subway. But that was a ways off.

For the moment, Halloween was here, and the girl leopard was being readied for the candy chase, the door-to-door trek for treats. But there was a basic problem. She had no concept of what it meant to receive this candy. I mean, these fundamentals of trick'r'treating had eluded her: take bag, go to door, knock, say "trick'r'treat" and receive candy. Oh, and say "thank you."

The year before, the "clown costume year," this had become all too apparent. Bringing her to a home, we'd walk her to the door, then stand on the sidewalk and wait while she was supposed to knock. Instead, she faced us. "Turn around and knock, honey." She'd go and knock, then come back to the top stop and stand with her back to the door, looking at us.

I think she got some candy, but the whole mechanics of it seemed, as I said, to elude her. Now in the year of the leopard, it was only worsening. How had I – trick'r'treater extraordinaire whose mother lodes of candy were still sung about in the hills – how had I failed her? You see, now at three and a half, she didn't even want to go out. She just wanted to stand at our door and give out candy.

Ye gads. We'd go next door to Grandma Cutshall's or across the street to the Griffins, and she'd plaintively ask, "Can we go home now?" Somehow the whole notion was escaping her, and I did not know what to say to tell her that all she had to do to get candy was to ask. So, home we'd go, where she'd gleefully race to the door and dispense goodies.

Somewhere during the evening, something, I'll never know what, struck her. She had just put candy into a bulging bag, when she stopped and looked hard at us. In about three seconds of rapid fire talk, she asked where all that candy came from and we said, "from trick'r'treating."

A light, a roaring fire of bright recognition, came into her eyes and she was out the door and running down the street, her leopard tail flying in breeze, father in hot pursuit. Together we arrived to the Charlebois' home, waylaid only by a cat accosting her tail. She stood eagerly at the door, saying "Trick'r'treat," then "Thank you" as the cat energetically munched on her tail.

We then covered the whole neighborhood, believe me. And I was ill for days from eating so much candy. Although I am happy to report that her delight in giving candy never disappeared and for years she was torn between the giving and the getting.

Which is, fundamentally, what life is about, isn't it? Happy Halloween.

"OVER MY SHOULDER" COLUMN FOR NOVEMBER 29, 1998
Sounds served as bookends for 1938

The recent *Post-Star* headline read "Crime down; Murder rate at 30 year low."

Could that be? Could it be that in the year that I graduated, the murder rate was as bad as now? I refused to believe it.

But thinking back to 1968, I recall my parents' lamenting the crime rate then. "Things were better in 1938," they'd say, "in spite of the Depression." And I would shoot back that as far as crime, maybe. There probably weren't enough wealthy people to rob and kill.

One thing we did both agree upon, 1938 foretold the future. The year had some absolutely wonderful and absolutely horrible aspects to it. On the wonderful side, swing, the music of Ellington, Goodman, Basie and all, had by 1938 come into its fullest bloom. The Benny Goodman Orchestra, the first major integrated swing band, made musical history at Carnegie Hall in February 1938. Even on a scratchy 78 RPM, the power of that night still makes your feet jump. From 1936 to 1946, the Big Bands would be the "soundtrack" for the end of the Depression and "The War," as World War II was always called by my parents.

There was horrendous turbulence in 1938. While things were financially better than in 1933, the depths of the Depression, locally unemployment was still high. Factories were open three or four days a week, most with one shift, not two or three. My father's stepfather, a fireman on the B&M Railroad, earned 16 dollars a week, and that was only if he did round-trips. Coal trains had shotgun-bearing guards to keep people from stealing. People would scavenge along the tracks to pick up the fallen pieces of coal. The number of hobos living along those tracks in this area was greater than in 1933.

In 1938, unions fought, literally fought, around the country to become established in major industry. Vilified, called communists and heaven knows what else, that year they made a beachhead for the rights of organized labor.

"The mob" was flourishing and the papers were filled with mob-related violence. It just didn't happen in "nice neighborhoods." Interestingly, I have never met anyone of my parents' age who didn't know someone who was "connected" with the mob.

Discontent was rampant. As I wrote last week, World War I veterans were still dissatisfied with the government's treatment of them. Moreover, veterans groups decried the long period of low funding for the defense budget that they felt had left the country unprepared. They were totally ignored by most of Congress.

Yet, if my copies of *The Post-Star*, *Glens Falls Times* and *New York Times* from

1938-1940 are any indication of public sentiment, the public was preparing for war, while most conservative politicians were isolationists. Newspapers deplored Hitler's advances in Austria and Czechoslovakia in 1938. In that year their language began to reflect the public itch to get back "over there" to finish what veterans started in World War I. Despite isolationist politics, newspapers from 1938 on covered events in Europe and Asia as if they expected war. It is no coincidence that the selective service system was instituted in 1940.

Still, few here had a glimmer of the real meaning behind one of 1938's most horrible events: the Nazi rampage against the Jews in November in which tens of thousands of synagogues, shops, and homes were destroyed. Our newspapers reported the tons of shattered glass that produced the euphemism "Kristallnacht." But no one could really understand it for what it was: a massive, very visible prelude on the road to the Holocaust.[lxxvii]

A year to remember, 1938, that started with joyous music and ended with the sound of shattering glass.

"OVER MY SHOULDER" COLUMN FOR DECEMBER 13, 1998
Strike up the band for a lesson in tolerance

After my graduation, a friend offered me a job in his family's brokerage house in the Wall Street area of Manhattan. I was "out in the world" now. December arrived and I realized that this would be my first holiday not spent with my family. I did not know it was also to prove for me a lesson in religious tolerance.

Our office, on the 17th floor of a building now demolished, had as many variations of people as the building had floors, a marvelous racial, ethnic, and religious mix. There were a variety of Christians, Protestants and Roman Catholics, and a variety of Jews, Orthodox, Conservative and Reform. Some practiced their faiths, some did not. There were also agnostics and atheists.

My gentile upbringing had left me totally ignorant of Judaism, notwithstanding my early childhood next door to the Caplans in Saratoga and playing with the Rosenberg boys in Fort Edward. My experiences in this brokerage house would be the beginning of my enlightenment.

Ironically, the firm's owner, Joe[lxxviii], a brilliant Italian-American, was a former Roman Catholic who viewed all religion with, at best, bemused skepticism. An agnostic or an atheist? Who knew? But I say ironically, because he celebrated every religious holiday observed in the office. The feast of St. Joseph? "Go up to little Italy and get the special cannolis." Passover? "Matzo brei for all."

The staff was about a third Jewish, among them Vic, the office manager; Eddy, a bookkeeper, Suzie, a cashier; and Max, a runner (a delivery person). Suzie, of Sephardic descent, taught me not only about Judaism, but of how limited my life had been in never having been a "minority" – which, in this city, she wasn't.

Max, a retired pharmacist, was a "Conservative" Jew. How Conservative? So much so in his religious observances, that one Sabbath (Friday) eve this elderly man had come within a hair of walking 10 miles home to the Bronx, because he almost did not get out of the office on time. His beliefs, I learned, would not have permitted him to ride in a train or car after sundown.

But the December office party for Christmas and Chanukah was my real awakening. Vic had asked Eddy to get a band for the office party and Eddy had called his cousin in Queens. The cousin arrived with the band...and a problem. The band only played for Jewish ceremonies, weddings, bar mitzvahs, and the like. They did not know one Christmas song.

I can remember Vic saying plaintively, "Eddy, they don't even know `Jingle Bells'?" To which Eddy replied, huffing through clenched teeth as he always did, "Hey, shoot me!" Their relationship filled books on office psychology.

Still, it went well as a party. We danced and drank to current rock tunes and sang along with Hava Nagila. But it did need a touch of "mistletoe and holly." Or even "Jingle Bells."

Some of us were standing in the front office when strains of "I'm Dreaming of a White Christmas" came wafting out. Puzzled, we went into the back office. There was Max and his wife, both devoutly Conservative Jews remember, leading the band.

Everybody sang, and I recall Vic even smiled at Eddy, as Max and his wife taught the band a dozen Christmas songs at least. But more importantly, they taught me a lesson of the breadth and depth of religious tolerance necessary to make our country work. I shall always remember the beautiful voice of Max's wife, raised in perfect tune, as she led the band in "Silent Night."

Unexpectedly, Joe sent me home on the train to spend the holidays with my family. And I took with me his gift – the one I had learned at the office party.

Happy Chanukah and Shalom.

"OVER MY SHOULDER" COLUMN FOR DECEMBER 20, 1998
A very special Santa

My mother had a little ornament that she placed on the Christmas tree each year, a tiny cotton Santa that she said she had placed on her tree from the time she was a little girl. The little Santa was, truthfully, in sad shape for its years of wear. But it was one of "those things," something given a special meaning when my mother was so little. Why, no one knew. Not even Mom.

As I grew older, with each Christmas I came to look forward to that Santa being placed gently on a high bough, nestled securely to prevent shrieking children, or cats, from knocking it to the floor. Without realizing it, a part of her childhood Christmases gradually became a part of her children's. It was a good feeling.

The tiny Santa moved a lot over the years. From my mother's birthplace in Mechanicville, it went to Saratoga, then to Fort Edward and then Ticonderoga, at each juncture adding children and years to its life. It sagged and it drooped and it faded. Yet it survived, tying each new Christmas into the ones that had passed.

The last time my mother put the Santa on her tree was in Ticonderoga in 1982. Shortly thereafter, she was diagnosed with cancer and on her next Christmas, which was to be her last, she decided she and my father would come to our homes instead. I remember her apology for not having a tree, which I later recognized as her way of saying, "I'm angry because I can't put up a tree, like I should."

So that year, 1983, for the first time in decades, the little Santa stayed in a box in my parents' cellar. At Christmas, 1984, my mother was gone and, again, the little cotton Santa stayed packed away. For that Christmas and the next two, my father would not decorate the house nor have a tree. The Christmas person in the King family was Mom and the Christmas person was gone.

About two and a half years after my mother died, Dad told us he was selling our family home in Ticonderoga. It was too big and too full of memories. "Come and take what you want," he told his children. The rest he would sell. For weeks upon weeks we helped him sort through the remains of a lifetime, as much a reward as a burden. For you must understand that Mom saved everything: family pictures and letters, dad's service records, the kids' report cards, canceled checks, even occupant mail. As I had before, I looked through acres of boxes of Christmas decorations. As before, I could not, amidst them all, find the tiny Santa.

Mom always was fond of saying, "What will be will be." I resigned myself to the fact that it was gone. "Things change," my father was always saying. Oddly, I think that while he knew that was true, in a way he never resigned himself to his own wisdom. Almost three years to the day after my mother's death, he died. Things had, indeed, changed.

For my wife, Sara, and I, that Christmas of 1987 in Glens Falls was, with my daughter being six, filled with expectations of Santa. It was also an oddly empty Christmas. We got out the boxes of decorations and frantically searched for our tree's special angel, fearful it had been misplaced and then found it packed snugly away. My daughter sighed a big sigh! Under our regular boxes were the ones I'd brought from Ticonderoga. I rummaged through them, looking at the bubble lights and other things from my childhood Christmas trees.

And then, I found it. A tiny box inside of which was my mother's faded cotton Santa wrapped up securely. Lost, but never really lost. Tenderly, I placed it on a high bough. And there it will go again this year, as we celebrate our Christmas and the memories that a special decoration carry with it.

From my family to you, a very merry Christmas.

"OVER MY SHOULDER" COLUMN FOR DECEMBER 27, 1998
New Year's Eve dance will spin on forever

For bacchanalian New Year's revelry no generation holds a candle to that of my parents, the "Kennedy generation," who grew up in the Depression and World War II.

I take you to New Year's eve in the mid-1960s — definitely not an era of standing at the bar with a white wine or seltzer while discussing working out or taking vitamins. The Kennedy generation was a crew that drank hard liquor like mother's milk and beer like chaser. Their New Year's celebrations were done in a way that made you think that they alone knew the secret that the world was ending the next day.

I've seen New Year's eve celebrations in large cities and small towns. Nothing, not even Mount Vesuvius, ever matched a North Country New Year's eve at that time. On a mid-1960s New Year's eve in Ticonderoga, you could literally feel the pulse of the night in the air. Every place was jammed with people. In homes were private parties, which everybody crashed, in between cruising from bar to bar, every one of which was absolutely jammed. And the fraternal organizations, such as the Elks Club or the Knights of Columbus, for example, were booked way in advance. They offered a combination of food, band and inexpensive booze. Oh my.

The bands that played on those nights in the mid-1960s, whether in the bars or fraternal organizations, were primarily those of my parents' generation. Take a place called "The Tavern," for example. There you'd expect to hear the bunny hop and Glenn Miller favorites. Their rock band was considered inconsequential by the forty-somethings, desperately clinging to the romance of their youth. We all do after forty.

Getting in was a challenge. The parking lot was jammed, and many car windows were already steamed up. You were careful about not appearing to look into any car.

You walked a few steps up into the Tavern. It took forever, huge lines of people oozing in and out of the main door, grunting, pushing, shoving. As you finally stepped in, by the horseshoe-shaped bar, the blast of laughing, shouting, singing, drinking people and the smog wall of cigarette smoke hit you before any music did. You shoved your way to the bar — barely able to see anything and suddenly roasting from the body heat of hundreds of people crushed into a space meant for far fewer — as Art Potter and his band played "Pennsylvania 6-5000," to which the dancers on the dance floor shouted the words.

There was a dark phone booth and a couple, to get privacy to neck, closed the door, forgetting in their passion that the light went on when you closed it. Everybody cheered, but nobody got to use the phone.

Meanwhile on the bandstand Marion stood up, belting out "Birth of the Blues," as she did twice a year, once after the bowling banquet and now. The band backed her with a racy, almost burlesque-style, rendition. The crowd went berserk. People on the dance floor fell over onto tables, drinks got poured down open neck dresses and three fights broke out simultaneously. Total success.

And there, amidst the kissing, screaming and turmoil, out on the dance floor and oblivious to all but the music, are my parents, having their little "warm up drink and dance" before heading to the Knights of Columbus hall. I see them, jitterbugging to "One O'clock Jump," Jane's eyes closed as she swirls, George, ever the hepcat, his face serene, his index finger swirling in the air to the music, and the words "Hubba hubba" forming on his lips.

The night is forever young, and they are again just newlywed on December 28, 1942, facing the world and war. Happy New Year, forever, George and Jane.

"OVER MY SHOULDER" COLUMN FOR MAY 29, 1999
The gradual transformation from a child to an adult

Let me tell you a story, my daughter, of all the children we've had, although your mother Sara and I have only had one.

I'll only tell you about some, for there have been eighteen, all girls. The first little girl came to our home on June 4th of 1981. She came at the same time the circus arrived in Glens Falls, definitely an omen of things to come.

She seemed so very little to me, as I rocked her in the hospital room, wondering what in heaven's name Sara and I had done. A nurse came by to say, quite seriously, that if I rocked her too much, I'd "spoil her." I chose to risk it and kept on rocking.

We took the baby home only to find the power company digging a trench through the new garden Sara had planted during her pregnancy. We fled the jackhammers for my mother-in-law's camp on Glen Lake. It was a cold and wet June, and everyone warned us we'd endanger the baby. We risked it and, so, have memories of that baby's beautiful dark eyes reflecting the flames in the camp's huge stone fireplace.

Then that baby went away. But another child appeared. She was able to sit up, crawl and coo, and blurble little words to her mother. When I read her Mother Goose, she would flip the pages mid-rhyme, so that I was convinced she'd only come to learn "Pease porridge hot, dickory dock, three men in a tub..." instead of one whole rhyme.

Then that child went away. Another came, a racing, screaming, squealing child of two, who said "No!" to perfection and enjoyed going next door to see Grandma Cutshall, with whom she shared what I call "a dedication to principle," because I would never say "stubbornness."

Then that child went away. Oh, but there was another, mischievous and wise beyond her years, wearing outrageous outfits from a clothing trunk her mom had, driving mom crazy by hoarding her underwear in numerous bags that she'd tote around like a miniature baglady.

She was birdlike and four, loving to be read stories, but starting to read on her own. Spending days with her sitter, Joann, while at night pretending with her Dad that the clown poster on the wall was a magic window through which she and her Teddy would climb each night during their dreams. How many trips that little girl and I took to our "special lands" through that poster!

I missed that child when she left, but so many other wonderful children came I couldn't stop to think about it. Like the 10-year-old girl who would become immersed in acting for years. We parents were a nervous wreck, but this girl went on stage for "The Sound of Music" as if she were Helen Hayes. We can still all sing "doe, a deer, a female deer," rising from a dead sleep.

Then one day – when was that? - all the children left, and a young woman came to our house. She could act, was an artist like her mother, could play the flute and bagpipes, and ride horses, just like all the other children, but she was a woman.

And she stepped into a sunlit room one day and I saw in her my mother and realized that more than just parents live on in their children. Julia, my daughter, you know of course that all of those children are you. None are gone. They are all here, living in our memories and our hearts. Now you are turning 18 and the other 17 children, your mother and I wish you Happy Birthday!

And we all wait to see to see what those future children will be.

For the best is yet to come.

"OVER MY SHOULDER" COLUMN FOR JULY 24, 1999
Remembrances of coming of age in Fort Edward

Summer's heat always brings out that peculiar smell of the cottonwood trees, and their cottony seeds which blanket the area. These tell those of us who grew up with them that summer is indeed here.

This summer's heat and that familiar cottonwood scent have brought back a vivid memory of standing as a child some forty years ago near the Hudson River's edge in Fort Edward, down by the "kee wall" as we pronounced the quay wall of the yacht basin.

When we moved to Fort Edward from Saratoga, I think those tall cottonwoods may have figured among my most prominent early memories.

We lived in an apartment over our family's pharmacy on Broadway. The building stands today, although many of the tall trees that made up the background vegetation of the area between our store and river are gone now, along with many of those buildings that were near the yacht basin.

Some of the cottonwoods[lxxix] were uprooted by hurricane in 1953, I think it was. Others were chopped down since then. The buildings that are now gone then defined back alleys and with the trees formed secret places perfect for adventure for my older brother, my sister and me.

The tall trees' scent mingled with the river smell. In my childhood, that smell was "enriched," shall we say, by the odor of chemicals from mills, untreated sewage and, of course, the bags of garbage people threw in the river with abandon. I didn't think much of it then. That was life.

But the stately cottonwoods softened anything bad. At school's end, the air grew hot and humid, and their scent wafted up to Broadway, filling the air in our store and apartment overhead. We kids would run down to see those huge yachts pull in. Oh, they were magnificent – elegant long things, most of them made of wood.

Especially beguiling was the extremely long excursion boat from New York City that had a galley, and even a living room with a television and a radio on board.

The "yacht people," were so friendly. It's a sign of how different things are now to realize how natural it was back then for us kids, anywhere from six years old and up, to go down to the yacht basin without adults to see the boats. The only thing our parents ever worried about back then – at least for us to hear – was our getting too close and falling in. "Don't get too close to the quay wall," Mom shouted, as we slammed down the stairs from the second floor.

We'd tear through the labyrinth of alleyways toward the river. Usually we'd start visiting at the Underwood Park end of the quay wall, then work our way northward from yacht to yacht. Sometimes a local person would treat us to a short boat ride. That open water between Rogers Island and the yacht basin was paradise, with the cottonwoods arched over the riverbanks, and sunlight glimmering on the water.

They rebuilt the yacht basin recently. I decided to visit it. It's lovely. Seeing it now, I wonder what yacht owners back then thought as they gazed on the backs of buildings with packing crates stacked high, some buildings in sad shape, and nearby barrels upon barrels of tar used by the state for road paving. It surely couldn't have been as inviting then as it is now.

I like the new yacht basin. It says "Welcome, friend."

But, still, there seems to be something missing that the yacht basin once held for a certain little boy many decades ago. Some of that adventure maybe?

Or maybe it just needs a few more cottonwoods around it.

"OVER MY SHOULDER" COLUMN FOR AUGUST 28, 1999
Old Saratoga racing brochure a family heirloom

Floating in my vast reservoir of what I generously call "memorabilia" – junk – there is a brochure for the 1946 Saratoga racing season.

The brochure came my mother's own vast reservoir, an odd piece, even among my mother's collection, which included a co-mingling of the sacred and the profane that defies comprehension.

I'm not one to cast stones. Like Jane, I too am a saver. Here I'd saved this brochure, 15 years after her death. But unlike her, I do pitch out junk mail. I mean, one must draw a line. Where would the souvenir restaurant menus from Cape Ann go if I didn't?

But when I first found it in her things in 1984, I wondered what would have possessed her to keep it. A racing souvenir of the track's first season after having been closed during the war? No. As much as my mother won at the races, and she did that, she was not a racing fanatic. If she went, she went. If not, not.

So, not knowing then, I promptly filed it.

I saw it again recently and pondered it again in a new light. That 1946 brochure had nothing to do with the 1946 racing season, but everything to do with moving to Saratoga Springs. It was a memory bookmark of a good time, a significant time.

World War II was over. "The war," as Jane and my father, George, called it. He was back after 4 years, a full lieutenant in the Navy, a man with a degree, ready to practice pharmacy. She'd greeted him with the son he barely knew.

She spent the duration in a small apartment in Mechanicville, waiting, writing him love letters and, when he went overseas, promising he'd return to love, a happy home, a beautiful baby.

He wrote back from exotic names – Hawaii, Australia, the Philippines. But these were ports from which he sailed his PT Boat and crew off to face enemy ships tons larger, throwing explosives at them and then scurrying off. And always hoping he'd live to scurry home.

When he did, he had injuries and spent time in the VA hospital. Then he began a career with E. R. Squibb. Jane had said that Dad had always wanted to move. He had proposed his staying in the Navy and their moving to California. In answer, she shot an empty baby carriage down two flights of apartment stairs at his head. He reconsidered.

He joked later that he had returned to Mechanicville just as the steam locomotive was replaced by diesel. He said the smoke and dust rose, he saw Mechanicville for the first time and wanted to leave. The reality was, he had traveled. She hadn't.

Nonetheless, they did share one motive for leaving. His mother. My father's mother – how shall we say this delicately? – could insinuate herself into one's affairs. Others may term it being over-bearing, pushy, perhaps "in-your-face." At any rate, not the mother-in-law made in heaven. Perhaps not even the mother.

So, in the spring of 1946, Jane and George and their two year old son moved to Saratoga Springs. Off to an independent life, near to, but not too near to, family. Off to a Saratoga filled with racing and gambling and a good time for a young couple making up for some stolen years.

They celebrated the move. Oh, I know they were happy about the move, for they spoke fondly of it in later years. But I mean, and feel confident in saying, that they actually celebrated the move.

For I was born nine months later.

So, I'll hang on to that racing brochure, a symbol of the beginning of my life. And thank my mother for that piece of "racing history."

"OVER MY SHOULDER" COLUMN FOR OCTOBER 9, 1999
Preparing for atomic bomb hard lesson to forget

Ask anyone of any age what they recall about elementary school and you'll hear answers like these:

"I remember clapping erasers" or "I remember practicing for the Thanksgiving pageant."

Me? I remember practicing for the atomic bomb.

It was in the heart of 1950s. I remember those wonderful days of Civil Defense drills with all the other little kids in my grade. In my mind's eye I still see them, same size as myself. But their faces are so young. The faces of little children in elementary school.

We were in the Powers Elementary School in Fort Edward, an 1890s beauty with thick inner and outer brick walls. Overall it resembled a national armory.

I can hear my second grade teacher's voice now as she read from her Civil Defense handbook and told us about "The Drills."

"The bell will ring twice boys and girls. This is a special ring. Do you understand?"

"Yes, Mrs. Boucher."

"Then we'll crawl under our desks." Now this was fun! I always waited for her to do that, but she never did.

Still reading she intoned: "And never look at the windows boys and girls. Because looking at the bright atomic cloud could harm your eyes."

Harm our eyes? We would have been molecules in a second. Even if it were distant, the cloud's after blast would have cleaned the room out like a strong toilet flush.

By third grade the Civil Defense wizards decided that we should "move quickly, but in an orderly fashion" into the hall and place our arms over faces and face the wall. Firing squad style. This the girls did in very orderly fashion, wanting to get in good with the principal, Mrs. Wagner.

We boys by that time only wanted to jump on each other in a "hogpile," and invariably fell on the floor in a massive heap, disentangled only by strong adult arms.

Teachers and janitors would chastise us, intoning how serious this was. We giggled.

But the reality of the bomb was beginning to sink in. We watched TV. We saw The Bomb blasting and the cloud rising. We heard talk of bomb shelters and saw articles in every magazine from Popular Mechanics to Ladies Home Journal. ("Making Crocheted Pillows for Your Shelter.").

By "junior high," it had sunk in. Many of us teenagers lived in varying degrees of fear of "The Bomb." Tom,[lxxx] in the same grade as my brother Mike, had a pathological fear. He said if he ever heard the air raid sirens "for real" he'd climb up on his mother's big china platter and stuff an apple in his mouth.

We walked home for lunch every day. One fall day, unbeknownst to us in school, a train had derailed and caught fire. The smoke rose in a huge mushroom cloud. As we were leaving the high school, Tom saw it and ran back inside, terrified. It took practically the whole lunch period to get him out of the building.

Our graduation session for The Bomb was the Cuban Missile crisis of 1962. Kennedy had issued his ultimatum to Khrushchev to remove the missiles from Cuba or else. While we waited for (and prayed that there wouldn't be an) "or else," I suddenly saw that most of my life could be obliterated by a bunch of adults playing with "The Bomb."

I think it was then that I first began to assume an attitude of "The hell with tomorrow. I'm alive right now."

While I would still have a fear of The Bomb, I gradually became a true member of the "Me Generation," and for too long followed these words of a now best forgotten rock song: "Tra la, la la la, let's live for today."

You could say that was my "Civil Defense."

"OVER MY SHOULDER" COLUMN FOR NOVEMBER 20, 1999
Memories of holidays gone by, via the back porch

My mother, Jane, had a special affinity for enclosed porches that were not winterized. They provided a holding space for a chaise lounge, crockery and other antiques, dried flowers, stacks of books, old *New York Times* magazines that rose like towers, and once a year, a Thanksgiving turkey.

The porch was her sanctum sanctorum. Of course, the whole house was Jane's to decorate as she saw fit. God knows my father had as much inclination toward interior decorating as a duck has for space travel.

But an enclosed porch was hers alone. My parents' last home in Ticonderoga, actually provided Jane with two unheated enclosed porches. The front porch had loads of window space, providing good sun. Here she had assembled various pieces of antique crockery and tinted 19th century medicine bottles that cast soft blue light when the sun shone through them. There were a few chairs and even a small bed that a guest could use.

The porch had been painted repeatedly and the chalky white paint took on a particular odor that gradually built into something hauntingly familiar. When dry flower arrangements and a few more antiques appeared, the realization came to me. Jane was carrying on a tradition. Here was a porch much like the unheated porch at her Aunt Kinks' house.

Aunt Kinks, given name Cornelia, occupied a special place in Jane's life and it was fascinating to see Kinks' porch – itself a place of warm memories for us all – re-emerging in our house in Ti.

However, it was the second porch off the kitchen that eventually became Jane's true sanctum sanctorum. The front porch was just too hot in the summer and, with the crockery and dried bittersweet, it developed as more of a room to behold than to occupy. The back porch had more shade. It was more of a cubbyhole, too, holding as it did the freezer and various large oven roasters, as our house sported the world's smallest kitchen.

Packed in there was also a chaise lounge. Summers, when hollyhocks grew tall outside the little porch, Jane would retreat there to read her books and newspapers and take the essential nap.

In the winter – mid-October to mid-April – the whole porch was a substitute refrigerator. It was very much like, I also saw, the back porch off Aunt Kinks' kitchen. It offered excellent cold storage for Thanksgiving and Christmas meals, when the variety and number of dishes Jane prepared surpassed anything offered by Julia Child.

I recall a particular Thanksgiving. It was a bit warmer than usual. Most of us kids were home, packed in the dining room with parents and grandmother. Between the number of bodies, the kitchen stove going round the clock and the fact that my father, George, had the thermostat cranked to 75, the house was unbearable. Occasionally to escape the heat, I'd step on to the front porch, which had received the overflow of relishes and rolls that no longer fit on the table or piano bench, already full with food. The smell would transport me to my aunt's house.

Thanksgiving dinner done, George ensconced himself in "his" chair in front of the football game, and was promptly snoring. We kids were ready to go out to visit friends. Mom, who should have been on the couch, was nowhere to be seen. Impulse guided me to the back porch. There, amidst the roaster pan with the turkey carcass, dishes of creamed onions and scalloped oysters, and stacks of magazines, lay the chef, asleep on her chaise with a coat on and a blanket pulled over her.

I let her be, but left the door open to let in the heat, allowing the sleeper to dream that it was summer again, with the hollyhocks in bloom.

"OVER MY SHOULDER" COLUMN FOR DECEMBER 18, 1999
Laundry and life lessons from the Christmas Cat

This is the story of the Christmas cat.

During the time when my family was living in Fort Edward in the 1950s, my father had a pharmacy that was the center of our life. For our first four years there, we lived in a second floor apartment above the store.

When we moved into a new home, our ties to the pharmacy didn't diminish. We kids all continued to work in it, spending a lot of time in the middle of a thriving business district, providing endless fascination for us kids. You must picture it as it was, especially in a December time, ready for Christmas.

Packed into only a few blocks near the Hudson River was incredible variety. Thereced was the A&P, Grand Union, other family markets and a bakery. There were other pharmacies, clothing stores, a shoe repair, barbers, a bank, churches, gas stations, a professional photographer, volunteer fire companies, doctors, dentists, lawyers, bars, restaurants, and more. Only a short alley away from us were single family homes, apartment buildings, trailers, and even a dilapidated shack. In short, a "downtown" in any small village in the mid-20th century. A thing of the past.

Directly between us and the river were buildings crammed along narrow, Dickens-esque alleyways, scurrying with dogs, river rats, and cats, in particular the Christmas Cat. The Hudson sent December's whipping winds and snows through the alleys, driving these animals into what shelter they could find.

Time could trick me, but I think I first met the Christmas Cat in December, for I don't recall him staying long around the store. That December was typical. Street decorations were up. Our pharmacy had special perfumes, watches, and candy beautifully displayed. Snow came right on time, a dusting in preparation for the main event. At home, Mom was getting ready for Christmas.

Toward the back of our store, a window looked out over the rear roof of the next building. Supposedly getting more soda for the cooler, I had stopped there to daydream, when I heard meowing.

On the roof sat a cat, a huge, muscular, tail-less Manx, with a grapefruit-sized head all marred with scars. Forgetting his fear, he came to me and, naturally, we "bonded."

Perhaps it was the season, but my normally sensible parents allowed him to be kept in the cellar of the back, unheated portion of the store. Their second mistake was allowing him to be brought home.

That was my mistake, too. For I had removed an alley cat from his world. Amidst a home with furniture, regular warmth and civilized rules of behavior, he was distinctly out of his element. Add to that a Christmas tree, and you have the seeds of discord.

The Christmas Cat came in only periodically to be fed. Otherwise, he had to stay in the garage. Now it was Christmas eve. With permission I let him in for food. In a twinkling, he was roaming the house. But where?

Where else? Having eaten, he needed the restroom. How thoughtful of our family to provide a tree.

My mother's shrieks pinpointed his location. I arrived in the living room just in time to see her pitching the Christmas Cat out the front door, with an added dexterity, his body arcing high in the air, the street light illuminating the twists and turns he took before landing. No one surpassed my mother Jane for cat pitching.

Jane marched to the tree, gingerly extracted the sheet from beneath it and thrust the now-pungent fabric into my arms with these words: "Go clean this." As we had no washer at that time, I knew what that meant.

And so, I spent a good portion of a picture-perfect snowy Christmas eve in a laundromat, within sight of our house, washing the soiled sheet until finally the Christmas "gift" of the Christmas Cat was removed. It is, shall I say, a lingering Christmas memory.

Oh, the Christmas Cat? He survived being pitched, but ultimately did not survive domestication. Out of his element, he had grown soft with love and affection. He was seriously injured in a fight and had to be put to sleep.

We cried. But of us, my mother cried the most, for that was Jane. She had come to love that big scar-faced Manx cat, who had left an enduring Christmas memory for us all.

"OVER MY SHOULDER" COLUMN FOR JANUARY 1, 2000
Lamenting what was gained, lost during the century

In my life...
Looking into the future on this first day of the year 2000, I look over my shoulder to see where my small world and the world as a whole have been in just my lifetime.

I was born in 1947, the year India became a free country; Jackie Robinson broke the color barrier in baseball; the transistor was invented; and a television set was first placed in a bar in Saratoga Springs, the city where I was born.

In my life I've seen India's 1947 population of 250,000,000 more than triple, and the world's population follow suit.

In my life, I have seen strides made toward racial equality, yet women, who make up 53% of the country, are so underrepresented in our representative government that I may never live to see a woman as President.

In my life the transistor moved from powering gimmick radios to powering the personal computer.

In my life radio was replaced by television, which went from broadcasting in black and white on two networks to color on scores of networks.

In my life, the computer graduated from the Univac, the size of a small room and programmed by paper cards to pocket-sized computers with the power of a thousand Univacs. I have seen the computer lead to the Internet, which has begun to eradicate TV as we know it.

In 1947, penicillin was mass marketed for the first time and it saved my life. In my life the DNA structure was discovered and virtually mapped, and medicine is moving toward the genetic eradication of disease.

In my life I have seen schools consolidate into mega-districts offering wondrous educational facilities, and offer services to the handicapped, previously under-taught or never taught. Yet I have seen our teachers stripped of their power to discipline and students living in fear of students.

In my life I have seen the forests protected and expanded. Yet now our logs are sold abroad, and the papermaking industry is moving to other countries. And I watch mobile homes growing in number because stick-built houses are unaffordable.

In my life too many of my generation went from chanting "Don't trust anyone over 30" to treating anyone under 30 as if they were imbeciles.

In my life I watched Vietnam tear my generation apart, while today most people couldn't find that country on a map.

In my life I've watched my Boomer Generation go from laying back and smoking "herbs," to exercising frantically while taking massive doses of herbal potions designed to postpone the inevitable.

In my life I saw rock'n'roll begin with Chuck Berry and Elvis and end with the creation of a rock'n'roll museum in Cleveland.

In my life I saw Ma Bell broken up in the name of progress. Yet today's call from my house in Cossayuna to Glens Falls is still "long distance."

In my life I saw the last steam locomotive run on the Delaware and Hudson Railroad, then watched railroads become obsolete as we put humans into space.

In my life I have seen with my own eyes in my own country families sleeping in the streets.

In my life I have seen toilet paper become cloud soft, while institutional toilet paper still appears to have small wood chunks in it.

In my life I have watched the majority of my state depopulate, its industry move to the south and west, and our leaders never grasping the fact that the 1990s boomtimes never came here.

In my life defeated Germany was split in two and the wall was built through Berlin. I saw wall fall in 1989 and Germany become one nation.

In my life I went from constant expectations of Soviet missiles to seeing the USSR end.

In my life I saw I saw a Marxist China emerge. Today it produces 7 out of the 10 capitalist products sold in America.

In my life I have seen the shopping center and mall invented and the downtown of my childhood atrophy like a withered arm, and farms vanish as suburbs grew.

Yet I have come to learn from this that change is inevitable and that someday, some person my age will look back up the vanished days of shopping malls and lament the passing of an era. Or, as the Beatles sang, "There are places I remember, all my life, though some have changed. Some forever not for better, some have gone and some remain."

And I have come to learn, most importantly, that it is ultimately the wonderful people I have cherished, many of whom are gone, who are the most important memories of my life.

As I travel into the next part of my life, I will take with me the memory of the places I have lived and the people I have cherished.

For, in my life I've loved them all.

"OVER MY SHOULDER" COLUMN FOR JANUARY 22, 2000
Days of enlightenment: Sampling the taste of paste

Whether to eat paste or not to eat paste, that was the question. Paste, I learned recently, stills forms an important element in the early experiences of school children. This is gratifying, as paste was so critical to my formative years.

Specifically, to first grade. I can see it now. Barely days in my new school and now Mrs. Green stood before us, ready to bring us to the next threshold of educational enlightenment, the Paste Ritual.

Picture my room in our older school: an 1890s brick wonder, with mile high ceilings and windows large enough to allow you to see to Kansas.

Everything in the room was huge. Like the enormous slate chalkboards that must have been lifted from the quarries by six men and a boy.

Our desks, the wood top and cast iron side variety, were lined up straight, military order. No circling around your teacher or sitting on floors with pillows. Namby-pamby stuff. We were Spartans.

Our general, Mrs. Bessie Green, stood to the front of the room, tall, round, with a benevolent smile, clutching a large jar of paste and a ruler. Ah, the ruler. That multi-purpose instrument of the teaching profession.

Under Mrs. Green, the black belt of ruler users, we saw its fullest potential. We sat in wonder as one moment the ruler measured, then baton like, directed us in song, then delivered a thwack on the knuckles of poor Pamela, caught counting on her fingers. The instrument of music was an instrument of fear.

Today her ruler was jammed into an enormous gallon jar of that white, gelatinous paste. Just before jamming it in, she had deftly used the ruler to rip sheets of the famed yellow paper with green lines into perfect squares. Amazing.

These squares she had given Douglas to bring to each seat, in which we sat bolt upright, our hands clasped together as in prayer, our excitement rising. Then, jamming the ruler into the paste like Arthur putting Excalibur back into the stone, she held the paste aloft signaling Douglas to pass it out.

She gave us our orders. Douglas would come to our desks. We would take the ruler and put an "exact" amount on the middle of our paper square. Here, in a deft move she demonstrated the procedure so swiftly it appeared the jar never left her hands. We were in awe.

Then she uttered these words that were to change our lives forever: "And I DON'T want to see a one of you eating that paste!"

Eating the paste? EATING it? We all sat blank-faced for a moment, then our eyes, glowing, shot furtively to our neighbors. None of us had ever thought of eating the paste.

The jar passed down from desk to desk. Skillfully we mastered extracting the right amount. Slowly our little sheets filled with a little white blob in the middle. Bessie, busy getting construction paper ready for the next phase, called over her shoulder, "I hope none of you is eating that paste."

Now the camera moves upward and pans the room, gliding swiftly from desk to desk, showing where every little paper has a finger mark gouged in the back side of the paste, where each child had snuck a little taste. All except that of Norman whose sheet betrayed the one, long, wet stripe where he had licked, in one fell swoop, the entire contents into his mouth, which was now working frantically to get that paste down before discovery.

But, no, he was not discovered! He was saved by Dennis, who had simply taken the ruler and placed the blob directly in his mouth, just as Mrs. Green turned to survey our progress.

He was dragged off into the "cloak room" where we heard his screams, while we patiently waited, furtively sticking our fingers in for yet another sampling of that delicious, wonderful, mysterious substance. Paste.

"OVER MY SHOULDER" COLUMN FOR APRIL 1, 2000
Way to grandma's heart - through your stomach

This is the story of the tuna salad sandwich.

Ask any of my siblings what they remember most about Grandma Fitzpatrick, and I'm sure it would be food. And guilt. For my father's mother, Ann Elizabeth Green King Fitzpatrick was a true grandmother in every sense of the word.

You must understand that to appreciate fully the story of the tuna salad sandwich, for great food and great guilt were among her most prized instruments of that high office.

After I had moved away and would come home to Ticonderoga for a visit, I'd always stop over to Grandma's little house that stood to the rear of my parents' home on Iroquois Street. As I'd enter, it was common for Gram Fitz, or "Annie," as my father always called her, to ask me three questions immediately as I stepped through her doorway. And I mean immediately.

They were: Have you eaten? Do you have enough money? Have you been to church? Sometimes the order of the last two would be reversed, but the question of whether one had eaten was always first. Always. I can see her to this day, sitting in a rocker that had been her great Aunt Hannah's, knitting or saying the rosary, but dropping a stitch or pausing mid-bead to ask, "Have you eaten?"

Now, the incident of the tuna salad sandwich is actually one of thousands of similar incidents, and what could probably be called forced feeding today. There never, repeat never, was a time when that woman did not have a five gallon bucket of freshly made tuna salad, and one of cole slaw, sitting in her refrigerator. I often said to my mother, Jane, that Annie lay in ambush at her front door with a tuna salad sandwich, the middle word of which Gram Fitz always pronounced like "solid." It was a legacy, I think, from having lived in the Boston area for a time with her first husband, my Dad's dad, who had died so tragically when my father was five.

My mother would sigh and say something like, "Oh that woman." Or "She's digging her grave with a spoon!" I think Jane's Presbyterian upbringing always imbued her, no slouch in the feeding department herself mind you, with a certain Calvinistic sense of what was proper by way of eating. Of course, the particular mother-in-law/daughter-in-law dynamic that fed, if you'll pardon the expression, Jane's comments about Annie would fill several volumes of psychological studies.

The lead-up to the tuna salad sandwich affair may have been born of a subconscious rivalry between the two women to see who would feed me breakfast. I don't know. But it was a lovely spring morning near Easter, which fell late that year. I awoke in time to join Jane and George at breakfast before they went to work. I feasted well.

Meanwhile, across the way, my grandmother awaited my arrival. For breakfast.

It wasn't agreed upon that I would have breakfast with her. But as she had assumed it, therefore it was so. The phone began to ring. And it rang, and rang. When was I coming over? Heaven forbid I should let the need for a bathroom stop interfere with getting there.

I arrived and she began the litany, "Hello, dear. Have you eaten?" and stopped dead when I answered, "Yes." This was a new wrinkle. I'd had the audacity to eat with my parents. A small cloud passed over her face, producing in me the obligatory guilt. Foolishly I thought that was that.

"Would you like a coffee?" she asked sweetly, knowing I love coffee. Sure. In a minute, out came a coffee. With a sugar cookie on the side. I reminded her that I had eaten.

"Oh, all right," she sighed with a sigh of ages. "I'll just have to throw it away." The old "I'll have to throw it away" gambit. There was my downfall. The thought of my grandmother throwing away even one crumb was absolutely preposterous. But already drenched in guilt, I caved in.

"Another coffee?" she asked a while later. Please, I said, "but no cookie." She agreed and came out with a coffee, and another cookie. Well, we had it out big time over that, I'll tell you. And she only got me to eat it with the promise that it would be the last.

Time went by. More coffee, dear? Yes, but... I gave her a look that meant business. She smiled and acknowledged it, saying, "No cookie."

And she was true to her word. She came back out with a cup of coffee – and a tuna salad sandwich. The sweet triumph shone from her eyes.

I looked dejectedly at the sandwich. It was, I felt, a form of Lenten punishment, but rather than fasting I was being forced to eat. I surrendered. I ate the sandwich.

And then the fruit cup, which normally would have come first.

And more coffee.

And, finally, a cookie. Just to make sure I'd had enough.

"OVER MY SHOULDER" COLUMN FOR MAY 27, 2000
Historical events create an eruption of memories

Volcanic dust, a plant commonly called bridal wreath, a tall man, and silk are among the many images that make up a very special memory for me.

The volcanic dust part of the memory you surely have guessed. Twenty years ago Mount St. Helens erupted and scattered its dust 3,000 miles away into our sunsets here, making them glowing spectacles.

I'll always remember those sunsets. My bride to be, Sara Cutshall, and I were traveling to Warrensburg to see her friend, minister Oren Lane. In the time before he would marry us, Sara and I would go to Warrensburg to talk with him about the ceremony, and the institution of marriage in general, something about which I am still learning.

In mid-May of 1980, Mount St. Helens erupted. I recall us sitting out by exit 23 of the Northway one evening. Oren, his wife, Sara, and I all watched as the sun set over the Adirondacks, the volcanic dust from Mount St. Helens creating a red glow that looked like something out of a Max Factor cosmetic ad.

Mount St. Helens would be a good symbol for the time surrounding any wedding. It's an emotional time to begin with. And then there are the details, which Sara, a master planner, took over, throwing herself into the process with passion. It was just as well. I can plan events, but detail is her forte.

I would say on the whole that the whole affair went stunningly. We wrote our own vows and added a touch of romance by going to MC Scoville Jewelers for our rings. I say that because, beyond the Scoville's' being jewelers, a year and a half before, Sara and I had met at a party in an apartment that Chris Scoville and Debra Vales had then on the third floor of the Scoville building.[lxxxi]

Several years later, Scoville's was selling items made from the volcanic glass retrieved from Mount St. Helens. Unbeknownst to each other, Sara and I both bought a volcanic glass gift from Scoville's as surprise presents for each other.

Now the bridal wreath part of this marriage memory. Our marriage was held on May 31 at the Unitarian Fellowship on Warren Street and we had the reception at the Glen Lake camp of Edna Cutshall, my mother-in-law. It was a lovely 1920 structure smothered in pines and filled with a two-story cobblestone fireplace that spelled romance.

Our friend Fred Fisher,[lxxxii] who at that time was the director of the Hyde Collection, offered to do the floral arrangements and I can see the camp filled with wild flowers and bridal wreath, the latter very symbolic as our home on Harrison Avenue was surrounded by it. I never see bridal wreath without thinking of Fred's gift to our marriage.

The tall man memory is that of Jack Wiberg, standing by the stone wall of the camp helping with details that made the reception go smoother. Twenty years have only strengthened a deep friendship.

The silk is the "surprise" memory, which I purposely saved for last. Sara had asked her dear friend, Pam Mikel Hayes, a wonderful artist with a gift for fabric, if she'd create an album for the wedding photos and memorabilia. Oddly, Pam seemed a little consternated at Sara's request, but she said yes and all went along as planned. Pam created an album with a quilted silk cover.

What neither of us knew was that Pam had already begun our wedding gift. She had fashioned an enormous silk quilt, on which she used all different fabrics to depict poignant scenes, memories of her friendship with Sara and of our friendship as a couple with her and her family. Memories that will live for as long as we do. It was "the" surprise of the wedding and is among our most cherished gifts.

There are other people and memories, of course. But those came to mind as I realized that, in what seems only a heartbeat, twenty years has passed and before another heartbeat went by I wanted to capture those memories to say: happy anniversary, Sara Cutshall.

Mount St. Helens may be dormant, but our volcano is still active.

"OVER MY SHOULDER" COLUMN FOR JUNE 17, 2000
Unexpected package conjures up Father's Day memories

Here's a father day story about the wonderfully strange ways life can surprise us.

The other day I received a large package from *The Post-Star*. In it was another package, mailed from Putnam Station.

The package came from Betty Lou Fuller. I'd recognized the name immediately but couldn't place the face.

Inside the package was a copy of John P. Marquand's novel *Point of No Return*.

I opened its cover and pasted on the inside was a bookplate with the inscription, "There is no frigate like a book to take us lands away." Below that was the handwritten signature "George A. King." My father. I smiled as I looked at it, because the signature was signed by my mother.

I knew the book. I knew the bookplate and even before I looked at the copyright date, I knew exactly when my mother had purchased the book and could place where we lived by it. It was Saratoga Springs, two years after I was born.

I stood stunned, holding a book that I'd just removed from an envelope, but a book that had sat on a shelf in my first home in 1949.

All of this recognition and calculation, of course, was happening more quickly than I am telling it now. Happening in seconds, literally. But the book was only the appetizer. Inside the book were also two greeting cards, both Father's Day cards. One, cut in the shape of a tee-pee had 6 cartoon Indians on the inside.

Laying those down for a moment, I read from the accompanying letter from Betty Lou, who wrote, "a few days I rescued a box of old books on the way to the dump. I just hate to see books being destroyed, such a waste when someone could enjoy them still....As I was thumbing through them, I was pleasantly surprised to see that some of them belonged to great old friends of mine, George and Jane King, " my mother and father.

I picked up the cards again. On the tee-pee one, four Indians were whooping around a grumpy-faced figure in a blanket. My mother had labeled the whooping Indians Mike, Martha, Bill and Joe, the children, and the blanketed figure "Fatha." She labeled the sixth, who was making smoke signals, "Mom." Certainly appropriate, as she was the one who always wrote the letters and made the calls.

From the look of the card and the fact that there were only 4 kids listed, I figured it was given during the mid-1950s, when we were living in Fort Edward. The last King child, Scott, came into the family in Ticonderoga.

The other card was from my brother Mike to my father. From the style of it and the mature signature, it appeared to be something out of the mid-1960s, by which time were in Ti. How strange. Objects in an envelope that had been in my three childhood home towns.

I returned to Betty Lou's letter. "About 30 years ago I worked the morning shift at Bunny Bevilacqua's Drug Store," the Burleigh Pharmacy in Ti. She worked behind the soda fountain and recalled "running around filling creams and sugars and making at least 6 full pots of coffee for the patrons, who were already queuing on the sidewalks out front."

Now I could recall her face. She was a part of what I call the Coffee Club, a gathering of morning regulars at the pharmacy. They were "waiting for your Dad to turn the door key so they could surge in on us. He and I used to tell each jokes and catch up on whatever gossip we missed the day before."

Ah, gossip. A Roman Catholic priest does not take to the grave as many secrets as does a pharmacist in a small town.

Betty wrote that she was holding the book when the two cards fell out and "I thought that you would enjoy having them returned to you and with Father's Day around the corner I hope you get a wink of joy and remembrance out of them."

I have indeed, Betty Lou, and thank you so much. Every Father's Day has been special since that month of June, 19 years ago, when I first became a father. This gift of yours from a long-ago father's day will make this year's all the more memorable, all the more special.

And to my brother Indians on the card from long-ago, Happy Father's Day to you, too.

"OVER MY SHOULDER" COLUMN FOR AUGUST 19, 2000
Warm and wild flashbacks to Summer in Saratoga

My daughter just came back from downtown Saratoga and, for reasons she'll never understand, I met the news with a reaction of envy and a shudder.

This is the season in Saratoga Springs. The ponies are here, the racing fans are here, and Damon Runyon's spirit lingers over the whole of the Spa City like too much cologne on a hot day. It conjures up some wonderful memories for me.

Whenever the words "the season" would be mentioned, my father would break into a litany of complaint about the days in Saratoga, when he was the manager of MacFinn's Broadway store, a large three-story Victorian structure that had a huge marble soda fountain with elegant seats, a balcony, cubic yards of women's cosmetics and swimming pools full of expensive perfume. In short, class.

It was the end of World War II. The economy was good, the gloomy days were over, and the track had reopened. Saratoga in the summer was again "the" place to be. The Piping Rock, Riley's, and other nightclubs swung with what remained of the Big Bands, plus the small combos. And they all featured non-stop gambling. It was the time before the crackdown of 1951 and Saratoga was wide open.

We lived on tree-lined Lincoln Avenue, three blocks from the track. My first memories are of Cadillacs and Olds with huge sun visors over the windshields depositing men and women who'd stroll the street in their finest on the way to the track. I was very little, but the sight of those two-tone brown and cream colored men's and women's shoes fills my memories. Men wore huge suits like Victor Mature in a film noir. The women were all Joan Crawford or Veronica Lake wannabes.

Real stars were everywhere, too. Just down the street from our house, the Williams Brothers rented a neighbor's house every summer and sung at Riley's out on the lake. Later, one brother, Andy Williams went on to become a major star.

Downtown along Broadway was filled with everyone who was and who wanted to be. It was possible to see actor Monty Wooley, of the "Man Who Came to Dinner" fame, sitting in the Colonial Restaurant with his drinking partner Frank Sullivan, writer for *The New Yorker* and a humorist counted among those of the Algonquin Round Table.

MacFinn's was, as every pharmacy was in those days, a place where one soothed one's soul. In the morning, the workout crews from the track could be seen sipping coffee side by side with the big winners and big losers, all magnificently hungover and quaffing bromo seltzers like magic potions.

During the season, hundreds came through daily to get a coffee, a prescription, or maybe "a little something to pick them up" or a "little something to calm them down." Or "a little something to pick the horse up" or a "little something to calm it down," things being a little, shall we say, more liberal in those days. Or to get a box of candy, a cosmetic compact, a wristwatch, or just to be seen in that magnificent place.

My father would go in early and stay until after midnight. In later years, he'd rant about the customers, demanding this or that, or making next to impossible requests. My mother would roll her eyes, laugh and say, "Oh, George." Or if the moaning got out of hand, "George!"

If most memories of MacFinn's brought smiles when retold later, one did not. "The Memory of the Impossible Customer" only brought shudders. An extremely wealthy woman in her mid-fifties had taken a fancy for my father, who was in his late 20s and very handsome. Well, let's be frank, it was more than a fancy. She suggested that for a very generous sum she was willing to pay, he could do more than fill her prescriptions. Oh, and no need for a divorce. That situation could all be worked out amicably.

At home on Lincoln Avenue, while my father related this as a humorous tale, although not without its ego-boost, my mother saw no humor, whatsoever, and a rip roaring fight ensued. Had my mother made contact with "the lady," she would have killed her on sight.

In later years, when we moved to Ticonderoga on Lake George, there were again tourists and there was again "a season," but for all my father's moaning, it simply was not the same. While the summer tourist wave could bring in the occasional impossible customer, none ever held a candle to – nor made an offer like – the original Impossible Customer.

"OVER MY SHOULDER" COLUMN FOR SEPTEMBER 30, 2000
Fall brings bright colors and warm memories

Odd, isn't it, how the most humble of plants will bring back a flood of memories?

The fall colors have finally arrived, delayed undoubtedly by the Noah's-Ark volume of rain that had tricked our plant life into thinking this is the tropics and therefore they could stay green year-round.

But it was the sight of a sumac turning red, of all things, that triggered waves of memories of a certain couple for whom fall was "the time."

It's only been in recent years that I've come to appreciate fall. When I was younger, even into my late thirties, the season depressed me, frankly, the very word expressing the downward motion of the leaves and my mood. It seems appropriate that this use of the word "fall" was coined by those stern early New Englanders for whom an economy of living meant an economy in their words. And so they shortened "autumn" to a symbolic single syllable. Or I should say a "blunt one word"?

Perhaps I've come to appreciate fall because it is so vivid here, but I think it has to do with age as well as esthetics. Whatever, I understand now the sense of enjoyment that my parents, Jane and George, derived from this season, which shows its most colorful face in the Northeast.

Each had a practical and a sensual appreciation of the season. George's stemmed from many things. He liked the crispness, the invigoration of the season. He also had a strong disliking for summer, prompted by spending almost three years in the South Pacific during "the war." There the heat and humidity, and insects often larger than his PT Boat, were motivating factors in his despising summer.

The other side of that was that "the season" would end when fall began. Gone were the summer tourists, from whom my father would gleefully extract money while craving their absence. Coming in were the "fall travelers," as he called them, generally older and wiser vacationers who preferred the off season, and were far more pleasant to serve.

He would say, "I like fall. It's the best season," but that was as far as direct comment went. Heaven forbid he should have ever directly expressed an unmanly sentimental notion to his children. But I suspect from things mentioned indirectly that George found in fall a return by memory to his days in college, while playing semi-pro basketball, working in the Watervliet Armory and dating my mother. Hard times fondly recalled by them both. He was fond of recalling, to her pleased embarrassment, that they enjoyed necking in Albany's Central Park, near the school.

That shared fall memory aside, Jane's enjoyment of the season was also motivated by a physical relief from the heat, although she enjoyed warmer weather and loved spring. Perhaps, too, fall symbolized her birthday in mid-September. But I only surmise that. She would say that she loved the sumac in the fall, and I'd look at her as if she were ready for intense psychiatric help. Sumac? That weed?

But fall was…well how can I express it? It was a visual time in the house, a time of Indian corn, pumpkins and squash. A time of motion, of picking fall flowers and of antique hunting. Jane gave a sense of nesting, to use a word my wife often uses, getting the hearth and home ready for the winter, for Thanksgiving and Christmas, the two holidays that were her crowning glories.

But under it all, I think they had in their own ways a restless nature that the fall accentuated. Both Jane and George discovered in fall the thrill of change. It was the relief from sameness that, oddly, grew in them as they aged and came to dislike what seemed to be the avalanche of change in their lives, with their "boomer" children becoming adults during the turmoil of the sixties and seventies.

It was a relief from sameness that grows and takes its expression in the enjoyment of a beautiful season that can only be called a brightly colored wake. I know, because I have discovered this in myself.

And it only takes the sight of the sumac turning a blazing red to start the pageant and the excitement—and the enjoyment that follows.

"OVER MY SHOULDER" COLUMN FOR NOVEMBER 4, 2000
Silence on politics keeps domestic bliss intact

My parents, Jane and George, never fought openly about politics that anyone could recall, in spite of the fact that they were registered in opposing political parties.

George was a Democrat, Jane a Republican. It should have made for tension, although there were enough other things in the relationship that easily overshadowed politics as a basis for connubial "non-bliss." We won't go there.

No, the relative political harmony that existed in King household is something to give wonder in these days when trashing the opponent is the norm. Of course, part of the secret was that they never discussed politics.

George hadn't always been a Democrat. His mother started him out as a Republican, surprisingly as she was totally of Irish descent. In the 1930s, it would have been more likely for her to be a Democrat.

However, when a Republican member of the state legislature was hiring students to be Capitol aids, a paid position in the Depression, money reared its lovely head. Grandma became a Republican party regular. She received a cast iron elephant bank and a job for her son. The die was cast.

Fast forward to 1960. John Kennedy is running for President. Kennedy was Roman Catholic, as was my father. But, more importantly, Kennedy had served in the PT Boat Squadrons, as had my father.

The die was broken. A Democrat was born.

When George and Jane married in 1942, both had been Republican. When he made the leap to the donkey, Jane stayed on the elephant.

Politics only became potentially divisive in the 1970s. Mom wrote me from Ticonderoga that George was running for office. I knew there would be problems.

In terms of his running for office in Ti, it wasn't that George was disliked. People really liked him. And it wasn't that he was not aggressive enough for politics. Not an issue with a pharmacist who could sell his famed Wild Indian Thyme cough syrup in the middle of summer to healthy people.

And it wasn't that he couldn't get the support of others. Whenever he became involved in anything, he just "drafted" people.

Maury Thompson of *The Post-Star* told me that his wife, Nancy, was a draftee. Trained as an artist, she was at that time working in Burleigh Pharmacy with George. One of his political cronies would be experiencing campaign trouble and George would race over to Nancy to tell her she had to whip up a sign or some kind of artwork to help the cause.

Self-assertion, then, was not an issue. But, there was a problem—actually two.

First, George was a Democrat. I don't think that I am revealing a secret of the universe by saying that the Republican Party is a fixture in the North Country. It was probably handing out campaign buttons when the Iroquois first arrived.

I talked about this recently with Virginia "Babe" Smith, a Ticonderoga Democrat who was the first woman mayor of the former Village of Ticonderoga and the Democrat Committee secretary for years. Babe summed up the Democratic experience in Ti by saying, "A Democrat in Ti never had a chance to win in office. We were always outnumbered 3 to 1."

So, here was my father running for town board from a distinctly underdog position. But, as Babe noted, "Your father was very stubborn," which she learned from their heated "discussions." One occurred when the Democrats wanted to back a Republican. Babe was against it, George for it. Babe said, "The party convened a meeting at Louis Morette's house. Your father and I got into an argument. We nearly bit each other's head off." Still, they remained friends.

Now, regarding the second problem, it was not on the home front. As Babe said, my mother was always good about going to any party the Democrats held. Probably pity for the underdog, but Jane wouldn't say that.

Actually, the second problem was that George wasn't a native son. In fact, the Kings were not even related to anyone in Ti, a distinct liability. No one knew what would happen, and few in our family had high hopes.

Election Day came. The results came in. George had won. Shock rippled through the community. For the first time in years—maybe for the first time ever—a non-native had won. And a Democrat at that. The world was crumbling.

Concerning that, my father's favorite story regarded a man who approached a Ti official to complain about my father's being elected. Bad enough, the man grumbled, that George was a Democrat, but wasn't it awful that he wasn't a native?

The man asked the official if the election could be reversed. After all, he wondered aloud, wasn't there something in the law that said if you were a native you couldn't hold office?

The official reminded the poor soul that that held true only for the presidency and told him to go away.

My non-native Democrat father continued to serve and to run for office.

But did his non-native Republican wife vote a "straight party line?"

I don't know. It was never discussed.

"OVER MY SHOULDER" COLUMN FOR NOVEMBER 18, 2000
Unforeseen results of picking the wrong president

"The election" has evoked a memory of another President, Eisenhower, and how it took me several years to stop blaming Ike. When each of the two "waiting to be Presidents" ends their speeches with "God Bless America," I am reminded of Dwight D. Eisenhower, the first President I can remember. Certainly, the first to make an impact upon my life, which he did with two words.

What led to my problem with Ike was that even as a child I grasped words differently. Grownups would use a big word or elaborate phrase and say, just memorize it. But I'd try to understand. My first tussles began with prayer. They were tough, compounded by my father's family being Roman Catholic, my mother's Presbyterian.

Take the Lord's Prayer. Raised Roman Catholic, I was taught, "Forgive us our trespasses." My cousins said, "Forgive us our debts." Debt I understood, not trespasses.

Starting at age seven, I'd pop into the confessional every week and the priest would ask what sins I had. Sometimes I felt as if the few I offered weren't enough to justify my having taken up the poor man's time, so I tried to think of others.

I constantly cut over the Gray's property. So, for three weeks in a row I confessed that. Finally, the priest, obviously confused, asked what I meant. I informed him gravely that I was "trespassing," as in the prayer.

There was a long silence and a sucking in of breath, which I'd recognize now as sounds of a man trying desperately not to burst into howls of laughter. Instead, he informed me, equally gravely, that "that trespassing isn't the same as the other trespassing." I walked out more confused than when I walked in.

As a child when you memorize a phrase, it sometimes becomes one word. Like the "Kingdom of Ferthyne." As kids, we spent part of summers with my mother's relatives. There I learned a different ending for the Lord's Prayer.

With Roman Catholics, the prayer ends, "…lead us not into temptation, but deliver us from evil. Amen." I dutifully memorized my relatives' version. But for several years I thought the kingdom that was to come was the Kingdom of Ferthyne. Because I heard the phrase "For thine" pronounced as one word, so it became "Ferthyne is the kingdom." I wondered where the Kingdom of Ferthyne was.

So, now we come to Ike. It is 1954. I had been in school two short years and had memorized, among poems and other things, the Pledge of Allegiance. My classmates and I all struggled with it, pronouncing "indivisible" as "invisible," making us think we lived in a land we couldn't see.

And the word "allegiance"? What, to kids, was a "legiance"? What were two "legiances"? So, in the mouths of children, the beginning of the pledge sounded like "I plejaleegence..." and the whole thing sounded like a giant chant with sounds that made no sense.

I dutifully memorized that. It was hard and I did not want to, but I did. That or be sent to the cloak room. So, I did. And then in 1954, the teacher solemnly told us that President Eisenhower had passed a wonderful law. The words "under God" were to be inserted in The Pledge.

I was dumbstruck. Devastated. Fuming. Two years of hard work and now this guy named Ike comes along.

Unfortunately, I protested, but fortunately did so at home. The roof blew off. But they had misunderstood. I was not a seven year-old protesting God being placed in the pledge.

I was seven, and to break the rhythm of the chant and insert two words was hard. But I did. And all my classmates did. The two words became part of the pledge chant, that ended sounding like this:

"....one-nation, unnergod, invisible, withliberdee anjustiss frall."

The nation became visible. God became invisible.

At least that we all understood.

"OVER MY SHOULDER" COLUMN FOR DECEMBER 23, 2000
Christmas, Sinatra, a store's end

Music played from an old Sinatra Christmas album I've had for years, and as I read the faded news clipping, I understood how only time brings us to an understanding of the joy that can come from sadness.

The newspaper clipping is dated December 2, 1961. It was an ad purchased by my father announcing our family's pharmacy, King's Pharmacy, had closed for good. All these years later, it was odd to look at those words on the yellowed newsprint, for they represent one of our family's most poignant, yet excellent, Christmases.

From the time our family moved to Fort Edward in 1952, life centered on the pharmacy – "the store" – open every day, Christmas being no exception. At first just Dad and Mom worked in the store. Then, as we children grew older, we worked, too.

A family owned business shapes the family around it. We first lived in an apartment over the store, then later in our own home nearby. Either way, the Christmas routine was the same: church, presents, store. We kids would awake Christmas morning, dying to know what we got. But, church first! We'd grumble, dutifully dress, and somberly walk past the Christmas tree. After services, we'd race home to unwrap presents, that is, to shred paper and make a chaotic mess.

Dad would then open the store. Mom would start dinner. As little children, we'd come down to show off our presents to the customers, who would "ooh and ahhh" like relatives. As we grew older and worked in the store, we'd still do the same. We grew up in the store. The store saw our joys, our heartbreaks.

After moving to our house, we added that Sinatra album, which became essential to the routine: church, presents, Sinatra, then store. In those ensuing years, the three older children worked in the store. But it affected us all. The store was like breathing – a part of life, done day in, day out, season after season.

But things did not go well financially. Debts mounted. Life became so very, very difficult. I can't express the worry and stress, and the horrible toll they took. Even so, though we knew it was coming, Dad's decision came as tremendous shock. The closing of the store was like a death in the family. Dad's newspaper notice was the obituary.

Afterwards, he went to work in Ticonderoga. We knew we would move there soon. Everything was over.

December was so strange without the store, Christmas Day simply bizarre. As always, we kids awoke, dashed downstairs, ready to be sent back to dress for church. Not today. We waited to attend a late service. This Christmas morning, we sat in our bathrobes, put on Sinatra and, while Dad and Mom sipped coffee, we opened presents, which were far fewer in number.

There is a photo of us that morning. My mother looking shell-shocked, Dad with a smile of what can only be relief. And we kids? Giddy. Relieved. Bewildered. This was bewildering. There wasn't that usual, normal, frantic quality about this Christmas morning. As he had past Christmases, Sinatra sang "I'll be home for Christmas," but we sat. We would not work in the store.

We laughed for no reason. If one rose, we all did, ready to get dressed and go to work. Then we'd all sit abruptly and smile in a slightly embarrassed way. Sinatra sang "Oh Come All Ye Faithful," but we would not work in the store. The store was gone, the stress from worry was gone, and frankly, the void was terrifying.

Yet, a calm sat between my two parents. The calm filled the house – and, gradually, filled us. I could not see then that the calm meant the beginning of a new life. I only saw an end, our last Christmas in this home.

Only later did I realize it might have been the end of the store and a way of life, but not life itself. We would have another home, another life.

That "Last Christmas" began teaching me what it's taking a lifetime to learn: in life there is no true ending, for every ending is a beginning.

May this be a beginning for you.

Merry Christmas.

"OVER MY SHOULDER" COLUMN FOR DECEMBER 30, 2000
Friend wrote annual poem for 'New Yorker'

When December comes, I always hope *The New Yorker* magazine's editors include the popular poem saluting the year's famous people and events.

When my family lived on Lincoln Avenue in Saratoga Springs, our neighbor was humorist Frank Sullivan, who wrote *The New Yorker*'s "Christmas poem" for many decades, making it an institution. I have an issue of that magazine from fifty years ago, December 23rd, 1950 to be exact. Why it was saved is the core of my story.

"Greetings, Friends," is the title of Sullivan's 1950 "annual Christmas card." The poem – sublime doggerel– was a tongue in cheek nod to those whose names had been on everyone's lips, famous folk Sullivan knew well. So, when he asked for blessings upon playwright "Anita Loos" and comedienne Fanny Brice, it was personal.

Many of the poem's hundreds of names are easily recognized today, many not. For example, he begins:
"We'll sing in cordial dithyramb,
"The praise of Philip Faversham,
"And Boris Karloff, Elswyth Thane,
"Phil Rizzuto, and Milton Crane."

Today, actor Faversham, author Thane, and short story anthologist Crane are not household names. However, every baseball fan knows Phil Rizzuto. And Boris Karloff is immortal, known as the king of horror movies and as the voice of the Grinch, in the classic cartoon TV special. However, here he was mentioned because he was starring on Broadway in the musical "Peter Pan."

Sullivan was as intimate with the "who's who" of Manhattan as of Saratoga Springs, his hometown. He split his living arrangements between the two. When not at his Lincoln Avenue home with his sister Kate, he lived in New York at the Cornell Club, a posh clubhouse dedicated to making Cornell alums feel more at home in the big city.

Sullivan's 1950 Christmas poem is also a history lesson. "Bless every distant khaki'd Joe" notes the Korean War, in full progress. The lines
"And hoist a beaker of Christmas punch
To sterling Nobelman, Ralph J. Bunche."
refer to the United Nations' chief mediator between the Israelis and Palestinians. For that, Bunche received the Nobel Prize for Peace in 1950. It's a work in progress.

Very significantly, Sullivan asks for
"Peace from broils and strikes and fission;
"Surcease from color television."
He was a visionary.

But Sullivan's poem focuses upon people, and not just the famous. *The New Yorker* gave him artistic license to weave in names of personal friends and Saratoga neighbors among those of the very famous. So, when he wrote "I mean to say we'll celebrate…With…

"Martha King, Robert Bliss,

"and William Faulkner, of Oxford, Miss."

he was writing a birthday greeting to my sister Martha, who had been born January 10, 1950. Here I've been writing all these years and my sister gets in *The New Yorker* the first year of her life. And with Faulkner.

The night Martha was born, Frank Sullivan appeared at the hospital to give greetings to my new sister, to congratulate my mother and to haul my father off for a celebratory "toddy." With Sullivan was his constant sidekick Monty Wooley, Yale professor turned actor, famed for "The Man Who Came to Dinner." Sullivan and Wooley took Dad down to the Colonial, their favorite Broadway watering hole.

Saratogians still sing folk songs in Congress Park about the drinking prowess of Frank Sullivan and Monty Wooley. While Dad's capacity for alcohol was fulsome, he was out-matched that night. One on each arm of my father, Sullivan and Wooley emerged from the Colonial, the picture of sobriety. They helped Dad into a cab, took him home, and then resumed their revelry.

Eleven months later, my sister's name appeared in "Greetings, Friends!" – in the company of

"…Helen Hayes,

"And the Roosevelts, including the Oyster Bays."

And so, in Frank Sullivan's spirit, I end with this birthday poem:

Now, Martha, you understand fully

Your entry, graced by Sullivan, Wooley.

Sullivan was a literary stork-er,

Announcing your birth in, gasp!, *The New Yorker*.

Afterward

Please pause for a moment, would you? These columns could only have come into existence because they were published in a newspaper, *The Post-Star* of Glens Falls, NY. The columns combined history and commentary, but they had to be grounded in fact. That was my editor's rule. *The Post-Star* always has been and is now about the factual, honest presentation of real news.

In my opinion, but one expressed by so many, newspapers are under siege and threatened with extinction. The onslaught of the internet has caused newspapers, daily newspapers especially, severe revenue losses resulting in shrinking staffs and truncated editions. Even publishing online, newspapers still face economic competition from internet advertising, and, far worse, competition from online opinion sites disguised as factual news sources.

The newspaper, on paper or online, remains unique as the central source for factual, vetted, unbiased news.

You could say that, today, I could easily start a "column" via a blog or some other internet format. You could say news is available everywhere on "The Net." But the reality is that no personal blog, no Facebook page, no Instagram, nor any form of social media devised as yet, can provide the newspaper's centralized, professionally edited, fact-based, open-to-scrutiny information.

In rural regions like that *The Post-Star* serves, the newspaper is the **only** central registry for community news—births, deaths, elections, upcoming cultural events, political infighting, school news, building projects, crime, stories of human interest and compassion, etc. The newspaper is not a perfect source. But as a self-governing gatherer and purveyor of facts, the best newspapers operate under ethical standards universally held by all true journalists. When I need the surest source for the facts, I turn first to a newspaper.

We are drowning in a sea of online opinion. We need to defend and promote factual information in all media, but especially the original bulwark of it, the newspaper. In my opinion, there is no replacement for the newspaper—the Fourth Branch of government, after the Executive, Legislative, and Judiciary. It is the guardian of our freedom.

We must support the newspaper—daily, weekly, and monthly—and help publishers find new ways of bringing young readers into the fold.

Whether your newspaper is printed on paper, delivered electronically, or sent by heaven knows what invention yet to come, support it. Agree or disagree with its news; love it or get angry with it; send in your critiques, corrections, commentary. But always cherish, defend, and promote your newspaper.

Your democracy depends upon it.

That is the view from *Over My Shoulder*.

OVER MY SHOULDER: EDITOR JULIA C. CUTSHALL-KING
DISCUSSING PLANS FOR THE BOOK WITH THE AUTHOR – 1996

INDEX

"Bootleg Trail" South St., Glens Falls.................43
"Hair," the musical...142
"Marjorie Morningstar" with Natalie Wood
    and Scaroon Manor..................................101
"Peter Pan," the musical
    and Boris Karloff.......................................178
"The Patriot," Mel Gibson movie
    and Saratoga Battlefields..........................126
100 Glen Street, Glens Falls
    Post-Star building.......................................32
1938 foretold the future....................................149
1980 Winter Olympics..5
54th Regiment of Massachusetts
    and Black veterans of................................38
    and Fort Edward Union Cemetery..........38
A&P building, Fort Edward
    Adirondack Pipes and Drums..................47
A&P supermarket
    on South Street, Glens Falls.....................45
Abe Wing's Tavern
    Glens Falls..26
Abolition movement, Greenwich, NY..............78
Abolitionist movement......................................78
    and Greenwich, NY..................................78
Abraham, Father C. Michael.............................24
Adirondack Chapter of the American Red Cross
   17
Adirondack Museum
    now The Adirondack Experience.............74
Adirondack Pipes and Drums...................46, 48
    founding members...............................46–48
Adirondack Regional Chambers of Commerce
    ....25, 35, 37
    and Glens Falls Civic Center......................3
Adirondack Regional Chambers of Commerce
    (the ARCC)..35
Aerosmith
    and Glens Falls Civic Center......................5
African American Revolutionary War veteran
   71–72
African American settlements of "Timbuctoo"
    and "Blackville".......................................122
Alaska
    Seward's purchase....................*See* Orange Ferris

Alcoholism..67
Alden's 6th Massachusetts Regiment
    Revolutionary War re-enactment group, & Joseph
    Norton..91
Alexandria, hamlet of, Ticonderoga.................72
Amendments, 14th and 15th.............................10
American Federation of Labor – the AF of L
    and Samuel Gompers...............................59
American Graffiti, movie
    and cruising...144
American House on Glen & South Sts.
    later Ruliff Hotel..43
American Legion Post 83, Whitehall
    and Joseph Norton...................................91
Aratare, Jerry
    movie theaters...38
ARCC
    Adirondack Regional Chambers of Commerce 35
Arthur, Chester A.
    and Erastus D. Culver...............................89
Arthur, President Chester A.
    and boyhood home Village of Greenwich.........14
Arthur, President Chester Alan
    and Greenwich, NY..................................15
Artists & chasm at Glens Falls..........................50
Associated Press
    night telegraph service.............................29
Atomic bomb, practicing for the....................158
Aunt Kinks
    Cornelia Cassedy Thierolf......................160
Austin, Hon. John, Warren County judge.......135
Austin, Judge John
    on Orange Ferris......................................12
B&M Railroad (Boston & Maine Railroad).....149
B. B. Fowler building
    Glen Street, Glens Falls.................27, 36, 60
Bail, Jean..18–20
Bail, Jean-Baptiste Bail................................18–20
Baille
    Bayle family history..................................19
Bain, Mrs. James H...8
Bald Mountain, Town of Greenwich
    George F. Bayle...19
Baldwin House in Fort Edward

and Sue Wade and William Hill..............................58
Baldwin House, Fort Edward
   1772 home, Justice Patrick Smyth............58
   now Old Fort House Museum......................58
Bank Square, Glens Falls...........................26, 42
Banker, Dr. Silas
   and Fort Edward Historical Association............135
Barnes, Martha..124
   and rural mail delivery in Washington County.124
Barrett, Nancy..22
Barrett, Nancy, of South Bay
   and Franklin Johndro, Congressional Medal of Honor recipient........................13
Barrymore Family............................See Empire Theatre
Barrymore, John, Ethel and Lionel
   at Empire Theatre, Glens Falls......................39
Bartlett, William Henry
   engraving of Glens Falls.....................................50
Bascom, Wyman, judge..................................135
Bascom, R. O...135
Bates, Loretta, Loretta, Deputy Historian, Washington County............................55, 133
Battenville
   Sallie Hollie speaks at..79
Battle of Bunker Hill......................................133
Battle of Chancellorsville, Virginia
   Civil War...23
Battle of Gettysburg, Pennsylvania
   Civil War...23
Bayle, George F...18–20
Bayle, George F., Sr.
   and Tri-County United Way..............................17
Bayle, Robert "Bob"......................................18–20
Bazinet, John...17
Beach Boys
   and Glens Falls Civic Center................................6
Beecher, Henry Ward
   and Erastus D. Culver..90
Benedict Arnold
   and John Knox..137
Benny Goodman Orchestra............................149
Bernhardt, Sarah..43
   at Empire Theatre..39
Berry Street, the former, Glens Falls..................3
Bicentennial of 1976
   and John Knox..137
Black history–Town of Kingsbury & Village of Sandy Hill.......................................94–97

Black Point on Lake George
   settled by African Americans..............................71
Black residents, Early, of Hudson Falls............94
Black Revolutionary War veteran
   Taylor, Prince, Tale of..................................71–72
Black Swan Image Works
   Michael George King, designer............................5
Black veterans, 54th Regiment of Massachusetts
   and Fort Edward Union Cemetery....................38
Black Watch, 42nd Regiment.............................47
Blackall, Mr. and Mrs. Edward
   and Fort Edward Historical Association..........136
Blair, Prime Minister Tony.................................54
Blakeney-Carlson, Chloe
   and Park Street Theater......................................38
Blow, David....................63, 64, 65, See David Blow
Bobby Kennedy..142
Bobby Kennedy, assassination..........................142
Bolton, Singer Michael.......................................97
Bolton, Town of, history.............................97–100
Bomb, The....................................See Atomic bomb
Border War in the Kansas Territory, 1854
   destruction of the Whig Party...........................80
Boris Karloff...178
Boston Store
   and Geo. F. Bayle...18
Bottskill Baptist Church
   and Underground Railroad................................78
Boucher, Mrs. Marie, teacher
   Powers Elementary School in Fort Edward.....158
Boy Scouts, Glens Falls.......................................18
Braydon and Chapman's....................................26
Bridge between Glens Falls & South Glens Falls
   ....46–48, 48–54
Bridges spanning Hudson River between Glens Falls and South Glens Falls.............48–54
Bridging the Years
   pictorial history of Glens Falls, NY.........6, 49, 50
Briggs, Frank, front page headlines
   The Post-Star..31
Broad Street School PTA...................................34
Broad Street, Glens Falls..............6, 7, 8, 34, 41, 63
Brown William H., Historian............................38
Brown, Asa, 1st Supervisor Town of Bolton.....98
Brown, Hubert..3
Brumagym, George and Henry
   Glens Falls-Queensbury Civil War monument 38
Buck, Colonel John, Hartford.........................133

and Battle of Bunker Hill 133
Bunche, Ralph J., UN 178
Burger King
    and Glens Falls Civic Center 4, 5
Burgoyne
    Burgoyne, General John 56, 58, 70, 81, 82, 83, 92,
        103, 107, 127, 128, 129
    Burgoyne at the Battles of Saratoga
        1927 observance 56
Burleigh Pharmacy 140, 169, 174
Burleigh's 1884 birds-eye map of Glens Falls 30
Buttrick, W. A.
    Glens Falls Chamber of Commerce 36
Byron Lapham 17
Cackener, Helen 7, 76
Calvin Robbins Blacksmith Shop 26
Cambridge
    Frederick Douglass speaks in 79
Cambridge Historical Society
    and Washington County Historical Society 130
Cantiello, Nicholas "Chuckie" 88
Caplans in Saratoga
    Cy and Vicki 150
Carota, Fred, "swing man"
    The Post-Star 31
Carter, Rob, collection
    Glens Falls Insurance Co. 64
Carter, Rob, officer of
    Glens Falls Insurance Co. 64
Carter collection
    Glens Falls Ins. Co. 64
Castleton, Vermont 127
Caswell, Mrs. Charles
    and Fort Edward Historical Association 135
Cederstrom, Harriet 7
Century Farms program
    Washington County, Sue Wade 58
Chambly, Province Quebec, Canada
    Bayle family history 19
Chapin's Farm 14
Chapman Historical Museum 2
    and Glens Falls Civic Center 5
Chapman, Dr. A.W.
    and Spanish Influenza 88
Charlie Kaulfuss' poolroom on South Street,
    Glens Falls 45
Charlotte County 48, 49, 73, 114
Chase, Seth, White Creek tavern-owner 86

Chatauqua County 61
Chautauqua 8
Chautauqua movement 8
Chester, Town of, history 100–101
Christians, Protestants and Roman Catholics . 150
Christmas 151
Christmas and Chanukah 151
Christmas cat, The 160
Cimo, Andrew
    Fort Edward Italian History Committee 57
City Hall, Glens Falls 26, 29, 31, 63
City of Glens Falls 6, 18, 20, 35, 53, 63
    founders 18
City Park, Glens Falls
    and Henry Crandall 17
Civil Defense 158
Civil War 7, 8, 12, 16, 17, 21, 22, 23, 27, 37, 38, 43,
    78, 90, 98, 99, 101, 120, 121, 122, 123, 132
Civil War Monument in Glens Falls 37
Civil War Monument of Town of Queensbury
    37
Civil War monument, Glens Falls 27
Clark, Dr. Billy J.
    and 1st American temperance society 67, 68
Clark, Hazlett N., 1st secretary
    Glens Falls Chamber of Commerce 36
Clark. William, First National Bank of Glens Falls
    President
    and the Glens Falls Civic Center 5
Clark's and Dennison's Lingerie
    on South Street, Glens Falls 45
Clarke, Joan Carswell 35
Clay, Henry
    and Erastus D. Culver 90
Clinton County 100
CNA Insurance
    Ferris and Yohn Collection 64
Cohan, George M.
    at Empire Theatre, Glens Falls 39
Collotti's Shoes, South & Broad Streets, Glens
    Falls 45
Colonel Williams monument, US Rt. 9 Lake
    George
    and Ephraim Williams 123
Colonial Restaurant
    Frank Sullivan's and Monty Wooley' favorite 170
Colotti, Frank 6
Colotti's Shoes Sales and Service 6

Columbia Street and South Street, Glens Falls..45
Colver, Attorney Erastus.*See* Colver, Attorney Erastus
Colvin, A.B. publisher and banker
   and Empire Theatre..39
Community Chest, Glens Falls
   Tri-County United Way......................................17
Company A of the 118th Regiment of the New York Infantry
   and Franklin Johndro...13
Condon, Bob, City Editor of *The Post-Star*...5
Confederacy..10, 121
Confederate Flag
   and Charley Reese..120
   and South Carolina Statehouse......................120
Confederate States of America..........................120
Confederates, Civil War.......................................23
Congregational Church of Greenwich
   and Corliss, Free Democratic League..............79
   and Free Democratic League.............................79
Congregationalism
   and Prince Taylor...72
Congress Park, Saratoga Springs.......................179
Congressional Medal of Honor...................13, 14
Continental Army, Captain Pillsbury
   and Prince Taylor...71
Cook, Dr. G. Peter..112
Cook, Joseph
   and Ticonderoga High School..........................93
Cool Insuring Arena...*See* Glens Falls Civic Center
Cool, Charles W., 1st mayor City of Glens Falls
   and Empire Theatre..39
Coon, Hannah, of Greenwich
   captured during Burgoyne's Campaign..........129
Cooper, James Fenimore
   artists and the chasm at Glens Falls..................50
Cooper's Cave...........................48, 50, 51, 52, 53, 54
   Lewis, Daniel Day, actor....................................51
Corbett, Lawrence
   The Idle Hour Club..132
Corliss, Hiram
   and Douglass, Frederick....................................80
Cormier, William "Al"
   Salem Town/Village Historian....................76, 77
Cossayuna (Lakeville)
   Frederick Douglass speaks in............................79
Cowhides, Spanish, to Wevertown......................74

Cowles Building
   Glens Falls...26
Coy, John J.
   Glens Falls Chamber of Commerce..................36
Crandall Free Library...................*See* Crandall, Henry
Crandall Park, Glens Falls
   and Monument as burial place..........................16
Crandall Public Library
   and Henry Crandall...17
Crandall, Bradshaw, American illustrator
   and Gladys Contryman Lapham.....................117
Crandall, Henry..28
Crane, Milton..178
Cronin, Glens Falls Mayor Robert J.....................4
Cronkhite, Frank
   and the Fort Edward Historical Association..136
Cronkhite, James
   Fort Edward Historical Association................136
Cronkhite, James R.......................................94, 96
Cruising in cars as teens, guide to................143–46
cruising, in a car...144
Cuban Missile crisis of 1962..............................159
Culver, Attorney Erastus
   in Easton...89
Culver, Attorney Erastus D.
   in Easton...86
Culver, Erastus Dean, Attorney
   and NYS Assemblyman, US Representative, Ambassador to Venezuela, Brooklyn City Court Judge..89
Cummings, Dedrick, and Huttons
   and other scottish settlers in Putnam................70
Cummings, Hannah Hutton
   and sister fending off attack..............................70
Cunningham, Colonel John, memoirs of..........13
Cunnion, Donald O., sports editor
   The Post-Star...31
Cutshall family, Glens Falls
   and Cutshall's Cleaners.....................................24
Cutshall, Edna, Glen Lake camp of..................167
Cutshall, Sara...167, 168
Cutshall-King, Julia C.......................................155
Cutshall-King, Julia Cornelia............................142
Cutshall-King, Sara..141
Czechoslovakia, Prague Spring, 1968................143
Daley, Fred
   and *The Post-Star*..2
Damon Runyon

and Saratoga 170
Daniel Chester French, sculptor
   and Crown Point Reservation 123
Daniel H. Cowles 17
Daniel Sickles 21
DAR Regent Glenna Shanahan
   and Jane McCrea Chapter DAR 93
Darwin's "Origin of the Species"
   and Friends in Council 8
Davenport, Daniel, US Rep
   and Samuel Gompers 59
David Blow 2, 6, 38
Davis, John S., 1st vice president
   Glens Falls Chamber of Commerce 36
Decharne, Stephen Pell 104, 105, 106
Decoration Day 13
Delaware and Hudson 53, 163
DeLong, Cutler J., Red Cross Treasurer
   and Spanish Influenza 88
DeLong, Daniel
   and Empire Theatre 39
DeMarce, Virginia, historian
   Bayle family history 19
Dennison's lingerie factory .... *See* Union Square
Depression, The Great 149
Dever, Dr. Francis X.
   on the 1913 demise of Glens Falls-South Glens Falls Bridge 53
Devil Dan Sickles Deadly Saliants
   by Gary Rice 23
Dineen, James, assistant sports editor
   The Post-Star 31
Dolan Building, The
   Glen Street 26
Dolan, Jr., Michael
   Building on 1 Broad St, GF 6
Donahue, Jack
   Adirondack Pipes and Drums 47
Doolittle, Will
   and *The Post-Star* 2
Dorchester Heights, fortifying of
   and John Knox 137
Douglass, Frederick .... *See* Ferris, Orange
   and Hiram Corliss 80
   and Quakers in Easton, NY 80
Douglass, Frederick, speaking Washington County, NY and Lakeville (Cossayuna) 80
Dr. Sherman Williams, Supt. Glens Falls Schools

and Crandall Public Library 16
Duke of Albany 73
Dunhams Basin 97
Dunn, Leo, Washington County copy
   The Post-Star 31
Dutchess County
   Quaker settlers from 85
Dylan, Bob 142
E.M. Wing Relief Corps 128, auxiliary to the GAR 34
Early Black residents of Hudson Falls 94
Easton Meeting of the Society of Friends 85
Edmond De Rocker Design 26
Edward Historical Association
   and founders of 135
Eisenhower, President Dwight D. 175
Elder Colver
   and Underground Railroad, Greenwich ... 78
Elementary School memories
   and eating paste 164–65
Elizabeth Deeb Joseph, aka Boe Joseph 25
Elks Club 153
Ellis, Mary Jane
   and Ft. Edward Historical Assoc. 57
Emergency Hospital at Glens Falls armory
   during Spanish Influenza outbreak 88
Emerson, Richard R. *See* History of Union Square
Empire Theatre, Glens Falls 27, 38, 39, 40, 41, 43, 45
Episcopalian church
   and Ticonderoga 72
Evergreen Bank
   originally First National Bank of Glens Falls ... 27
Excelsior Brigade of New York
   Civil War 23
Faherty, Gregory E., copy editor
   The Post-Star 31
Fairfield, Vt.
   Chester A. Arthur birthplace 15
Fall, the season 171
Faulkner, William 179
Faversham, Philip 178
Feast of St. Joseph 150
feeder canal connecting Glens Falls and Kingsbury
   Completed 1832 74
Feigenbaum, Minna, society editor
   The Post-Star 31

Feingold, Dr. Joseph
    and the Fort Edward Historical Association.....136
Ferris and Yohn collection
    Timothy Weidner's role in saving..................63
Ferris and Yohn collection of the old Glens Falls
    Insurance Company..................................63
Ferris, John A.
    and building on Glen Street........................65
Ferris, Mortimer, NYS Senator..............110, 111
Ferris, Orange..................................10, 11, 12
Finch Pruyn & Co.....................................21
First Lodge, Boston's Masonic lodge
    and John Knox....................................137
First National Bank of Glens Falls..............26, 198
Fisher, Alvan
    artists and chasm at Glens Falls...................50
Fisher, Frederick.....................................168
Fitzgerald's Restaurant................................35
Fitzpatrick, Ann Elizabeth Green King
    (Grandma Fitzpatrick)...........................165
Flat track, first in Glens Falls and Queensbury
    Mile Track...30
Flick, Hugh..................................57, 130, 131
Flick, Hugh, Acting New York State Historian 56
Ford over Hudson River below Wing's Falls
    Between Queensbury and Moreau................48
Fordham College, The Bronx.....................142
Fort Ann, Burgoyne Campaign.....................127
Fort Ann, NY
    and Queen Anne..............................72–73
    began as Fort Anne...........................72–73
Fort Edward
    and childhood in..................................155
    and John Knox...................................139
    description of downtown 1956..................160
Fort Edward Advertizer...............................132
Fort Edward Collegiate Institute............56, 92, 102
Fort Edward Historical Association 6, 54, 56, 58,
    130, 135
Fort Edward Town Historian....................57, 58
Fort Edward Union Cemetery
    and Black veterans, 54th Regiment of
    Massachusetts..38
Fort Miller
    and John Knox....................................139
Fort Ticonderoga......................................127
    and John Knox....................................137
    and Pell Family.....................................104

Fox, Jehial, Chestertown's first settler...............100
Francis Scott Key......................................22
Franco-Prussian war of 1870..........................19
Frank Scully's Wonder Bar.............................35
Frank Sullivan....................................170, 179
Frederick Douglass
    and John Brown Farm State Historic Site.........121
    in Union Village (Greenwich)....................78
Free Democratic League..............................79
French and Indian War
    and Ephraim Williams............................123
French and Indian War..............20, 70, 72, 73, 127
French Canadian, Irish immigrants
    Wevertown..75
French, sculptor Daniel Chester
    and Crown Point Reservation....................123
Freshet..52
Freshet at Glens Falls 1810............................50
Friends in Council
    Quaker term..8
    Study club for women in Glens Falls................7
Fuller, Betty Lou......................................168
Gail, Jane [aka Ethel Magee]
    silent movie star................................76, 77
Gail, Jane-Silent Films of..............................77
Galesville
    Frederick Douglass speaks in......................79
    Sallie Hollie speaks at..............................79
Garrison, William Lloyd
    and Dr. Hiram Corliss.............................78
General Burgoyne.................................73, 92
General Philip Schuyler................................20
Gettysburg saved as national park
    and Daniel Sickles..................................24
Gibbs, Leonard
    of Greenwich Free Democratic League...........79
Gill, Islay V. H.
    and Washington County Historical Society......131
Girl Scouts, Glens Falls................................18
Glassbrook, Judge Howard............................47
Glen Park Hotel
    formerly "The Club House".......................30
Glen, Colonel John
    buys rights to Wings Falls..........................49
Glen, Joahannes..........................*See* Glen, John
Glen, John
    Glens Falls...20

Glens Falls (now Adirondack) Chapter of the American Red Cross ... 18
Glens Falls Academy ... 11, 21, 31
Glens Falls Chamber of Commerce ... 35, 36, 37
Glens Falls City School System ... 9, 16
    and Eva Judkins ... 9
    and Henry Crandall ... 16
Glens Falls Civic Center ... 3–6, 141
    and Ringling Bros. ... 141
Glens Falls Civic Center Heritage Hall of Fame .3
Glens Falls Fire Department ... 63
Glens Falls fire of 1884 ... 4
Glens Falls Hospital ... 6, 17, 18, 43, 69, 88, 141
    and Dr. Lemon Thomson ... 43
Glens Falls Hospital Guild ... 34
Glens Falls Hotel
    Wait S. Carpenter ... 65
Glens Falls Ins. Co. collection
    Chapman Historical Museum ... 64
Glens Falls Insurance Company 63, 64, 65, *See* Egbert W. West
    and Cooper's Cave logo ... 52
    and Tri-County United Way ... 17
Glens Falls Insurance Company building at Bay and Glen building
    Razed 1976 ... 64
Glens Falls Lion's Club ... 48
Glens Falls National Bank and Trust Company
    and Henry Crandall ... 16
Glens Falls Opera Festival
    and Glens Falls Civic Center ... 5
Glens Falls Operetta Club ... 34
Glens Falls Portland Cement Company ... 18, 19
Glens Falls Urban Renewal
    and Glens Falls Civic Center ... 3–6
Glens Falls Urban Renewal at Warren & Glen Sytreets
    and business/buildings removed by ... 3–4
Glens Falls, Burleigh's 1884 birds-eye map of ... 30
Chapman Historical Museum 6, 7, 24, 28, 40, 50, 115
Glens Falls, virtual historical tour of downtown ... 25
Glens Falls/Queensbury volunteer fire companies
    on South Street, Glens Falls ... 42
Glens Falls' first Labor Day ... 60, 58–61
Glens Falls-Queensbury Historical Assoc. 40, 135

parent org. Chapman Historical Museum ... 64
Glens Falls-South Glens Falls Bridge ... 48–54
Globe and Diamond Cab
    on South Street, Glens Falls ... 45
Godine, Amy
    and John Brown Farm State Historic Site ... 122
Gompers, Samuel ... 59
Goodman, Samuel ... 26
Grandma Moses
    and Washington County Historical Society ... 131
Granger, Marcus E.
    and The Club House ... 30
Granville Free Library ... *See* Pember Library
Granville, Village of ... 101
Grateful Dead
    and Glens Falls Civic Center ... 5
Great Depression ... 10, 56
Great Fire of 1864 ... 26, 62, 65
Greeley, Horace
    and Culver, Erastus Dean, Attorney ... 90
Green, Joey, murder, South St., Glens Falls ... 44
Green, Joseph P. (Joey) Albany "gunman, burglar, muscleman'"
    and South St. murder ... 44
Green, Mrs. Bessie, teacher
    Powers School, Fort Edward ... 164
Greenwich Baptist Church ... 15
Greenwich Village
    Frederick Douglass speaks in ... 79
Greenwich, Village of ... 78, 123
    Chester A. Arthur boyhood ... 15
    Washington County, NY ... 14
Grenadier Regiment Erbprinz, or Grenadier Regiment Crown Prince, for the Crown Prince of Hesse-Kassel
    Bayle family history ... 19
Greyhound and Trailways bus station
    on South Street, Glens Falls ... 45
Guiteau, Charles J.
    and James A. Garfield and Chester A. Arthur ... 15
H. J. and George H. Rockwell
    and Lake Luzerne, NY ... 66
    and Rockwell House, Glens Falls ... 66
Haddassah, Glens Falls ... 34
Hague, Joan, NYS Assembly woman
    and Glens Falls Civic Center ... 3
Halloween trick'r'treat ... 147
Hampton, Bertha, visiting nurse

and Spanish Influenza................................88
Harper's Ferry, Virginia
   and John Brown................................122
Harris, Fred
   Adirondack Pipes and Drums..............46
Harrisena Church
   and Henry Crandall..............................16
Harrisena, Town of Queensbury
   and Henry Crandall..............................16
Hava Nagila..151
Hayes, Helen..179
Hayes, Rev. Pam Mikel..............................168
Haymarket Square, Glens Falls
   now Union Square................................27
Heidorf, Chris...37
Helen Hayes..179
Hemlock bark & tanning
   Wevertown...74
Henry Crandall..............................16, 17, 28
Henry Hudson Townhouses on South Street,
   Glens Falls...45
Hesse Hanau Regiment................................19
Hide tanning
   Wevertown...74
Hilfinger, Alex
   and Fort Edward Historical Association...136
Hill, Mrs. A. P.
   and Fort Edward Historical Association...135
Hill, William, Historian
   and the Fort Edward Historical Association...136
Historian A.W. Holden................................37
   Civil War Monument............................37
History of Queensbury
   Dr. A. W. Holden, auth......................198
History of the Town of Queensbury
   Dr. A. W. Holden, auth........................11
History of Warren County................11, 74, 100
Holden, Dr. A.W. "History of Queensbury" 198
Holden, Dr. A.W. *History of the Town of Queensbury*\................................11
Holden, James, New York State Historian
   and Empire Theatre..............................39
Holley, Sallie...79
   Abolitionist, educator............................79
Holocaust
   and 1938...150
Hoosick, Town of
   Rensselaer County, NY..........................14

Horne, Field, Historian
   researches history of Patt Smyth's House (Old Fort House Museum)................................83
Horton, Beecher
   Glens Falls Chamber of Commerce........36
Hotel Ruliff
   and Empire Theatre..............................39
Hudson Avenue, Glens Falls
   creation at Glen Street..........................65
Hudson Falls 34, 37, 39, 40, 46, 47, 48, 55, 59, 96, 108, 114, 123, 129, 131
   and John Knox..................................139
Hudson River
   and John Knox..................................139
Hull, Hon. Edgar..55
Hutton, William
   and settlement of Putnam.....................70
Hyde, Louis F..17
Idle Hour Club, The, Fort Edward............133
Impeach President.......................................10
Impeach President Johnson.........................10
Intemperance..67
Irving, Arthur P., general manager, *The Post-Star* 31
James A. Garfield
   and assassination..................................15
   and Chester A. Arthur..........................15
   and Union College................................15
James Fenimore Cooper
   artists and the chasm at Glens Falls.........50
   The Last of the Mohicans......................50
James, Atticus Siddell..................................96
James, Ethel Van Alstyne
   and Atticus Siddell James......................95
James. Atticus Siddell..................................95
Jane Gail's Silent Films................................77
Jane McCrea..128
Jane McCrea Chapter of the Daughters of the American Revolution........................91–93
   and Capt. Joseph Norton.......................90
Jane McCrea Monument
   and Jane McCrea Chapter DAR............92
Jerome Lapham Engine Company No. 3.......62
Jessup Brothers..41
Jews, Orthodox, Conservative, Reform......150
Jim Crow laws...10
John Adams
   and John Knox..................................137
John Brown Farm State Historic Site

and Lake Placid 121
John Glenn, Colonel 20
John Kennedy is running for President 173
Johndro, Franklin
   and Congressional Medal 13
Johnsburg
   Wevertown a part of 74
Johnson, Lewis
   and Mrs. Matilda Johnson 96
Johnson, Matilda 96
Johnson, President Lyndon 142
Jones, Daniel, Loyalist
   and Quaker Wing Familys 85
Jones, Linda
   Post-Star Educational Services Director in 1999 31
Joseph, Bill and Jeff 25
Joseph, Doc 25
Joseph, Jean 25
Joseph, William and Elizabeth Deeb 25
Joseph's Restaurant, Glens Falls 24
Joy, Robert, architect 7
Judkins, Eva 9
Judkins, Eva (aka "Mrs. Charles O. Judkins")
   and Friends in Council 9
Julius – "Former Slave"
   Hudson Falls obituary of 94
Justice Patrick Smyth, home of
   American & British Rev. War HQ 58
K Locksmith on South Street, Glens Falls 45
Kansas-Nebraska Bill 80
Karloff, Boris 178
Kathryn O'Brien 7, 8, 10
Kayaderosseras Patent 20
Kennedy, Bobby, assassination 142
Kennedy, William, author, Pulitzer Prize winner
   The Post-Star 34
Kettler, Frederick, NYC architect
   and Empire Theatre 39
Key, Philip Barton
   son of Francis Scott Key 22
King, George A. 168
   and Valentine's Day 140
King, George and Jane 154
King, Jane 159
King, Jane and George, my parents 172, 173
King, Martha
   and The New Yorker 179
King, Martha J. 169

King, Martin Luther, assassination 143
King, Michael (Mike) 169
King, Michael George, Black Swan
   Image Works 5
King, Mrs. Josephine Mary Clements
   Jane McCrea Chapter DAR 91
   King, Dr. Joseph E. 91
King, Scott B. 169
King, William (Bill) 169
King's Pharmacy 176
Kingdom of Ferthyne 175
Kingsbury
   and John Knox 139
Kinner Cemetery
   Town of Whitehall 90
Kirkpatrick, Dr. Harold
   Adirondack Pipes and Drums 47
Knight, H. Ralph managing editor
   The Post-Star 31
Knight, Ralph, associated editor The Saturday
   Evening Post 32
Knights of Columbus 34, 61, 153, 154
Knox's trek, 1775 137–39
Konafsky, Sid
   and South Street, Glens Falls 45
Kristallnacht
   Nazi rampage against the Jews, November 9-10,
   1938 150
Ku Klux Klan
   and John Brown Farm State Historic Site ... 122
Laakso, Oliver, president Kamyr
   and Glens Falls Civic Center 4
Laaskso, Oliver
   and Glens Falls Civic Center 3
Labor Day 58, 60, 61, 146
Labor Day, Glens Falls' first 60, 61
Labor union membership
   and Roman Catholics 61
Labor unions
   and Knights of Columbus 61
Labor unions of villages of Glens Falls, Sandy Hill
   & Fort Edward, 1900 60
LaHaise, A. Gustave, Wevertown church
   designer 75
Lake George 6, 34, 40, 42, 50, 72, 73, 81, 97, 98, 99,
   104, 105, 117, 138, 139, 144, 145
Lake George's Mossey Point
   and John Knox 139

Lake Placid
   and John Brown Farm State Historic Site.........121
Lakeville (Cossayuna)
   Frederick Douglass speaks in.........................79
Lamb, Wallace. historian...99
Lane, Oren, Methodist minister, Warrensburg
  167
Lapham, Byron...17
Lapham, Gladys.............................115, 116, 118
LaPointe, Elizabeth Ferris...................................111
LaPointe, John Putnam Town Supervisor.........71
LaPointe, Karl J..111
Lauder, Harry
   at Empire Theatre, Glens Falls..........................39
Laverty, Jeannine...84
Leggett, Isaac, Quaker "Minister"
   and prisoner of Iroquis in Revolution..............85
   Quaker Springs..85
Lewis, Daniel Day, actor
   Cooper's Cave..51
   Last of the Mohicans...51
Lewis, L. R.
   and Washington County Historical Society.......131
Lincoln Avenue, Saratoga.................................178
   and King family..170
Lincoln, Abraham
   and Erastus D. Culver.......................................89
Lincoln, President Abraham................................10
Linus Barnes & Jarret Thomas
   and Wevertown's first tannery.........................75
Little Round Top
   Civil War..23
Lloyd Garrison, William................................78, 79
Lodewick Shear, surveyor, Putnam
   and Prince Taylor..72
Loding, Paul, Kingsbury Town Historian............90
   and Joseph Norton..90
Log drives' origins, controversy over
   Wing, Abraham II and Fox brothers................100
Lonergan, Theresa
   Ticonderoga Town Historian............................93
Loomis, John R..17
Lord, Ben, Glens Falls Country Club pro
   Spanish Influenza outbreak..............................88
Lord's Prayer..175
Louis F. Hyde...17
Louis M. Brown...17
Lumber industry

and Henry Crandall...16
Luzerne...41, 66, 88
M. B. Little Hose Co..62
Mabb, Kingsbury Town Clerk Holly..................96
MacFinn's Drugstore, Saratoga Springs..........170
Mackintosh, Jane, historian....................74, 75, 76
MacMorris, Mary M. "Molly"
   Washington County Historian.........................55
Madden Hotel, South St., Glens Falls.................43
Magee, Ethel
   silent movie star...........................See Gail, Jane
Marbles, game of...146
   and alleys, aggies, cats eyesshooters...............147
MarcAntonios barbershop on South Street,
   Glens Falls...45
Mason, A. E.
   Glens Falls Chamber of Commerce..................36
Masons
   and John Knox..137
Massacre of Jane McCrea
   1927 observance of..56
Matochik, Dr. John
   and Fort Edward Historical Association........136
MC Scoville Jewelers
   and Mount St. Helens....................................167
McCarty, R. Paul, Historian..73, 83, 108, 135, 136
McClellan, Mrs. Robert
   and Washington County Historical Society.....131
McCrea, Jane, Massacre of
   1927 observance of..56
McCrea, Patriot John
   brother of Jane..127
McCreery, B. F.
   Glens Falls Chamber of Commerce..................36
McEachron, Doris
   Washington County Historian.........................54
McGillicuddy, T. J..17
McGinley, Francis W...3
McIlvaine, Florence....................29, 31, 32, 34, 35, 146
McIlvaine, Florence Webster,.............................31
McPhillips, James...17
Me Generation...159
Mel Gibson
   and "The Patriot" movie.................................126
Melucci's Restaurant
   South Street, Glens Falls.............................40, 43
Memorial Day..13
Mender, Mike

and *The Post-Star* 2
Merchants Bank 26
Messinger, Alice M.
   and Atticus Siddell James 95
Metivier, Don, *Post-Star* Editor
   and the Glens Falls Civic Center 5
Metz on Moselle River, France
   Bayle family history 19
Michael Dolan, Jr.
   Building on 1 Broad St., GF 6
Milbert
   artists and chasm at Glens Falls 50
Mile Track, Glens Falls & Queensbury
   subdivided for Broadacres 30
Mile Track, The 31, 61
Mill Creek
   Wevertown 74, 75
Mohawk River
   and John Knox 139
Monahan-Chase Caterers 26
Montcalm Street, Ticonderoga
   Cruising in cars on 145
Monty Wooley 170, 179
Monument Square, Glens Falls 27, 42, 43, 46
Morette, Louis 174
Morgan, Robert, Vice President
   Glens Falls Ins. Co. 64
Moss Street Cemetery, Kingsbury 97
Motown 142
Mount St. Helens eruption 167
Mozelle family
   and South Street, Glens Falls 45
Muhlig, Betty, *Post-Star* Correspondent 126
Mullen, Charles
   The Idle Hour Club 132
Murray, Anna 8
NAACP
   and John Brown Farm State Historic Site .. 122
National Black History Month 94
Native Americans, Quakers, ... 83
New Deal 56
New Year's eve in Ticonderoga 153
New York State circuit court
   and unions and Gompers 59
New York State Historical Association 57, 113
Niagara Mohawk 7
North Pownal, Vermont
   and Chester A. Arthur 15

North Star, abolitionist newspaper
   Frederick Douglass in Greenwich 80
Northumberland
   and John Knox 139
Norton, Captain Joseph, Revolutionary War
   Town of Whitehall 90
NuWay Lunch on South Street, Glens Falls ... 45
Old Brownstone, The 26
Old Fort House Museum 54, 57, 58, 83, 94, 96,
   105, 107, 116, 118, 135, 136
   Susan E. Wade 1st Curator 136
Oppenheim, Mrs. Monroe
   and Fort Edward Historical Association ... 135
Ordway Hall, Glens Falls 27
Ossie Davis as Frederick Douglass
   and John Brown Farm State Historic Site . 121
Paddocks and the Wevers .... *See* Wevertown
Paisley, Scotland
   and Putnam's settlers 70
Palace Lunch, Glens Falls
   Tony deJulia 35
Palmer, Estelle, Director of Red Cross
   and Spanish Influenza 88
Parke family 21
Parker, Whitehall Judge
   and Culver, Erastus Dean 89
Passover 150
Paste, eating of 164
Patt Smyth House 54
Patton, Doris 74
Pearsall, Glen 74
Pell Family
   and Fort Ticonderoga 104
Pember Library. *See* Pember Museum of Natural
   History and the Pember Library
Pember Museum of Natural History and the
   Pember Library 101, 102
Pember Opera House Block 102
Pember, Franklin 101, 102
Pendleton Civil Service Reform bill
   and Chester A. Arthur 15
Penn Yan 61
Peoples, Pearl 112
Peoples, Pearl Torrey 113
Peter's Diner
   and Peter Demas 45
   South Street, Glens Falls 45
Peters, C.V.

Glens Falls Chamber of Commerce 36
Philo, Emeline
    wife of Franklin Johndro 13
Piping Rock, Saratoga Springs 170
Pitcher, NYS Governor Nathaniel
    and Mrs. Matilda Johnson 96
Platt, Charles A.
    architect Crandall Library 28
Pledge of Allegiance
    change in 1954 175
Porter District Schoolhouse, Town of Hebron
    and Pember 102
Post-Star building, former, corner of Park and Glen 26
Post-Star column "Historical Museum Notes."
    Van Dusen, Richard 64
Potter, architect E. B.
    and Empire Theatre 39
Pottersville 100, 101
Powers Elementary School, Fort Edward 158
Prague Spring, Czechoslovakia 143
Presbyterian church of Hudson Falls
    and Mrs. Matilda Johnson 96
President Chester A. Arthur 15
Prince Taylor, Tale of
    Revolutionary War veteran 71–72
Priscilla Lee Baker's dance recitals 34
Prohibition
    and South Street, Glens Falls 45
Prostitution, Glens Falls
    Glen Park Hotel, aka The Club House 30
Province of New York 48
PT Boat 172
PT Boat Squadrons 173
Purcell, Bill, Red Wings coach 5
Putnam, Town of
    early settlement of 70
Quaker meeting-houses, Easton
    Sallie Hollie speaks at 79
Quaker persecution by Patriots and Loyalists in Revolution
    Quakers' impact on our region 85
Quaker Springs
    Sallie Hollie speaks at 79
Quakers
    and Queensbury 48
Quakers & Abolition, Saratoga & Washington Counties 78–80

Quarantines
    Spanish Influenza outbreak in Glens Falls Region 88
Queensbury
    and John Knox 139
Queensbury Hotel 36, 66, 142
Queensbury Patent, the original 1762
    and Dorothy Wing 136
Rabble in Arms 71
Racing season in Saratoga Springs 170
Radical Republicans 10
Red Cross Chapter (Glens Falls)
    and Eva Judkins 9
Red Wings, hockey franchise 5
Reese, Charley, columnist
    and Confederate flag 120
Revolutionary War 20, 23, 67, 68, 71, 84, 91, 92, 93, 118, 133
Rhode Island
    and White Creek Quakers 86
Richards, William Lee 89, 113
Riedesel, Baron & Baroness
    in Burgoyne Campaign 81
    in Fort Edward 81
Riedesel, Baron & Baroness von
    at "Red House" 81
Riedesel, Baron von 19
Riedesel, Frederika Charlotte Luisa von Massow, Baroness von Riedesel 81
Riley's, Saratoga Springs 170
Ringling Bros. Barnum and Bailey Circus 141
Ringling Bros. Circus
    elephants won't cross bridge at Glens Falls 53
Ringling Brothers Circus 5
Rite-Aid Pharmacy on South Street, Glens Falls 45
Rizzuto, Phil 178
Road to the Feeder Dam
    South Street, Glens Falls 42
Rob Carter collection
    Glens Falls Insurance Co. 64
Robbins, Janice, Crown Point historian 109, 111, 113
Robertson, Daniel L.
    Glens Falls Chamber of Commerce 36
Robinson, Willard
    and Fort Edward Historical Association 135
Robson, Mary Blackall

and Fort Edward Historical Association 136
Rockwell House, Glens Falls
   and H. J. and George H. Rockwell 66
Roden, William, writer/naturalist 99
Rogers Island, Fort Edward 132
Roosevelt, Franklin D., Governor 110
Roscoe Conkling
   and Chester A. Arthur 15
Rosenberg boys in Fort Edward, Alan and Fred
   150
Rt. 9 Bridge between Glens Falls & South Glens
   Falls 48–54
Ruliff Hotel on Glen & South Sts.
   formerly American House 43
Russert, Michael, historian, author, editor ... 57, 131
S. R. Stoddard
   and John Brown Farm State Historic Site 122
Salter, John, runaway slave
   and Underground Railroad, Greenwich 78
Salvation Army 18, 32
Sandy Hill 29, 53, 59, 60, 95, 96
   now Hudson Falls 94
Sandy Hill Herald 94, 95, 96
Sara Cutshall 168
Sarah Bernhardt .... *See* Empire Theatre
Saratoga County 2, 20, 50, 51, 52, 67, 68, 79, 83, 85, 123
Saratoga National Historic Park 56
Saratoga racing season, 1946 156
Saratoga Springs
   Saratoga racing season, 1946 156
Saratoga Springs, "the season" 170
Savage, Robert
   and Fort Edward Historical Association 135
Scaroon Manor
   "Marjorie Morningstar" with Natalie Wood 101
Schenectady
   Chester A. Arthur 15
Schenectady Pipe Band 47
Schuylerville
   and John Knox 139
Scoville, Chris and Debra Vales
   and MC Scoville Jewelers 167
Second Fair Oakes 14
See"
Seward, William H.
   and Erastus D. Culver 90
Seward, William H., US Secretary of State 12

Seward, William, as Gov. NY State
   and Orange Ferriss 11
Sgt. Peppers Lonely Hearts Club Band 142
Shapiro, Ralph 7
Sharp, Cathy, Greenwich Town Historian 14
Sherman, Edward J., city editor
   The Post-Star 31
Sherman, Henry L.
   during Spanish Influenza outbreak 88
Sherman, Hermine, *Post-Star* Women's Editor .. 3, 198
Sherwood, Thomas Adiel
   and Patt Smyth's House 83
Shushan
   Frederick Douglass speaks in 79
Sickles, Daniel 21
Silent Films of Jane Gail 77
Sinatra Christmas album 176
Singleton, J. Edward 36
Singleton, James E. 17
Slavery 59, 78, 79, 95, 96, 120, 121, 122
Slavery in the Empire State
   as a quote in obituary of Matilda Johnson 96
Smalley, Frank M. 17
Smith, Al, NYS Governor 110
Smith, David, sculptor 99
Smith, Virginia "Babe"
   1st woman mayor of former Village of Ticonderoga 174
Smiths Basin 131
Smyth house, saving of in 1943
   Susan E. Wade and William Hill 136
Smyth, Justice Patrick
   Home of, 1772 58
Society of Friends & Abolition, Saratoga &
   Washington Counties 78–80
Society of Friends, Quakers, Easton 83
Society of Friends, Quakers, Feathers of Peace 83
Society of Friends, The
   Quakers' impact on our region 86
Soldiers' Monument Restoration Committee
   Chris Heidorf 37
South Glens Falls 21, 34, 48, 53, 54, 68, 69
South Glens Falls mills
   post-Revolution 21
South Street in Glens Falls 38, 40, 43, 45
South Street School, South St., Glens Falls 46
South Street speakeasies, gambling 44

South Street, Glens Falls 40–46
   aka the Street of Dreams 27
Southard, Mildred
   Washington County Historian 55
Spa State Park, Saratoga Springs 110
Spain, South America and California
   and Wevertown's first tannery 75
Spanish American War 60, 92
Spanish Influenza 1918
   in Glens Falls Region 87–88
Speakeasy, Jerry Linehan's, South St.
   & Joey Green murder 44
Starbuck, Archeologist David 83
Stoddard, Seneca Ray
   and Cooper's Cave 51
   artists capturing the chasm at Glens Falls 51
Stott, Earl
   Adirondack Pipes and Drums 47
Street of Dreams, Glens Falls
   South Street 27
Street of Dreams, the
   South Street, Glens Falls 40
Streetcar line on South Street, Glens Falls 43
Study clubs for women in New York State ...... *See*
   Friends in Council
Sullivan, Frank
   and Algonquin Round Table 170
Sullivan, Frank, author
   and *The New Yorker* 178
summer of love, 1967 142
Sumner, Walter K.
   Hazlett N. 36
Swan, Martha
   and John Brown Farm State Historic Site ... 122
Syria, Lebanese immigration to Glens Falls
   Region *See* Joseph, William & Elizabeth Deeb
Syrian community, Glens Falls, First Ward 24
Tait, George
   Glens Falls Chamber of Commerce 36
Tammany Hall 22, 23
Tasker, V. K. Malcolm
   and Susan E. Wade, the first Washington County
   Historian 57
Taylor, Prince, Tale of
   Black Revolutionary War veteran 71–72
Temperance society 67, 68
Temporary insanity, Sickles
   first citing as a defense 22

Terp, Gail 5
Thane, Elswyth 178
Thanksgiving 160
The 41 Worst Predictions of All Time. *See* Ferris,
   Orange
The Adirondack Civic Center Coalition 3
The Bomb .... *See* Atomic bomb
The Boston Store 19, 60
The Club House, Sanford St., Glens Falls 30
The Colonial, restaurant, Saratoga Springs 179
The Glens Falls Times 33
The Great Depression 149
The Hyde Collection
   and Glens Falls Civic Center 5
The Idle Hour Club 132, 133
The Last of the Mohicans
   James Fenimore Cooper 50
The Liberator
   article by Dr. Hiram Corliss 78
   William Lloyd Garrison's Boston newspaper 78
The Morning Post
   The Post-Star 26, 28, 29, 31
The Morning Star 28, 29, 59, 60, 61
The New Yorker
   and Frank Sullivan 170
The New Yorker magazine 178
The New Yorker's "Christmas poem"
   and Frank Sullivan 178
   and Martha J. King's birthday 178
The Post Company 29
The Post-Star 3, 4, 5, 6, 2, 7, 20, 26, 28, 29, 31, 32, 33,
   34, 35, 36, 48, 54, 59, 60, 70, 72, 88, 110, 116,
   122, 123, 126, 130, 168, 174, 180
The Post-Star, 1936 editorial staff 31
The Saturday Evening Post .... *See* Ralph Knight
The Star Building 1892 26
The Tavern
   Michalik's Tavern, Ticonderoga 153
The United States of America
   Constitution of, 1789 .... 115, 120
Thomas Nast's political cartooning
   and Tweed Ring 90
Thompson, Maury 38, 70, 109, 112, 113, 174
Thompson, Nancy 174
Thomson
   and John Knox 139
Three Years with the Adirondack Regiment
   memoirs of Colonel John Cunningham 13

Threehouse and Thurston's Inn.................65
Thurman, John....................................74
   Wevertown, origins........................74
Thurston's History
   and Dr. Hiram Corliss.......................78
Ticonderoga
   post-Revolutionary War....................71
Ticonderoga Democrat.........................174
Ticonderoga on Lake George................171
Ticonderoga, parents' last home in.........159
Ticonderoga's first high school................93
Tidmarsh's Orchestra
   The Idle Hour Club.........................132
Tilford, Ernest
   and Washington County Historical Society......131
Tingley, Ken, Managing Editor of *The Post-Star*........................5, 2, 31
Tom Calarco.......................................78
Tony deJulia's Palace Lunch....................35
Towers Hotel, Glens Falls
   formerly Rockwell Hotel....................66
Town of Hoosick..................................14
Town of Moreau....................21, 50, 53, 67
Town of Putnam..................................70
   and Prince Taylor............................72
Town of Queensbury...6, 10, 16, 21, 37, 49, 50, 105, 136
   and Queensbury Patent, the original 1762......136
Town of Westfield............................72, 73
Town of Williamstown, MA
   and Ephraim Williams.....................124
Travelway..40
Travelways...40
Trick'r'treating on Halloween................148
Tri-County Association for the Blind........18
Tri-County United Way....................17, 18
   founders of....................................17
Tuna salad sandwich, eating of
   and Grandma Fitzpatrick.................165
Turney, Mrs. Ferdinand (Blanche)
   and Fort Edward Historical Association......135
Tweed Ring
   and Culver, Erastus Dean, fights against....90
Typewriters used at *The Post-Star*, 1936........33
Underground Railroad................78, 80, 122
Union Carriage Works
   on South Street, Glens Falls................43
Union College, Schenectady

Chester A. Arthur................................15
Union School No. 2............................6, 7
Union Square, Glens Falls.......6, 7, 27, 43, 45, 46
Union St. School
   Union School No. 2, GF......................8
Unionization efforts in Canada and US
   and Samuel Gompers........................59
Unions in Greater Glens Falls Region
   and Samuel Gompers........................59
Unitarian Fellowship, Warren St., Glens Falls.167
University of Vermont......................11, 89
Urban Renewal....................................45
   Glens Falls.....................................66
Urban Renewal Glens Falls
   and Glens Falls Civic Center..............3–6
Vales, Debra, and Chris Scoville
   and MC Scoville Jewelers.................167
Van Dusen, Richard
   Chapman Historical Museum co-founder.....64
   Glens Falls Insurance Co. officer..........64
   Post-Star column "Historical Museum Notes"....64
Viele, F.C.
   Glens Falls Chamber of Commerce.......36
Village of Fort Edward..47, 81, 106, 107, 108, 109
Village of Glens Falls.....6, 11, 13, 16, 30, 39, 51, 58
   and Henry Crandall.........................16
Village of Granville.............................101
Village of Greenwich............................14
Village of Ticonderoga..........................72
Virtual Bus Tour of Glens Falls................26
virtual historical tour of downtown Glens Falls 25
Vreeland, E.B. (R) Chatauqua County
   and 1st Labor Day Glens Falls............61
W. T. Grant Company
   Glens Falls.....................................66
W.C.T.U. (Women's Christian Temperance Union)..8
Wade, Susan E.
   and the Fort Edward Historical Association....136
   Washington County Historian............54
Wade, Susan E., first Washington County Historian..55
Wade, US Senator Ben
   and Frederick Douglass........*See* Ferris, Orange
Wagner, Mrs. Ann
   principal of Powers Elementary School....158
Wall Street, Manhattan.........................150
Wall, L, Glens Falls engraving by.............50

Walter Winchell, columnist on Warren County, a place to "get away with murder" 44
Walters, Frances, Queensbury Supervisor and Glens Falls Civic Center 3
War Chest, Glens Falls 18
  Community Chest 18
Warren County Centennial 24
Warren County Fairgrounds
  Glens Falls 30
Warren County Fairgrounds, Glens Falls subdivided 30
Warrensburg 167
Warrensburgh, Warren County's first tannery .. 74
Washington County 6, 2, 18, 19, 20, 31, 34, 49, 50, 51, 54, 55, 56, 57, 58, 59, 70, 71, 72, 73, 78, 83, 86, 100, 109, 114, 115, 126, 130, 131, 135, 136
Washington County Clerk's office 55
Washington County Historian 54, 55, 56, 57, 130, 131, 136
Washington County Historical Society 54, 57, 130, 131, 136
Washington County Town Historians in 1940 and Washington County Historical Society 130
Wasson and Watson
  and Wevertown's first tannery 75
Way Down East
  and Empire Theatre 39
Weeks, John E., Vermont Governor 110
Weidner, Timothy, Executive Director
  Chapman Historical Museum 40, 63, 65
West Mountain, Queensbury 36
West Point 22, 23
West, E.
  possibly Egbert or Elmer 17
West, Egbert W., 1st president
  Glens Falls Chamber of Commerce 36
West, Elmer C.
  Glens Falls Chamber of Commerce 36
Western Union and Postal Telegraph messengers
  The Post-Star 32
Wevertown, first tannery 74
Whiteface Mountain road 110
Whitehall, Town of 90, 91
Wiberg, John ("Jack") 27, 168
Williams Brothers
  and Riley's, Saratoga Springs 170
Williams College
  and Ephraim Williams 123

Williams College alumni
  and Ephraim Williams monument 124
Williams, Ephraim
  and Williams College 123
Wilmarth, C.M. 17
Wilmarth, M.L.C. 36
  Glens Falls Chamber of Commerce 36
Wilson, Hugh Allen, musician/conductor 99
Wilson, Mrs. Roscoe
  and Washington County Historical Society .. 131
Wing, Abraham 38, 41, 48, 49, 85
  sawmill 21
Wing, Abraham II and Fox brothers
  and controversy over log drives' origins 100
Wing, Abraham, sells rights to Falls 49
Wing, Asa R.
  and Fort Edward Historical Association 135
Wing, Dorothy
  and the Fort Edward Historical Association .. 136
  and the Queensbury Patent 136
Wing, Lieutenant Edgar M.
  Civil War Monument 38
Wing's Falls
  renamed Glens Falls 21
Wing-Northup House in Fort Edward
  and Washington County Historical Society .. 131
Witherbee Sherman Co., Mineville 112
Women's Civic Club, Glens Falls 9, 34
Wonder Bar, Frank Scully's
  Rogers Building, Glens Falls 35
Wooley, Monty 179
Woolworth's Store, Glens Falls 27
York Shirt factory ...... 6, *See Union Square, Glens Falls*
Youngken, Richard
  1980 Glens Falls Natl. Register nomination ... 39

Endnotes

i Hermine Sherman was the last "women's editor" at *The Post-Star*. For a loving memorial to her, see Irv Dean's "Hermine Sherman was the personification of perseverance" in the April 20, 2002 edition of *The Post-Star*.

ii Frances Walters, the first woman to serve as Supervisor of the Town of Queensbury.

iii Heritage Hall's materials eventually ended up gracing the walls of The Wood Theatre in Glens Falls, thanks to the late Bill Woodward, its Director. An avid history lover, Bill captured not only the Heritage Hall materials, but also the original box office of the Paramount Theater, which had been demolished in 1978.

iv Don Metivier (1937-2007). Journalist, raconteur, historian, and ardent booster of his native Glens Falls, Metivier began at *The Post-Star* in 1961 as city police reporter. He went on to be sports page editor and by the time he left the paper in 1980, editorial page editor. In addition, he broadcast sports and a yearly show of Christmas memories on WWSC AM, wrote several histories, and published a collection of his columns *Saturday Morning*. He went on to be publisher of *Ski Racing Magazine*.

v Founded in 1962, the Glens Falls Opera Festival performed summers at Queensbury High School's auditorium. Despite proposals to renovate the old Empire Theatre, or incorporate it in the Civic Center, or in a new theatre on the Urban Renewal site, or build a new performance shed on West Mountain, nothing materialized. It was moved to Saratoga Springs and now operates under the name Opera Saratoga.

vi Bridging the Years Glens Falls, New York 1763-1978. King, Robert N.; Austin, John D.; Buffington, Susan E.; Fisher, Arthur S.; King, Florence M.; McAndrew, Elizabeth S.; et al. (1978). The Glens Falls-Queensbury Historical Association, publisher.

vii That pharmacy recently ceased operations there.

viii There never was a part two. Frank Colotti later died. Architect Gary McCoola purchased the building and beautifully restored it. It is listed as "3 Broad Street."

ix All quotes are from Kathryn O'Brien's 1974 history.

x Holden, Dr. A. W. *History of the Town of Queensbury, New York*. (1874).

xi Cathleen Sharp Barber (1947-2007). Cathy was Greenwich Town Historian from 1992 to 2003. A native of Greenwich, Cathy dedicated herself to her work and made lasting contributions to the history of Greenwich and Washington County.

xii Evergreen Bank began as The First National Bank of Glens Falls in 1851. Evergreen was purchased by TD (Toronto Dominion) Bank of Toronto in the 1990s.

xiii Dr. Sherman Williams was the first Superintendent of what is now the Glens Falls City School System. An early leader in, and advanced thinker regarding, education, Williams went on to serve as the Chancellor of The New York State Education Department and pushed for the addition of local and state history in New York State public school curricula. Not enough scholarship has been done on him.

xiv A log mark was a brand, usually applied to the cut end of a cut tree using a hammer bearing the brand. An excellent book on the topic is *Log Marks on the Hudson* by Richard C. Merrill (2008). Dick Merrill—Dr. Richard C. Merrill—was an engineer with GE and led the team that invented the biodegradable replacement for PCB. Dick, who was an ardent historian and collector of artifacts, served as Chairman of the Board of the Chapman Historical Museum in the late 1970s and early 1980s. Together with this author, at that time the museum's director, he led the Board to purchase the Seneca Ray Stoddard Collection, a major collection of that 19th photographic legend's works.

[xv] See column "A family's twisting history" for more on the Bayle family history.

[xvi] Bazinet would also serve as Mayor of Glens Falls.

[xvii] An excellent study in late 19th-early 20th century power in the region would have to focus on Brown, an attorney who sat on more Boards and had more power than a mere endnote can convey.

[xviii] Louis F. Hyde was a Boston native, and Boston Brahmin, who was attorney for the Boston Elevated Train Co. He met his wife Charlotte Pruyn Hyde when she was taking courses at Harvard from the famed William James. They married and lived in Boston until Charlotte's father wooed her to return to Glens Falls with the promise of a position at Finch Pruyn & Co. for Louis and of a house built on Warren Street to their specifications. The couple, ardent collectors, designed it around their collection, which included works of Botticelli, Rembrandt and Picasso. It is now The Hyde Collection.

[xix] Lapham was a descendant of Stephen Lapham, co-founder of the Town of Queensbury. In 1923, Lapham was also president of The First National Bank of Glens Falls, aka The White Bank, so named for its 1914 white marble headquarters on Glen Street, immediately south of Crandall Public Library.

[xx] Smalley was for many years an officer of The Glens Falls Insurance Co. The rug from his office was donated to the Chapman Historical Museum alone with cases of historical artifacts collected by Rob Carter, another officer of that company. See the column, "Celebrating paintings' homecoming."

[xxi] Tait was the founder and President of Imperial Wallpaper and Chemical Co.

[xxii] This could be Egbert W. West, President and Chairman of the Board of The Glens Falls Insurance Co., or Elmer West, President of Adirondack Power and Light Co. In the author's opinion it is the latter. The former, when using initials, is most often referred to as "E. W. West."

[xxiii] The Wilmarth family came to Glens Falls in the 1840s to start a furniture business. By the 1920s, they had become an extremely wealthy and influential family.

[xxiv] This is the same George F. Bayle, Sr. described in the July 26, 1998 column, "One good effort leads to another."

[xxv] DeMarce, Virginia. *Settlement of the Former German Auxiliary Troops in Canada after the American Revolution.* 1984.

[xxvi] Rice, Gary. "Devil Dan Sickles Deadly Salients" (in the November 1998 issue of "America's Civil War" and now online at www.historynet.com).

[xxvii] Leech, Margaret. *Reveille in Washington.* (1942).

[xxviii] Sickles mustered out as a Major General.

[xxix] Rice, Gary. "Devil Dan Sickles Deadly Salients."

[xxx] Harland Cutshall (1907-1969) and Edna Johnson Cutshall (1907-1991) originally hailed from Indiana. They first established Cutshall's Cleaners in Whitehall, NY, in

1931, but after a disastrous flood, moved to Warren Street, Glens Falls in the mid-1930s. Cutshall's was renowned for the quality of its work. The family name is still widely recognized and respected throughout the area. I am proud to carry it.

[xxxi] Chapters in a future history of Glens Falls will discuss the tortured trail to success in finally building a stunning addition to the Library. The name Christine McDonald, the Crandall's Director, will be prominent in that victory.

[xxxii] Founded in 1879 by Colvin as *The Glens Falls Daily Times*. At the time, Addison Beecher Colvin was 21.

[xxxiii] In 2009, Mark Mahoney, *The Post-Star*'s Editorial Page Editor, won the 2009 Pulitzer Prize for editorial writing. Mahoney is now Editorial Page Editor of *The Daily Gazette*.

[xxxiv] Lieutenant Edgar M. Wing (1841-1864) was also honored by having the Grand Army of the Republic Post named for him. The GAR was an organization of Union Civil War veterans. His portrait is in the Chapman Historical Museum in Glens Falls.

[xxxv] Brown, William H. *History of Warren County, New York*. Publisher: [Queensbury, N.Y.]: Board of Supervisors of Warren County, 1963.

[xxxvi] The Empire Theatre's exterior was designed by Manhattan architect J.B. McEphattrick.

[xxxvii] Hyde, Louis Fiske. *History of Glens Falls, New York*. (1936). Louis F. Hyde died in 1934. His friend William H. Hill, a historian and author from Fort Edward, revised and edited the book for publication in 1936.

[xxxviii] Harris, Fred. "Highland Echoes, a History of the Adirondack Pipes and Drums."

[xxxix] Jacques Gérard Milbert published an engraving of the chasm in 1828. The chasm was painted by W. G. Wall and engraved by I. Hill in 1821. William Henry Bartlett produced an engraving in 1840.

[xl] Regrettably, I never mentioned that Charles Reed Bishop, considered a Founder of modern-day Hawaii, was born in 1822 in the tollhouse his parents tended on the bridge. A champion of his memory is Hawaiian-born Kaena Peters, who is planning a celebration in Glens Falls in 2022 to mark the 200th anniversary of Bishop's birth.

[xli] A large terra cotta representation of that logo is now prominently displayed at the Chapman Historical Museum in Glens Falls.

[xlii] Loretta Bates graduated from volunteer to a paid position in 2006 when the Washington County Clerk Deborah Behan was officially designated as Clerk/Historian. In 2008, under Washington County Clerk Dona Crandall, Loretta was given the title Deputy Historian. In my five years as Washington County Historian, I relied heavily on the on Loretta's immense knowledge of county history and genealogy. She was a joy to work with. Loretta is a published historian. She researched the records of the Washington, NY, Poorhouse records and published *Those Called Paupers* (2013). She also published *Memories of Early Sandy Hill* (2017) from records of Orson Richards.

[xliii] Timothy Weidner, now in his 21st year at the Chapman Historical Museum, holds the distinction of being the museum's longest serving Executive Director.

[xliv] Lape, Jane M. (ed.). *Ticonderoga: Patches and Patterns from Its Past*. Ticonderoga Historical Society (N.Y.), 1969. I was fortunate to know Jane, whom I met while working at Fort Ticonderoga.

xlv Kenneth Roberts' *Rabble in Arms*. (1936).
xlvi Johnson, Crisfield. *History of Washington County*. (1878).
xlvii The Village of Ticonderoga was unincorporated in 1992.
xlviii Joseph Cook, born 1838 in Ticonderoga, NY; died 1901 in Ticonderoga. Cook, a world-famous author, writer, and intellect, was the only son of a Ticonderoga farmer, who sent Joseph to be educated at Phillips Andover, Yale, Harvard, and German universities. Based in Boston, he gained fame as the "Boston Monday Lecturer," according to Worldcat (http://worldcat.org/identities/lccn-n81067894/). Cook's "talks on subjects ranging from theology and science to current events and world history attracted thousands of listeners every week and were reprinted in newspapers around the world." A liberal Protestant, Cook embraced and explained such movements Transcendentalism and Evolution.
xlix After ten years at the Adirondack Museum, historian, author, and film producer Jane Mackintosh a she left to pursue independent projects. Among them, she wrote and co-produced the WMHT PBS video *Seneca Ray Stoddard: An American Original*. She also has been instrumental in creating exhibits and publications for several museums and individuals. and continues to be passionate about the region's history.
l Smith, H. P. 1886 *History of Warren County*.
li St. Charles Borromeo (1538-1584) Roman Catholic archbishop of Milan from 1564 to 1584; a cardinal; and a leader in the Counter Reformation. The Wevertown Roman Catholic church ceased as such in the 20th century.
lii William "Al" Cormier was William "Al" Cormier is a native of Webster, MA. Al moved with his family to Salem NY in 1965 to be Assistant Superintendent of Schools. He retired from the school system in 1992 as its Superintendent. He served as Town of Salem Historian from 1983-2019 and Village Historian from 1983-2017, the year of the Village's dissolution. In that time, Al did herculean work as historian, preservationist, and advocate for the history of Salem, especially its role in the American Revolution. He is currently Deputy Historian for his successor, Judy Flagg.
liii Thomas Calarco went on to author and co-author numerous histories on the Underground Railroad (UGRR) in the United States.
liv David Starbuck, PhD is, as his biography on the Plymouth State University website notes in part, "an historical and industrial archaeologist, specializing in the archaeology of America's forts and battlefields" and "has published or edited nearly 20 books" and hundreds of other scholarly works. As of 2019 David is again doing archeological work on Rogers Island, Fort Edward, one of the nation's most important historical sites.
lv William Lee Richards (1926-2013) was a born historian. Son of William Lee Richards, Sr., a charter founder of The New York State Historical Association, he shared his father's passion for the history of this region, especially the Colonial and early Federalist periods. A cofounder of the Warren County Historical Society, Bill published *Three Related Tales* (2001), and produced a concordance of A. W. Holden's 1874 *History of the Town of Queensbury, NY*.
lvi Paul Loding (1949-2016) was Historian for the Town of Kingsbury and the Village of Hudson Falls from 1990 to 2016. His book *Kingsbury and Hudson Falls* was published

in 2001. He was an avid re-enactor as Lieutenant Colonel of the 53rd Regiment of foot in North America.

[lvii] Nathaniel Pitcher (1777–1836), eighth Governor of New York (1828); born in Litchfield, CT, he was raised in, lived in and died in Sandy Hill, now Hudson Falls, NY.

[lviii] Brown, William H. *History of Warren County, New York*. Publisher: [Queensbury, N.Y.]: Board of Supervisors of Warren County, 1963.

[lix] Stephen Pell Dechame (1947-2013) was the second of three sons of Stephanie Pell and Roger Dechame. Steve served as a Juvenile Defender in the Massachusetts Juvenile Justice System. Like the rest of the Pell family, so deeply associated with Fort Ticonderoga, he loved history.

[lx] Charley Reese (1937-2013), was a nationally syndicated columnist. Reese called himself a "conservative." I believed him a reactionary, especially regarding the Confederacy. He glorified the Confederacy. under the cloak of "states' rights."

[lxi] Amy Godine is an independent scholar who has done seminal research in, and published scores of articles about, Adirondack ethnic and social history. She has also curated several exhibitions, among them the "John Brown Lives!" exhibition about the Abolitionist John Brown;-and the traveling exhibition, "Dreaming of Timbuctoo," about an abolitionist-founded black settlement near North Elba.

[lxii] Martha Sears Barnes (1914-2000) died in December 2000. As of 2019, her grandson still does Martha's rural delivery route for the Cossayuna Post Office.

[lxiii] Matthew Rozell is an award-winning history teacher, author, speaker and blogger on World War II and the Holocaust. There is not room enough to describe the wonderful work he has done as a high school teacher, and in his own books, lectures and other educational endeavors to make the Holocaust remembered and understood, so it will never be repeated. He has been rightly honored and awarded for that work.

[lxiv] Isabella Weer Brayton was Hartford Town Historian for many years and was later succeeded by her daughter Sylvia Brayton Van Anden. Both were remarkable advocates for Hartford and the County. In 1929, Isabella Brayton and John B. Norton published *The Story of Hartford: a History*. Published on the eve of the Great Depression, it has some insightful commentary on the authors' perception of the declining financial conditions of Hartford after 1890.

[lxv] Michael Russert is a noted authority on the American Civil War, member of the North Shore Civil War Roundtable and the Company of Military Historians.

[lxvi] Mullen, Charles. *The Idle Hour Club*. Charles Thomas Mullen Jr. (1926-2010) was born in Fort Edward. Having served in WW II, he first taught in Hartford, NY. He then went to Fort Edward Public Schools, serving, in this order, as Junior High Social Studies teacher, Media Supervisor, Junior High School Principal, Elementary School Principal, and lastly as Superintendent of Schools. He retired in 1988 and died in his hometown. See also Volume 1 of *Over My Shoulder*.

[lxvii] Brayton, Isabella; John B Norton. Publisher: Hartford, New York. 1929.

[lxviii] The Hon. John Austin (1931-2019), Warren County judge was so instrumental in the preservation and dissemination of our region's history. Space does not permit a listing here. I was privileged to meet Judge Austin when I was hired as Director of the

Board of the Chapman Historical Museum of the Glens Falls-Queensbury Historical Association. John was on the board of the museum, which he helped cofound.

[lxix] Dr. Joseph Feingold (1913-2005) was a wonderful physician, an ardent historian, and beloved friend to many people. He was our family doctor in Fort Edward. He took his degree from University of Michigan's Medical School. During World War II, Dr. Feingold was a Major the U.S. Army Medical Corps in the European Theater. When I was researching my book *Hospital By the Falls*, Dr. Feingold told of being at the Battle of the Bulge in 1944. He said it was becoming known by then what the Nazis were doing to the Jews and that he knew if captured he would have been executed. Aside from his work as Founder of the Old Fort Museum, he also preserved for posterity many acres of land in the Town of Moreau fronting the Hudson River.

[lxx] Robert Frederick Vorreyer (1924-2016) was our longtime friend. Bob attended the University of Illinois, the Brooklyn Museum Art School, the Royal Academy in London, and studied under various artists. An incredible artist, he did all the designs for Charles R. Woods' Storytown and Gaslight Village.

[lxxi] Edna Johnson Cutshall (1908-1991).

[lxxii] Jane King—Martha Jane Kalbaugh King (1918-1984).

[lxxiii] George A. King— George Augustine King (1919-1987).

[lxxiv] Students for a Democratic Society (SDS).

[lxxv] Che Guevara (1928-1967), Marxist who helped lead the 1959 Cuban Revolution.

[lxxvi] The Game of Marbles flourishes, as a quick search on the internet will show the reader hundreds of games of marbles, played by adult and child alike.

[lxxvii] The scourge of antisemitism has been seen again and again, and it has now erupted again in the United States and Europe. Only through remembering the Holocaust and its causes, and then teaching each new generation its lesson, can we hope to avoid its repetition. We must never forget. Ignorance breeds hate and death.

[lxxviii] Joseph P. Carucci was founder and CEO of Carr Securities on 17 William Street, Manhattan. Brilliant, multi-lingual, and a financial wizard, he worked his way through NYU (1938), then onto Wall Street. After WW II, he started his own firm. His son Wally (Walter) and I graduated from Fordham in 1968. Joe was kind enough to give me a job. From 1969 to 1971, I worked all jobs from runner (who delivered stocks and bonds) up to the trading table. I was not J. P. Morgan. Despite his protests, I left. Wally succeeded his father as President of the firm. Joe died in 1989, Wally in 2013.

[lxxix] Also called poplars.

[lxxx] "Tom" is Thomas Rogers, who graciously allowed me to reveal his identity.

[lxxxi] The wedge-shaped building, former business and home of Christopher Scoville and Debra Vales, stands at the intersection of Glen and Ridge Streets in Glens Falls.

[lxxxii] Frederick J. Fisher, Executive Director, 1977-1990, of The Hyde Collection, a Glens Falls museum created from the home and fine arts collection of Charlotte Pruyn and Louis Fiske Hyde. He transformed the Hyde, professionalizing its operations, physically expanding the museum, and drawing further national attention to this treasure. From 1990 to 2010, he was Executive Director of the Hillwood Estate, Museum & Gardens, a decorative arts museum in Washington, D.C., and former residence of Marjorie Merriweather Post. As with the Hyde, he transformed the Hillwood into the vibrant cultural jewel it is today. He is now retired and lives with his wife Rebecca in Pennsylvania.

Made in the USA
Las Vegas, NV
03 December 2023

82021267R00118